Howard Walter Caldwell

Studies of American History

A Survey of American History

Howard Walter Caldwell

Studies of American History
A Survey of American History

ISBN/EAN: 9783743400467

Manufactured in Europe, USA, Canada, Australia, Japa

Cover: Foto ©ninafisch / pixelio.de

Manufactured and distributed by brebook publishing software (www.brebook.com)

Howard Walter Caldwell

Studies of American History

STUDIES

IN

American History

A SURVEY OF AMERICAN HISTORY

SOURCE EXTRACTS

BY

HOWARD W. CALDWELL, A.M.

LINCOLN, NEBRASKA, U. S. A.
J. H. MILLER
PUBLISHER

Copyrighted, 1898,
BY
J. H. MILLER.

PRESS OF
JACOB NORTH & COMPANY,
LINCOLN, NEB.

CONTENTS.

	PAGE.
Introduction	i.
The Founding of the Colonies.	1
The Development of Union Among the Colonies	25
Causes of the American Revolution	47
Steps in the Formation of the United States Constitution	71
Interpretation of the Constitution; Nationality	99
Slavery in the United States, I	123
Slavery in the United States, II	147
The Civil War and Reconstruction	171
A Study in American Foreign Relations and Diplomacy	195
A Study in Economic History	219

AMERICAN HISTORY STUDIES.

INTRODUCTION.

METHODS of teaching history are in process of transformation. With the change in method comes the demand for new books; so if anyone asks the reason for this little collection of sources on American history, the answer is believed to be found in this change. The compiler is pleased to know that these studies have been received with favor by many progressive teachers. He feels that the lack of proper and available material is one reason that the "laboratory method" has not found more ready acceptance in the past by a larger number of teachers. In the belief that this collection will in part supply the demand, it is now sent forth to the school-world in this more permanent form.

In many Normal schools and in some high schools brief reviews are demanded and given In such cases it seems to the writer to be a waste of time to hurry through some text book, repeating the work that has been done in the grades, in perchance even a less efficient way. It is hoped and believed that the following ten "studies" help to solve the problem of such reviews. A few suggestions are made in regard to the method of handling this material. A note-book should be in the hand of every pupil. It is desirable to have this made up of loose sheets of paper, perforated, so that they may be bound together, or removed and changed in place at the will of the pupil. A cover should be made or purchased in which to keep and preserve these sheets.

The next and most important matter is to bring the students into contact with the original material as often and as completely as possible. For this purpose, of course the "sources" must be accessible, and as far as possible in the hands of every pupil. It should be noted here again that it is not expected that the larger part even of the facts of history can be obtained from these sources, so a good narrative text must be at hand, and in constant use. The "sources" are to be used for the purpose of illustrating how the narrative history was formed; but more especially for the mental training which may be obtained from their use. The same document or illustrative extract should be in the hands of every member of the class that each may have the benefit of the criticism of all.

With the material then in the hands of the class, the first question will be to determine as far as possible its value. To do th s necessitates that we find out whether the document is what it purports to be; then to determine whether we have a correct copy of it. Next we must find out who wrote it, and under what circums ances. Finally, the character of the author will come under discussion. Did he have the opportunity to know? Was he able, honest, educated? Was he writing for parti-an ends, or did he attempt to tell the exact truth? These are a few of the tests we must apply to our material, if we are to know its real value. Perhaps the most important question of all will be, did the writer know of his own personal knowledge, or did he gain his information from hearsay? After we have determined the value of our "source," we next proceed to analyze it, and to find out just what the writer meant. Here we must notice the use and meaning of words at the time the document was written, and note any changes at the present time, so that we may get just the idea intended to be conveyed. A series of questions will often greatly help in this analysis. The ones given in the text are only intended to be suggestive, and so may be supplemented by others, or limited by omissions.

The next step will be to classify and arrange our knowledge. In the writer's opinion this is the hardest, as well as the most important, part of the work. A logical arrangement must be insisted on. A careful outline must be prepared, containing a page reference to every point in the notes. It is only by this careful preparation that accuracy in thinking or in writing can ever be secured. When this work is completed, then the last step in the plan can be taken with great ease and facility, for then the whole mind and strength can be concentrated on the composition. The memory under such circumstances is not burdened with carrying all the details. They are indicated in the outline and in the notes to which it refers. It goes without saying that every piece of student work when completed should be tested by comparing it with the best narrative texts, or with the teacher's knowledge.

One final idea should be suggested. Each of these studies covers many years of time. The evolution of the topic has been kept in mind in making the extracts. In working up the material then into papers and reports, the teacher should see that the pupil has noted and understood the changes and the reasons therefor. For example, if the topic be the "Economic History" of the United States, great pains should be taken to call the attention to the changes in belief in regard to the tariff, or internal improvements. Let every effort be bent to discovering the causes of these changes. If Webster cease to be a free-trader, the reason for the change should be found if possible. If the South oppose internal improvements, let the cause be unearthed.

These studies, then, are committed to my fellow teachers in the hope that they may aid them a little in solving the difficult problem of how to get our children to understand their own history, and to get such an understanding in such a way as to make them mentally and morally stronger, that they may be better prepared to meet the exceedingly difficult questions which will confront the coming generation. The writer has no extravagant ideas or expectations in regard to the transforming power of these studies. He simply hopes and believes that they will be found to be an aid.

H. W. C.

November 25, 1898.

NOTE.—It will be seen that the following material is merely a reprint of the articles that appeared in the North Western Monthly for the year 1897-98; many references that are not appropriate for the present purpose find their explanation in this fact.

American History Studies

No 1.   SEPTEMBER, 1897.

THE FOUNDING OF THE COLONIES.

SELECTIONS MADE FROM THE SOURCES

BY

H. W. CALDWELL,

UNIVERSITY OF NEBRASKA.

J. H. MILLER, Publisher,
LINCOLN, NEBRASKA.

PUBLISHED MONTHLY, EXCEPT JULY AND AUGUST.

Entered as second-class matter at the Post Office, Lincoln, Nebraska,
U. S. A.

AMERICAN HISTORY STUDIES.

EDITOR'S PREFACE.

VERY little space will be given this year to narrative text, or to method. Copious extracts will be made from the sources. The aim will be to choose the extracts in such a way that they may to a great extent tell their own story. In the ten numbers of the MONTHLY it is intended to illustrate ten phases of American history by calling in contemporaries to speak for themselves. Of course these extracts are expected to do little else than whet the appetite for more. It is hoped that the spirit of original research may be intensified in this way to such an extent that the reader may wish to go to the more extended compilations of sources. Professor Hart's new work, "American History as Told by Contemporaries," in four volumes, will meet the want of many. Many extracts may be found in the MONTHLY which could not have been laid before its readers had not this compilation been available. Niles' "Documents Illustrative of the American Revolution" is also a valuable and convenient collection of sources bearing on the American Revolution. Professor Woodburn's revision of Johnston's "American Orations" has increased the usefulness of that valuable work. It now consists of four volumes of the best speeches on all political topics made by American statesmen. The reader of these articles will thus recognize that they contain only an insignificant fraction of the available material, but it is hoped that these papers may throw light on a few of the many great questions in the development of the life and thought of the American people. May we not at least hope that those who cannot have access to the more elaborate works, or those whose time is too limited to use them, may find something to aid them in these briefer extracts?

To get the greatest value from this work the writer believes that definite, systematic work is necessary. On the whole, the plan outlined in the September and October numbers of the JOURNAL of last year is believed to be a desirable one. Questions will accompany each paper this year. They will aim to direct the thought to the most important points in the extracts, and to bring out the hidden meanings. The new reader may perhaps understand the method from a few explanatory sentences. In the first place, a written answer should be prepared for every question, accompanied by the page reference to the proof for the answer. Then an outline should be prepared arranging in proper and logical order the knowledge which has been accumulated in answering the questions. This second step is followed by the third, which consists in writing a paper following the "outline" and based on the answers to the questions for the "material" or matter which it contains. In brief, we first gather our "material," then make an "outline," and finally write our "narrative" history. It is believed that those who will conscientiously follow this plan will by the end of the year have gained much in power, in knowledge of method, and in general culture and information.

More or less explanatory matter will be introduced into the extracts, but in all cases it will be inclosed in brackets [ ]. The editor will, however, in general leave the contemporary writers to tell their own story. Last year it seemed necessary to argue for the use of the sources. In Nebraska at least the acceptance of the principle is now so nearly universal that it would be like carrying a feather bed downstairs at a fire to elaborate further on the subject. The only question now is to make the sources available to the teachers and students of the state. Time will determine the success of this experiment.

Teachers who wish credit in the University of Nebraska may secure it by keeping a note-book, and at the end of the year submitting it for inspection. The note-book should also show the time given to the work from day to day. The amount of credit will, of course, vary with the quantity and quality of work done.

THE FOUNDING OF THE COLONIES.

The planting of the colonies may be said in general to extend from 1600 to 1700. By the latter date they were firmly established and the lines of their movement well determined. The social, religious, political, educational, and industrial life must all be considered in our study. Also the purposes of colonization and the character of the emigrants, as well as the Indians, are factors in our study. Selections, therefore, have been made to illustrate each of these problems.

1. *Reasons for colonization.*

Then shall her Majesties dominions be enlarged, her highnesse ancient titles justly confirmed, all odious idlenesse from this our Realm utterly banished, divers decayed towns repaired, and many poor and needy persons relieved, and estates of such as now live in want shall be embettred, the ignorant and barbarous idolaters taught to know Christ, the innocent defended from their bloodie tyrannicle neighbors, the diabolicale custome of sacrificing humane creatures abolished. . . .—*1582. Sir Geo. Peckham in Hakluyt; Voyages, etc.*

. . . ayming at the glory of God, the propagation of the gospell of Christ, the conversion of the Indians, and the enlargment of the King's Majesty's dominions in America. . . . —*Hart, I, p. 190.*

2. The emigrants: Class, laws concerning.

1582.—Sir Geo. Peckham proposed to get rid of a great number of men which do now live idely at home, and are burthnous, chargeable, and to the common annoy of the whole state.—*Hakluyt.*

1637.—No persons being Subsidy Men [liable for taxes] or of the value of Subsidy Men shall emigrant.—*Proclamation, Chas. I.*

You are to take . . . such a course . . . that vagrants and others who remain here noxious and unprofitable, may be soe transplanted to the generall advantage of the publique as well as the particular commoditie of our Forraine Plantacons.—1660. Instructions for the Councill for Forraigne Plantacons. *From Documents relating to New York History.*

And probably many vagrants agreed with Charles II., for, in 1679, two bright Dutch travelers tell us of a "Godless Emigrant Ship" bound for New York.

In fine it was a Babel. I have never in my life heard of such a disorderly ship. It was confusion without end. I have never been in a ship where there was so much vermin, which was communicated to us. . . . There were some bunks and clothes as full as if they had been sown. But I must forbear.—*Long Island Hist. Society, Memoirs.*

On the other side, hear Rev. Francis Higginson, 1629:

The passage was through God's blessing . . . short and speedy—6 weeks and 3 days, healthful to our passengers, being freed from the great contagion of the scurvie and other maledictions, which in other passages . . . had taken away the lives of many; and withal, a pious and Christian-like passage; for I suppose passengers will seldom find a company of more religious, honest and kynd seamen than we had. We constantly served God morning and evening by reading and expounding a chapter, singing, and prayer. And the Sabbath was solemnly kept by adding . . .

preaching twice and catechising. And in our great need we kept 2 solemn fasts . . . Let all that love and use fasting and prayer take notice that it is as prevailable by sea as by land, whensoever it is faithfully performed.—*Quoted in Hart, I, p. 194, from Thomas Hutchinson's Collections.*

3. *The Indians.*

Peckham, 1582, says:

All Savages . . . *as soon as they shall begin but a little to taste of civility* will take marvellous delight in any garment, be it never so simple . . . and will take incredible pains for such a trifle. . . . Now to the end it may appear that this voyage is not undertaken altogether for the peculiar commodity of ourselves . . . it shall fall out in proof that . . . if in respect of all the commodities they can yeelde us . . . that they should but receive this only benefit of Christianity, they were more than fully recompenced. . . . Wee got for trifles neer 1100 Bever skinnes, 100 Martins, and neer as many Ottus.—*Captain J. Smith in "A Description of New England."*

Governor Winslow, 1621, says they were "very trusty, quick of apprehension, ripe-witted, just."

Penn, in 1683, testifies that

he will deserve the name of wise who outwits them in any treaty about a thing they understand. . . . Do not abuse them, but let them have justice and you win them.—*Quoted from Janney's Life of Penn.*

4. *Mechanism of colonization.*

The colonization companies in England were certainly rare enthusiasts. It is amusing to notice in the proceedings of the Council for New England, 1622, the following item:

It is agreed that ye Councell meet the Morrow . . . at Sr. Ferd: Gorges Lodgings for conferring about ye forme of a patent *betweene 7 and 8 o'clock in ye morneing.*

The royal generosity of the kings in giving away continents is well illustrated by this account of how the above company disposed of New England, 1623:

There were presented to the Kings most excellent Matie a Plot of all the Coasts and lands of New England devided into twenty parts each part conteyning two shares, And twenty lotts conteyning the said double shares made upp in little bales of waxe, And the names of twenty Pattentees by whom these lotts were to be drawne.—*From Proceedings American Antiquarian Society.*

Having given the lands to the companies, these must settle them. The proposal of the proprietors of Carolina in 1663 illustrates the method, and the expectations:

'Wee will grante to every present Und^{r}taker for his oune head, 100 acres of land, to him and his heires forever, to be held in free and common Soccage, & for every man Sarv^t y^t he shall bringe or send thith^r y^t is fitt to bare Armes, armed wth a good fierlocke Musket, performed boare, 12 bullets to ye pound, and wth 20 lb. of powder & 20 lb. of Bullets, 50 acres of land.—*Hart, I, 297.*

The charters show the crude geographical ideas and the dangers inherent in promiscuous grants. In the instruction given by Charles II., in 1660, to the first Council for Foreign Plantations we find the following unconscious estimate of this chaos:

You shall informe yourselves *by the best wayes and meanes you can* of the state and condicon of all Forraigne Plantacions, and by what comissions or authorities they are and have bene governed and disposed of; and are to procure . . . copies of all such comissions and graunts . . . that you may be the better able to understand judge and administer.—*Documents, New York.*

In 1621 the Virginia Company, of London, tells us how they sent over fifty young women to be given in marriage for "one hundred and fiftie pounds of the best leafe tobacco for each of them;" for, they add, "we have used extraordinary care and diligence in the choice of them, and have received none of whom we have not had good testimony of theire honest life and cariadge."

In 1660 Charles II., in his instructions for the first Council for Foreign Plantations, has the following:

You are to apply your selves to all prudential meanes for the rendering those dominions usefull to England and England helpfull to them, and for the bringing the severall Colonies and Plantacons, within themselves, into a more certaine civill and uniforme of goveremt and for the better ordering and distributeing of publique justice among them.—*Documents, New York.*

5. *Political life.*

James, by the Grace of God, King of England, Scotland, France and Ireland, Defender of the Faith, &c., whereas Sir Thomas Gates . . . (and others) consisting of certain Knights, Gentlemen, Merchants, and other adventurerss, have been humble suitors unto us, that We would vouchsafe unto them our License, to make Habitation . . . in that part of *America* commonly called Virginia, . . . situate . . . between four and thirty Degrees of Northerly Latitude . . . and five and forty Degrees of the same Latitude, . . . We, greatly commending, . . . their Desires . . . which may . . . hereafter tend to the Glory of his Divine Majesty, . . . and in time bring the Infidels and Savages . . . to human civility, and to a settled and quiet government: Do, &c., agree. . . .—*Poore, II, 1888. Charter, 1606.*

We . . . do . . . Give, Grant and Confirm to our trusty and well-beloved subjects, Robert, Earl of Salisbury, . . . Robert, Lord Viscount Lisle, . . . Sir Humphrey Weld, Lord Mayor of London, . . . George Piercy, Esq., Sir Edward Cecil, Knight, . . . Dr. Meadows, . . . Captain Pagnam . . . Geo. Bolls, Esq., Sheriff of London, Wm. Crashaw, Clerk, Batchelor of Divinity, . . . Thomas Harris, Gentleman, . . . Geo. Walker, Sadler, John Swinhow, stationer, Wm. Brown, shoemaker, . . . Frances Binley, minister, Richard Shepherd, preacher, William Shirley, haberdasher, Wm. Gibbs, merchant, Thomas Gypes, cloth-maker, John Dike, fishmonger, . . . Christopher Vertue, vintner, . . . the Company of Goldsmiths, the Company of Brewers . . . Robert Chening, yeoman, . . . that they shall be one Body or Commonalty perpetual "having that part of America called Virginia . . . " [description follows, but it is too long to quote].—*Charter, 1609. Poore, Charters.*

1610. Virginia.—Sir Thomas Gates draws the character of the first settlers. There was

a great shipwrack in the continent of Va. by the tempest of
dissention: every man overvaluing his own worth, would be a
Commander; every man underprising an others value, denied
to be commanded. . . . The next fountaine of woes was
secure negligence, and improvidence, when every man sharked
for his present bootie, but was altogether carlesse of succeeding
penurie. . . . Unto idlenesse you may joyne treasons,
wrought by those unhallowed creatures that forsooke the Colony. . . . Unto Treasons, you may joyne covetousnesse
in the Mariners, who . . . partly imbezzled the provisions, partly prevented our trade with the *Indians*, making the
matches in the night, and forestalling our market in the day.

Cast up this reckoning together: want of government, store
of idlenesse, their expectations frustrated by the traitors, their
market spoyled by the Mariners, our nets broken, the deere
chased, our boats lost, our hogs killed, our trade with the Indians forbidden, some of our men fled, some murthered, and
most . . . weakened, and indanngered, famyne and
sicknesse by all these meanes increased.—*Hart, I, 206-208.*

1619. Virginia.—We have an official "Reporte of the ... General Assembly convened at
James City, in Virginia, July 30, 1619, consisting of the Governor, the Counsell of Estates,
and two Burgesses elected out of eache Incorporation and Plantation, and being dissolved
the 4th of August."

The most convenient place we could finde to sitt in was the
Quir of the Churche Where Sir George Yeardley, the Governor, being sitt down in his accustomed place, those of the
Counsel of Estate sate nexte him on both handes, except
onely the Secretary then appointed Speaker, who sate right
before him, John Twine, Clerke of the General assembly,
being placed next the Speaker, and Thomas Pierse, the Sergeant, standing at the barre, to be ready for any Service the
Assembly should command him. But forasmuche as men's
affaires doe little prosper where God's service is neglected . .
a prayer was said. . . . Prayer being ended, to the intente that as we had begun at God Almighty, so we might proceed with awful and due respecte towards the Lieutenant,
our most gratious and dread Soveraigne. . . . [The
Assembly proceeded immediately to pass laws "Against Idleness, Gaming, durunkenes & excesse in apparell" within
three days.]—*Colonial Records of Virginia.*

1620. Massachusetts.—Rev. John Robinson wrote his advice after the Pilgrim colonists, whom he could not accompany.

Whereas you are to become a Body Politick . . . and are not furnished with Persons of special Eminency . . . to be chosen by you into Office of Government; Let your Wisdome and Godliness appear not onely in choosing such Persons as do intirely love . . . the common Good; but also in yielding unto them all due Honour and Obedience in their lawful Administration, not beholding in them the Ordinariness of their Persons, but God's Ordinance for your Good; . . . and this Duty you may the more willingly, and ought the more conscionably to perform, because you are . . . to have them for your ordinary Governours which you yourselves shall make choice of for that Work.—*Hazard, Collections.*

1620.—Mayflower Compact.

This day, before we came to harbor, observing some not well affected to unity and concord . . . it was thought good there should be an association and agreement . . . to submit to such government and governors as we should by common consent agree to make and choose. . . .

In ye name of God, Amen. We . . . the loyall subjects of our dread Soveraigne Lord King James . . . haveing undertaken, for ye glorie of God, and advancemente of ye Christian faith and honour of our king & countrie, a voyage to plan ye first colonie in ye Northene parts of Virginia. Doe by these presents . . . in ye presence of God, and one of another, covenant & combine our selves togeather into a civill body politick; for our better ordering, and preservation & furtherance of ye ends aforesaid; and by vertue hearof to enacte, constitute and frame such just & equall lawes . . . as shall be thought most meete & convenient for ye generall good of ye colonie: unto which we promise all due submission and obedience. In witness whereof we have hereunder subscribed our names at Cap-Codd ye 11 of November . . . Anº Dom. 1620.—*Winthrop, History of Mass.*

1632.—Governor Winthrop tells us in his Journal that (2-17-163⅔)

The governour and assistants called before them divers of Watertown. . . . The occasion was, for that a warrant being sent to Watertown for levying of £8 . . . the pastor and elder, etc., assembled the people and delivered their opinions, that it was not safe to pay moneys after that sort, for fear of bringing themselves and posterity into bondage. . . After much debate, they acknowledged their fault. . . . The ground of their error was, for that they took this government to be no other but as of a mayor and aldermen, who have not power to make laws or raise taxations without the people; but understanding that this government was rather in the nature of a parliament, and that no assistant could be chosen but by the freemen . . . and therefore at every general court . . . they had free liberty . . . to declare their grievances . . . they were fully satisfied; and so their submission was accepted, and their offence pardoned." . . .

1634.—The general court came to a deadlock.

So when they could proceed no farther, the whole court agreed to keep a day of humiliation to seek the Lord, which accordingly was done, in all the congregations. [And then when they met again] although all were not satisfied . . . yet no man moved aught about it; . . . [and thus Puritan theology ruled and softened Puritan politics].—*Winthrop's Journal.*

1635.

At this court, one of the deputies was questioned for . . . affirming that the power of the governor was but ministerial, etc. He had also much opposed the magistrates, and slighted them, and used many weak arguments against the negative voice, as himself acknowledged upon record. He was adjudged by all the court to be disabled for three years from bearing any public office.—*Winthrop, History.*

1637.—For an interesting case of political division and party manipulation, see Hart, I, pp. 378-9.

1639.—Governor Winthrop gives us this very interesting view of theocratic government:

When the people have chosen men to be their rulers, and to make their laws, and bound themselves by oath to submit thereto, now to combine together . . . in a public petition to have any order repealed, which is not repugnant to the law of God, savors of resisting an ordinance of God . . . amounts to a plain reproof of those whom God hath set over them, and putting dishonor upon them, against the tenor of the fifth commandment.—*Winthrop, History.*

1646.—The Presbyterians demanded a share in the government.

We therefore desire that civill liberty and freedom be forthwith granted to all truely English, equall to the rest of their countrymen . . . and as all freeborne enjoy in our native country. . . . Further, that none of the English nation, who at this time are too forward to be gone, and very backward to come hither, be banished, unless they break the known lawes of England in so high a measure as to deserve so high a punishment . . . and we likewise desire that no greater punishments be inflicted upon offenders than are allowed and met by the laws of our native country.—*Hutchinson.*

1653.—In this year Massachusetts furnished the first American example of the nullification of a federal act—*i. e.*, of the New England Confederation.

It can be noe lesse then a contradiction to affeirme the Supreame power; which wee take to bee the Generall Courts of every Jurisdiction Can bee commanded by others an absurditie in pollicye; That an Intire gov'r'ment and Jurisdiction should prostitute itselfe to the comaund of Strangers; a Scandall in Religion that a generall court of Christians should bee oblidged to acte and engage upon the faith of six Delligates against theire consience all which must be admitted.—*Plymouth Records.*

1639. Connecticut.—"Fundamental Orders" made by "a Gen'all Cort at Harteford."

This constitution consists of eleven articles, but the lack of space necessitates very brief quotations.

. . . we . . . the Inhabitants and Residents of Windsor, Harteford and Wethersfield . . . doe . . . conjoyne our selves to be as one Publike State or Commonwealth . . to mayntayne . . . the liberty and purity of the gospell . . . as also in our Civill Affaires to be guided and governed according to such Lawes, Rules, Orders and decrees as shall be made . . . as followeth:

(1.) It is ordered . . . that there shall be yerely two generall Assemblies; . . . the first shall be called the Courte of Elections [to choose officers]. . . .

(5.) Also the other General Courte in September shall be for makeing of lawes. . . .

(10.) It is Ordered . . . that every Generall Courte . . . shall consist of the Governor . . . and 4 other Magistrats at lest, with the major p'te of the deputyes of the severall Townes legally chosen. . . —*Poore, Charters and Constitutions; also Hart, I.*

New York had a reform party and movement in 1650, and their leaders have left us their ideas of reform and good government. Colonization was not begun properly; for it was merely accidental, and was not intended. . . . Trade . . . is more suited for slaves than freemen, in consequence of the restrictions upon it and the annoyances which accompany the exercise of the right of inspection . . . [For years, too, not] any thing large or small,—worth relating, was done, built or made, which concerned or belonged to the commonalty, the church excepted.—*New York Historical Society, Collections.*

Care ought to be taken of the public property as well ecclesiastical as civil. . . . There should be a public school, . . . so that first of all in so wild a country, when there are many loose people, the youth be well taught and brought up, not only in reading and writing, but also in the knowledge and fear of the Lord. . . . There ought also to be an alms house, and an orphan asylum, and other similar institutions . . . the country must also be provided with godly, honorable and intelligent rulers who are not very indigent, or indeed, are not very covetous. . . .—*Documents relating to New York Colonial History.*

That none shall be admitted freemen or free Burgesses within our Town . . . but such Planters as are members of some or other of the Congregational Churches nor shall any but such be chosen to Magistracy or to Carry on any part of Civil Judicature, or as deputies or assistants, to have power to Vote In establishing Laws, and making or Repealing them or to any Chief Military Trust or Office. Nor shall any But such Church Members have any Vote in any such elections; Tho' all others admitted to be Planters have Right to their proper Inheritance, and do and shall enjoy all other Civil Liberties and Privileges. . . .—*Records of the Town of Newark, N. J.*

6. *Characteristics of colonial life.*

Massachusetts.—John Endicott wrote to Charles II. in 1661:

Your Servants are true Men, Fearers of God and of the King, not given to change, zealous of Government and order, orthodox and peaceable in Israel; we are not seditious as to the Interest of Cæsar, nor Schismaticks as to the matters of Religion; We distinguish between Churches and their Impurities, between a living Man, though not without Sickness or Infirmity, or no man; Irregularities either in ourselves or others we desire to be amended. [A most excellent description.]—*Hazard, Historical Collections.*

Samuel Newall, in 1692, enters in his diary the ominous note that

A Bill is sent in about calling a Fast and Convocation of Ministers that may be led in the right way as to the Witchcrafts. [And the next page we read about] 7 Balls of Fire that mov'd and mingled each with other. . . .—*Diary of Sewell in Mass. Hist. Society Collections.*

In 1631 Winthrop's diary gives us this item:

At this court . . . a servant . . . being convict . . . of most foul, scandalous invectives against our churches and government, was censured to be whipped, lose his ears, and be banished the plantation, which was presently executed.

Connecticut.—In the true Blue Laws of 1672 we read:

If any Man or Woman be a Witch . . . they shall be put to death.

[And] *forasmuch as the good education of Children is of singular behoof and benefit to any Colony, and whereas many Parents and Masters are too indulgent and negligent,* . . . If any man have a stubborn or rebellious Son . . . *sixteen years of age,* which will not obey . . . his Father or . . . Mother . . . then may his Father or Mother, being his natural Parents lay hold on him, and bring him to the Magistrates assembled in Court, and notifie . . . that their Son is Stubborn and Rebellious, and will not obey their voice and chastisement, but lives in sundry notorious Crimes, such a Son shall be put to death.

No man shall exercise any Cruelty towards any Bruit Creatures which are usually kept for the use of man. . . .—*Laws of Connecticut.*

John Josselyn, in 1674, after enumerating a number of punitory laws, sums up New Englanders:

Their great masters, as also some of their Merchants are damnable rich; generally all of their judgment, inexplicably covetous and proud, they receive your gifts but as an homage or tribute due to their transcendency, which is a fault their Clergie are also guilty of, whose living is upon the bounty of their hearers. . . . The chiefest objects of discipline, Religion, and morality they want, some are of a *Linsie-woolsie* disposition, of several professions in Religion, all like *Æthiopians* while in the Tent, only full of ludification and injurious dealing, and cruelty the extreamest of all vices.—*Hart, I, 495.*

Virginia.—In 1622 Capt. Nathaniel Butler tells us how he

found the plantations generally seated upon meer salt marshes, full of infectuous boggs and muddy creeks and lakes. Their houses are generally the worst that ever I saw, the meanest cottages in England being every way equal (if not superior) with the most of the best.

Tobacco only was the business, and for ought that I could hear every man madded upon that little thought or looked for anything else.—*Virginia Historical Society, Collections.*

Governor Berkeley, in his official report of 1671, tells us, too, that of

commodities of the growth of our country, we never had any but tobacco. Now for shipping we have admirable masts and very good oaks; but for iron ore I dare not say there is sufficient to keep one iron mill going for seven years.—*Berkeley's Report, Henning's Statutes of Va.*

Rev. John Clayton, writing on Tobacco Culture in 1686, tells us that in Virginia

'tis only the barrenest Parts that they have cultivated, by tilling and planting only the High-Lands, leaving the richer Vales unstirr'd, because they understand not anything of Draining. Therefore every three or four years they must be for clearing a new piece of ground out of Woods, which requires much Labour and Toil.   . Thus their Plantations run over vast Tracts of Ground, each ambitious or engrossing as much as they can, that they may be sure to have enough to plant . . . whereby the Country is thinly inhabited; the Living solitary and unsociable; Trading confused and dispersed; besides other Inconveniences. [And moreover] resolute they are and conceitedly bent to follow their old Practice and Custom, rather than to receive Directions from others, tho' plain, easi'e and advantageous. . . .—*Force's Tracts.*

Maryland. 1666.—Alsop's description.

He that desires to see the real Platform of a quiet and sober Government extant, Superiority with a meek and yet commanding power sitting at the Helme, steering the actions of a State quietly, through the multitude and adversity of Opinionous waves that diversely meet, let him look on Maryland . . . *the Miracle of this Age.—Hart, I, 263.*

Maine.—John Josselyn, in 1675, tells us of the Maine group:

The people . . . may be divided into Magistrates, Husbandmen, or Planters, and fishermen; of the Magistrates some be Royalists, the rest perverse Spirits, the like are the planters and fishers. . . .

The planters have a custom of taking tobacco, sleeping at noon, sitting long at meals sometimes four times a day, and now and then drinking a dram of the bottle extraordinarily: *the smoking of Tobacco, if moderately used refresheth the weary much, and so doth sleep.* . . .

If a man . . . came where they are roystering and gulling in *Wine* with a dear felicity, he must be sociable and *Roly-poly* with them, taking off their liberal cups as freely, or else be gone, which is best for him. . . .—*Josselyn, in Hart, I, 430.*

7. Religion.

The charters from 1584 on put religion as one of the chief motives of the crown in furthering colonization. Nor was this wholly a spiritual spirit with some, as the extract from Peckham given above shows a most keen appreciation of the commercial value of Christianity. But at any rate we always find the crown zealous for conversion—

it being the hon'r of our Crowne, [wrote Chas. II. to the Council in 1660,] and of the Protestant Religion, that all persons in any of our Dominions should be taught the knowledge of God, and be made acquainted with the misteries of Salvation.

William Bradford, in 1607, tells us how the English Puritans,

seeing themselves thus molested and that ther was no hope of their continuance ther [in England] . . . resolved to goe into ye Low-countries, wher they heard was freedom of Religion for all men.

FOUNDING OF THE COLONIES 17

[And from their wanderings and travels it came that] by these so publick troubls, in so many eminente places, their cause became famous, and occasioned many to look into ye same; and their godly cariage and Christian behaviour was such as left a deep impression in the minds of many. And though some few shrunk at these first conflicts, and sharp beginnings [as it was no marvell] yet many more came as with fresh courage, and greatly animated others.

When they resolved to leave Holland for America, to the thousand fears and ill prophecies,
it was answered that all great, and honorable actions, are accompanied with great difficulties; and must be, both enterprised, and overcome with answerable courages. It was granted ye dangers were great, but not desperate; the difficulties were many, but not invincible. For though their were many of them likly yet they were not certaine. . . . Their condition was not ordinarie; their ends were good and honorable; their calling lawfull, and urgente; and therfore they might expect ye blessing of God in their proceeding. . . .—*Bradford's History of Mass.*

We foresee from the above what Rev. Peter Bulkeley, in 1651, expressed as that to which New England was called.
There is no people but will strive to excell in some thing; what can we excell in, if not in holinesse? If we look to number, we are the fewest; If to strength, we are the weakest; If to wealth and riches, we are the poorest of all the people of God through the whole world; . . . and if we come short in grace and holinesse too, we are the most despicable people under heaven *. . . strive we therefore herein to excell and suffer not this crown to be taken away from us. . . —*Hart, I, 452.*

Massachusetts—The Massachusetts Company, in 1629, wrote to their colonists regarding their ministers that
because their Doctrine will hardly bee well esteemed whose persons are not reverenced, wee desire that both by your owne Example and by commanding all others to do the like, our Ministers may receive due Honor.—*Am. Antiquarian Society Proceedings.*

Only eight years later Governor Winthrop, when examining Anne Hutchinson, says to her:

Your conscience you must keep or it must be kept for you — [a most comprehensive critique on Puritan theology]— *Hutchison, History of Mass. Bay Colony.*

No time was lost in passing laws by which the church forced reverence from all. And things went on this way until, in 1660, Edward Burrough, an English Quaker, gained the king's ear for the miseries of the Massachusetts Quakers. One horrible example is enough:

Two beaten with *pitched ropes*, the blows amounting to *an hundred thirty-nine*, by which one of them was brought near unto death, much of his body being beat *like unto a jelly*, and one of their own Doctors, a Member of their Church, who saw him said, 'It would be a Miracle if ever he recovered, he expecting the flesh should rot off the bones'; who afterwards was banished upon pain of death.—*Hart, I, 484.*

In 1659 Mary Dyer, a condemned Quakeress, wrote a justification to the General Court:

Was ever the like Laws heard of among a People that profess Christ came in the flesh? And have such no other weapons but such Laws, to fight against *Spiritual Wickedness* withall, as you call it?—*Hart, I, 479.*

John Cotton, as sketched by John Norton in 1652, illustrates perfectly the solid and attractive parts of the Puritan minister:

He was a general Scholar, studious to know all things, the want whereof might in one of his profession be denominated ignorance. . . . He was a man of much Communion with God, and acquaintance with his own heart, observing the daily passages of his life. He had a deep sight into the Mystery of God's grace, and man's corruption, and large apprehensions of these things. . . . He began the Sabbath at evening [on Saturday]; therefore then performed Family-duty after supper, being larger than ordinary in Exposition, after which he Catechised his children and servants, and then returned into his Study. . . Upon his return from Meeting he returned again into his Study . . . unto his private devotion : where (having a small repast carried him up for his dinner) he continued till the tolling of the bell. The publick service being over, he withdrew for a space to his prementioned Oratory for his sacred addresses unto God as in the forenoon; then came down, repeated the sermon in the family, prayed, after supper sang a Psalm, and towards bed-time betaking himself again to his Study, he closed the day with prayer. . . . In his Study he neither sat down unto, nor arose from his meditations without prayer: whilst his eyes were upon his book his expectation was from God. He had learned to study because he had learned to pray.—*Hart, I, 337-38.*

Two entertaining Dutch travelers in New England in 1680 give us a very amusing, but rather caustic, account of religion in Boston. One of the ministers being sick, a day of fasting and prayer was observed.

In the first place a minister made a prayer in the pulpit, of full two hours in length; after which an old minister delivered a sermon an hour long, and after that a prayer was made, and some verses sung out of the psalms. In the afternoon, three or four hours were consumed with nothing except prayers, three ministers relieving each other alternately; when one was tired, another went up into the pulpit. There was no more devotion than in other churches, and even less than at New York; no respect, no reverence; in a word, nothing but the name of independents; and that was all.

The ministers seemed to be persons who seemed to possess zeal but no just knowledge of Christianity. The auditors were very worldly and inattentive. The best of the ministers . . . is a very old man, named John Eliot. . . .

They are all *Independents* in matters of religion, if it can be called religion; many of them perhaps more for the purposes of enjoying the benefit of its privileges than for any regard to truth and godliness. . . . All their religion consists in observing Sunday, by not working or going into the taverns on that day; but the houses are worse than the taverns. No stranger or traveler can therefore be entertained on a Sunday, which begins at sunset on Saturday, and continues until the same time on Sunday. At these two hours you see all their countenances change. Saturday evening the constable goes around into all the taverns of the city . . . stopping all noise and debauchery, which frequently causes him to stop his search, before his search causes the debauchery to stop. There is a penalty for cursing and swearing, such as they please to impose. . . Nevertheless, you discover little difference between this and other places. Drinking and fighting over there not less than elsewhere; and as to truth and true godliness, you must not expect more of them than of others.—*Long Island Hist. Society, Memoirs.*

Alas, the children were not all they should be, either. Chief Justice Sewall tells us how for

his playing at Prayer-time and eating when Return Thanks he whipped his boy Joseph "pretty smartly." [We do not wonder that even Puritan theology failed to repress hunger, but it is a shock to find that there was enough juvenility left to assert itself at such a critical moment.]

Rev. Nathaniel Wood, in 1647, sums up best the Puritan view of toleration in its most virulent form.

To tolerate more these indifferents is not to deale indifferently to God. The power of all Religion and Ordinances, lies in their purity: their purity is their simplicity; then are mixtures pernicious. That state is wise, that will improve all paines and patience rather to compose, then tolerate differences in Religion. He that is willing to tolerate any religion, or discripant way of Religion, besides his own, unless it be in matters meerly indifferent, either doubts of his own, or is not sincere in it. He that is willing to tolerate any unsound Opinion, that his own may also be tolerated, though never so sound, will for a need hang God's Bible at the Devills girdle. Every toleration of false Religion, or Opinions hath as many errors and sins in it, as all the false Religions and Opinions it tolerats and one sound one more. That State that will give Liberty of Conscience in matters of Religion, must give Liberty of Conscience and Conversation in their Morall Laws, or else the Fiddle will be out of tune. . . . There is no rule given by God for any State to give an affirmative Toleration to any false Religion, or Opinion whatsoever; *they must connive in some cases, but may not concede in any.—Hart, I, 394-95.*

Maryland.—It is a relief to turn from this to a colony where toleration was more worthily conceived of. In 1633 Lord Baltimore summed up his long instructions to the colonists with the injunction:

In fine . . . bee very carefull to do justice to every man w'th'out partiality [and the result was, as Alsop wrote in 1666, that] here the Roman Catholick and the Protestant Episcopal . . . concur in an unanimous parallel of friendship, and inseparable love infugled unto one another.

. . . The several Opinions and Sects . . . meet not together in mutinous contempts . . . but with a reverend quietness obeys the legal commands of Authority.

In 1649 the Maryland Assembly ruled that blaspheming, cursing, denial of or "reproachfull speeches, words or language concerning" the Trinity should be punished with death and forfeiture of goods. But in the same proclamation we read that

noe person . . . professing to beleive in Jesus Christ, shall from henceforth bee any waies troubled, Molested or discountenanced for or in respect of his or her religion nor in the free exercise thereof . . . nor any way compelled to the beleife or exercise of any other Religion against his or her consent, so as they be not unfaithfull to the Lord Proprietary, or molest or conspire against the civill governem't.
. . . —*Archives of Maryland*, by Browne.

Virginia.—

In Virginia the families . . . being seated . . . at such distances from each other, many of them are very remote from the House of God, though placed in the middest of them. Many Parishes as yet want both Churches and Gleabes, and I think not above a fifth part of them are supplyed with Ministers, where there are Ministers the people meet together Weekly, but once upon the Lord's day, and sometimes not at all, being hindered by . . *. the length or tediousness of the way, through extremities of heat in Summer, frost and Snow in Winter, and tempestuous weather in both. . . . —*Hart*, I, 295.

Rhode Island.—To be contrasted with Ward on toleration we have R. Williams, writing in 1670.

Forced worship stinks in God's nostrils. In these flames about religion . . . there is no other prudent, christian way of preserving peace in the world but by permission of differing consciences. . . . —*Mass. Hist. Society, Collections.*

And Governor Peleg Sandford, in his official report, in 1680, writes:

We leave every Man to walke as God shall persuade their hartes, and doe actively and passively yield obedience to the Civill Magistrate and doe not actively disturb the Civill peace

. . . and have liberty to frequent any meetings of worship for their better instruction and information. . . . —
Greene, History of Rhode Island.

Connecticut.—Blue laws of 1672:

If any person . . . Blaspheme the Name of God the Father, Son or Holy Ghost . . . or shall curse in like manner, he shall be put to death.

New York.—Governor Thomas Dougan, of New York, in 1687, writes:

Here bee not many of the Church of England; few Roman Catholicks; abundance of Quakers preachers men and Women especially; Singing Quakers, Ranting Quakers, Sabbatarians; Anti sabbatarians; some Anabaptists some Independents; some Jews; *in short of all sorts of opinions there are some, and the most part of none at all.—Documentary History of New York.*

Before this, in 1679, Dankers and Sluyter went to religious service in New York.

As it is not strange in these countries to have men as ministers who drink, we could imagine nothing else than that he had been drinking a little this morning. His text was, *Come unto me all ye*, etc., but he was so rough that even the roughest and most godless of our sailors were astonished.

QUESTIONS ON THE TEXT.

1. Name the reasons given for colonizing. 2. What class of emigrants came, judging from the text? 3. What change between 1637 and 1660 in regard to allowing emigration? 4. What do the accounts in regard to ocean voyages show in regard to character of emigrants? 5. What did the early voyagers say regarding the Indians? 6. How did the king dispose of part of the land? 7. How were settlers enticed to come to America? 8. How did the settlers in Virginia get wives? 9. What land was granted in the first charter, 1606? 10. What classes were stockholders in the second charter, 1609? 11. When did the first House of Burgesses of Virginia sit? *12. What contest in regard to taxes between the people of Watertown and Massachusetts Bay? 13. What can you learn from the Mayflower compact? 14. Meaning of the punishment of a deputy for questioning the right of the governor to the "negative voice." 15. What did Winthrop believe in regard to his power as governor? 16. What religious denominations complained of their treatment? 17. When and what was the first popular constitution? 18. Can you find any indications of a spirit of rebellion? 19. Were the Puritans superstitious? 20. Were their laws harsh? their punishments? 21. Name the industries you find men-

tioned. 22. Were they good farmers? 23. Trace the journey of the Pilgrims from England to Plymouth. 24. Were the Puritans tolerant? 25. What kind of a man was Rev. John Cotton? 26. What does the testimony prove in regard to the morals of the colonists? 27. What peculiar attribute do you find in Maryland? 28. What colony would you have preferred to live in? why?

SUGGESTIVE QUESTIONS.

a. How would you explain the intolerant spirit so often manifested? *b.* Point out institutions existing now that had their beginning in 17th century. *c.* Did the theory and the practice of the Puritan coincide? *d.* Trace the development of witchcraft. Do you find its basis in life depicted in above extracts? *e.* Name the lessons you may learn from this study?

American History Studies

No 2. OCTOBER, 1897.

THE DEVELOPMENT OF UNION AMONG THE COLONIES.

SELECTIONS MADE FROM THE SOURCES

BY

H. W. CALDWELL,

UNIVERSITY OF NEBRASKA.

J. H. MILLER, Publisher,
LINCOLN, NEBRASKA.

Yearly Subscription, 40 cents.   Single Copy, 5 cents.

PUBLISHED MONTHLY, EXCEPT JULY AND AUGUST.

Entered as second-class matter at the Post Office, Lincoln, Nebraska, U. S. A.

AMERICAN HISTORY STUDIES.

DEVELOPMENT OF UNION AMONG THE COLONIES.

I.

THE several colonies were planted at different times, by different interests, and in some cases by different races. The geography of the country was such that there was very little communication and intercourse between the various colonies for many years. The soil and climate also tended to produce divergent interests and civilizations. The intolerant religious spirit of the age lent itself also to the same tendency. On the whole, one sometimes wonders that the colonies came together as easily as they did in support of interests that were not always clearly in common.

It is very difficult frequently to find an extract that is sufficiently condensed and pointed, which may be cited, to bring out some force that tended to prevent union or was, on the other hand, aiding it. Especially have I found it difficult to get quotable extracts on the effects of geography. In general it is by inference only that one gathers his conclusions. In the extracts given it has in general seemed best to give those that brought out the salient movements looking toward union, rather than to give those that emphasized the divergent tendencies of the time. I wish to emphasize the fact that the study of sources means that every word and phrase is to receive careful consideration. The value of the training consists to a considerable extent in acquiring the ability to read between the lines, to draw inferences, to find the spirit or motive which prompted to word or act.

It is hoped that the extracts quoted this month may illustrate not only the fact that various attempts to unite were made, but also drive home the character of the union possible, and the kind of union which the colonies sought and which the mother country attempted to force on them. It will be an interesting exercise to trace the expansion of the idea of union and to classify the factors which were at work; also to follow the changes in the nature of the union which were outlined in the various proposals from 1643 to 1776. Less weight has been given to the congresses of 1765 and 1774 than might seem necessary from their prominence. The reason for this is that the union movement then was rather unconscious, an accessory to the more palpable thoughts,—first that of a redress of grievances, and later that of independence. The Causes of the Revolution, which will be our subject for next month, will give us the opportunity to study this period as it deserves.

The extracts this month are taken largely from the colonial records as reprinted by the various states. Massachusetts began this work as early as 1792 and has developed it till now her various historical publications are numbered almost by the hundreds. New York has also reprinted, or printed from manuscript, thousands of pages of letters, laws, reports, and other documents. The same is true of Connecticut and other states. It is from these documents that we can draw and yet scarcely make an impression in the limited space at our command.

I wish to thank the many who write words of encouragement concerning the work which we are attempting to outline. Certainly the idea that history may be studied in part from the sources in our graded schools is spreading. In some cases it is well done, as I know by receipt of the results in the form of papers. I desire to call the attention of teachers elsewhere to the plan of the West Superior, Wis., schools, where the papers are printed in a neat little volume, 100 copies printed, costing less than $16. The local paper published each student paper as it was completed, then put them together at a mere nominal cost. I doubt not that every town has some local paper that would do likewise. Principal Griffin has evidently found an added incentive to good work, and even to real contributions to local history in some cases.

But I wish also to say that some criticisms come to me. One teacher suggests that the spelling of her pupils is not improved by working over the old manuscripts. Shall the spelling be modernized, or shall we have the old flavor of our forefathers, trusting to some device to avoid the evil, if such it be, of which mention has been made? Will not the teachers discuss this question pro and con in letters to me? Perhaps a more serious danger is suggested by another who says: How do we know that Mr. Caldwell can or does make extracts in such a way as to give a true picture of the times? How do we know that the writers he cites are representative, are good witnesses? Well, the mere fact that such questions can be asked shows that in part, at least, our work is done. The critical faculty is awake, and the word of any one text will perhaps not necessarily be unhesitatingly followed hereafter. I can only answer that I try to be fair. My judgment is not infallible, and my knowledge is not encyclopædic, so I can only ask such confidence as an honest desire deserves. By all means correct me by every available source, and the end that we seek will be gained.

II.

As early as 1637 references may be found in the colonial records pointing to a desire for union among the colonies. The following extracts will afford some insight into the motives and spirit that animated them in their actions at this time:

It is ordered that the letter lately sent to the Governor by Mr. Eaton, Mr. Hopkins, Mr. Haynes, Mr. Coddington, & Mr. Brereton, . . . , shalbee thus answered by the Governor: that the Court doth assent to all the ppositions (propositions) layde downe in the aforesaid letter, but that the answere shalbee directed to Mr. Eaton, Mr. Hopkins, & Mr. Haynes, onely excluding Mr. Coddington & Mr. Brenton, as men not to bee capitulated wthall by us, either for themselves or the people of the iland (Rhode Island) where they inhabite, as their case standeth.℮ [Oct. 7, 1640.]—*Massachusetts Colonial Records, I, p. 305.*

1. At this court (7 Mo. 22 day 1642) the propositions sent from Connecticut [to Massachusetts] about a combination, &c were read, and referred to a committee to consider of after the court, who meeting, added some few cautions and new articles, and for the taking in of Plimouth (who were now willing,) and Sir Ferdinando Gorges province, and so returned them back to Connecticut, to be considered upon against the spring, for winter was now approaching, and there could be no meeting before, etc.—*Winthrop, History of New England, II, pp. 102–103.*

2. At this court (Mo. 8, 10, 1643) came the commissioners from Plimouth, Connecticut and New Haven, viz: from Plimouth Mr. Edward Winslow and Mr. Collins, from Connecticut Mr. Haynes and Mr. Hopkins, with whom Mr. Fenwick of Saybrook joyned, from New Haven Mr. Theophilus Eaton and Mr. Grigson. Our court chose a committee to treat with them viz: the governour [John Winthrop] and Mr. Dudley, and Mr. Brodstreet, being of the magistrates; and of the deputies, Captain Gibbons, Mr. Tyng the treasurer and Mr. Hathorn. These coming to consultation encountered some difficulties, but being all desirous of union and studious of peace, they readily yielded each to other in such things as tended to common utility, &c, so as in some two or three meetings they lovingly accorded upon these ensuing articles, which, being allowed by, our court,

and signed by all the commissioners, were sent to be also ratified by the general courts of other jurisdictions; . . .—*Winthrop, History of New England, vol. II, p. 121f.*

By reason of ye plottings of the Narigansets, . . . the Indians were drawn into a general conspiracie against ye English in all parts, as was in part discovered ye yeare before . . . ; [this caused the Colonies] to thinke of means how to prevente ye same, and secure them selves. Which made them enter into this neu union & confederation following. [The articles follow.]—*Bradford, History of Plymouth Plantation, p. 416.*

ARTICLES OF CONFEDERATION.

WHEREAS we all came into these parts of America with the same end and aim, namely, to advance the kingdom of our Lord Jesus Christ, and to enjoy the liberties of the gospel in purity with peace; and whereas by our settling, by the wise providence of God, we are further dispersed upon the seacoast and rivers than was at first intended, so that we cannot, according to our desire, with convenience communicate in one government . . . : and whereas we live encompassed with people of several nations and strange languages, which hereafter may prove injurious to us or our posterity; and for as much as the natives have formerly committed sundry insolences, . . . and have of late combined themselves against us, and seeing by reason of the sad distractions in England (which they have heard of,) and by which they know we are hindered . . . of seeking advice, and reaping . . . protection, which at other times we might well expect; we therefore do conceive it our bounden duty, . . . to enter into a present consociation . . . for mutual help and strength . . . , that, as in nation and religion, so in other respects, we be and continue one, . . . :

I. Wherefore it is fully agreed . . . between parties above named, . . . that they . . . be called by the name of the United Colonies of New England.

II. These united colonies . . . enter into a firm and perpetual league of friendship and amity . . . both for preserving and propagating the truth and liberties of the gospel, and for . . . safety . . .

III. It is further agreed, that the plantations which at present are or hereafter shall be settled within the limits of the Massachusetts, shall be forever under the government of the

Massachusetts, and shall have jurisdiction among themselves in all cases as an entire body; [same provision follows in regard to Connecticut, Plymouth, and New Haven.] . ; provided that no other jurisdiction shall . . . be taken in as a distinct head or member of this confederation, nor shall any other . . . be received by any of them; nor shall any two . . . join in one jurisdiction, without consent of the rest, . . .

IV. It is also . . . agreed, that the charge of all just wars, . . . shall, both in men and provisions . . be borne, . . , in manner following, viz. [in proportion to number of males from 16 to 60 years of age.]

V. It is further agreed, that if any of these jurisdictions, . . . be invaded by any enemy whatsoever, upon notice and request of any three [or two under conditions] magistrates of that jurisdiction so invaded, the rest of the confederates, . . . shall . . . send aid . . . [as follows:] Massachusetts one hundred men [furnished] . . . , and each of the rest 45 men so armed . . .

VI. It is also agreed, that for the managing . . . of all affairs . . . concerning the whole confederation, commissioners shall be chosen [as follows:] two for the Massachusetts, two for Plimouth, two for Connecticut, and two for New Haven, all in church fellowship with us, . . . to hear . . . and determine . . . all affairs of war or peace, leagues, aids, charges, . . [This section also specifies place of meeting, etc.]

VIII. . . . It is also agreed, that if any servant run away from his master into any of these confederate jurisdictions, . . . upon certificate of one magistrate in the jurisdiction out of which the said servant fled, . . . the said servant shall be delivered to his master . . . [In general the same provision in regard to criminals.]

XI. [The last article pertains to breaches of the articles.]

Lastly, this perpetual confederation, and the several articles and agreements . . . were . . . certified [as completed] at the next meeting held in Boston, (7.) 7, 1643. —*Winthrop, History of New England, vol. II, p. 121f.*

The English Commissioners to New England, in 1665, pass the following, among other resolutions:

There is no power in the charter [of Massachusetts] to incorporate with other colonies, nor to exercise any power by that association: both belongs to the kings prerogative. If there be any other undecent expressions & repetitions of the word "commonwealth," "state," and the like, in other pages, wee desire they may bee changed.—*Massachusetts Colonial Records, vol. IV, pt. 2, p. 213.*

To this the General Court of Massachusetts sent the following reply:

. . . And also considering that they were severall colonjes under one king, & come from their native country for one & the same end, & were here scattered at a great distance amongst the wild salvages in a vast wilderness, had no walled tounes or garrisons of souldjers for their defence, they apprehended the least they could doe was to enter into a league of amity and union one with another, ingaging, . . . jointly to assist each other . . . , this being the end of their then confœderating, . . . to the end that as our distance of place one from another rendered us weake, & layd us open to their rage and violence, so our union might be as well to them a terror as to us strength; & through the goodness of God, wee have hitherto had large experience of the great good that by this confœderation hath redounded, not only to all his majesties subjects here planted, but even to the natives themselves, it having been a means to prevent much trouble & bloodshed among themselves, so that although since that warr [the Pequod] some of them have . . put us to a considerable charge . . , yet no massacre hath beene among us from that day to this, blessed be God for it.—*Massachusetts Colonial Records, vol. IV, pt. 2, p. 231.*

Again, the General Court says that the commissioners seem to desire

to make a flame in the country . . by their high favors to discontented persons, & great countenance given to the Road Islanders, whose first rise and continuance hath beene such to the other colonjes as is not unknowne to any discreet observer in these parts; and on the other hand, calling . . . the United Colonjes that usurped authoritje contrary to the light of reason, . . . which therefore made it seeme to be their speciall design to disunite the colonjes & so to bring us unto ruine.—*Ib., pp. 233-34.*

To the Assembly of Maryland, by Jacob Leisler.

A. D. 1689: 29th September in the fort of New York.

GENTLEMEN—I have received your acceptable letter the

18 of this instant & communicated as directed, wee have considered the contents with due affection, & . . . embrace with all our hearts your offers of a mutuall & amiable correspondence with you, which we shall labor to keep & preserve inviolable towards you, and without fail shall omitt nothing that may appeare any wayes to your intrest peace & welfare as we also doe with Boston & Connecticutt collony being of the same opinion with you, that it is the onely means to preserve . . . their majestie's interests. [King William and Queen Mary]. . . [Similar letters sent to Mass., Conn., etc.]—*Documentary History of New York*, vol. II, p. 19.

Agents of four colonies and several Indian chiefs met in 1684 to consider union. One of the sachems addressed the Massachusetts agent as follows:

We all, namely, our governor, the governor of Virginia and the Massachusetts Coloney, and Maquese, are in one covenant. We do plant here a great tree of peace, whose branches spread so far as the Massachusetts Coloney, Virginia, Maryland, and all that are in friendship with us and do live in peace, unity, and tranquility, under the shade of said tree.—*Mass. Archives*, *XXX*, *p. 303*, *cited in Frothingham.*

Governor Treat, of Connecticut, wrote to Governor Bradstreet, July 31, 1689, in part, as follows:

I hope we shall be willing in the season of it, to revive the ancient confederation upon just terms and articles, holding forth a right consideration of our state compared with the other colonies.—*Frothingham, Rise of the U. S. Republic*, p. 87, note.

Governor Bradsteet wrote, February 3, 1689-90, in the same spirit:

All true Englishmen [ought] to lay aside their private animosities and intestine discords, and to unite against the common enemy.—*Ib., 88.*

Circular to the Governors of the several provinces:

NEW YORK, Aprill 2d, 1690:

HONBLE SIR:—[After stating danger from French and Indians, Governor Loister says, we] have likewise communicated the same to the Governor of Boston, & the gentlemen of Connecticutt are likewise advertised thereof, in so much that wee propose for a generall assistance that such persons as to you shall seem meet may be commissioned to treat with them of New England, Virginia, pensilvania and Jerseys, . . that we may conclude what may conduce most to the King's intrest, wellfare of the provinces. . . .—*Documentary History of New York, vol. II, p. 117.*

A. D. 1690 ye 30 Apprill : in N. Yorke.

GENTLEMENS—Last monday arrived heer the Comintioners off [of] Boston Plimouth en Caneticot who have been taking [talking] off several businis concurning the Indian war. . . [Signed Jacob Leisler.]—*Ib., p. 133.*

N. YORKE, Primo May 1690.

At a meeting of ye commissioners of ye Province of New York & ye collonies of ye Massachusetts, Plymouth & Connecticut,

It is concluded . . . that each of ye Collonies aforesd shall Provide and furnish ye undermenconed proporcons of Souldiers with Answerable Provisions at their own Charges to Be sent with all Speed:—

viz :

By New Yorke four hundred...................... 400
By Massachusetts Colony one hundred & sixty...... 160
By Connecticut Colony one hundred & thirty five.... 135
By Plymouth Colony sixty........................ 60
By Maryland by Promise one hundred.............. 100

In all eight hundred fifety five................. 855

Further agreed [various things mentioned] That ye Officers Be required to maintain good order Amongst ye Soldiers to discountenance & Punish Vice & as much as may be to Keep ye Sabbath and Maintain ye Worship of God.

JACOB LEISLER.
WILLIAM STOUGHTON.
SAML SEWELL.
P. D. LANCY.
JOHN WALLEY.
NATHAN GOLD.
WILLIAM PETKIN.

—*Massachusetts Archives,* XXXVI, 47.

Leisler in a letter to the governments of New Jersey, Pennsylvania, and Rhode Island, attempting to secure additional aid, said:

I hope you will not be wanting so blessed a work at this time to please God and our gracious king. Losing the opportunity and neglecting the season may cause the next generation to curse us.—*Frothingham, p. 93.*

Though the French colony contains, perhaps, not 30000 men capable to bear arms; yet these are all under the despotic command and sole direction of their Governor-General, . . . The strength of our colonies, on the other hand, is divided, and the concurrence of all necessary both for supplies of men and money. Jealous they are of each other; some ill constituted; others shaken with intestine divisions, and if I may be allowed the expression, parsimonious even to prodigality. Our assemblies are diffident of their Governors; Governors despise their assemblies, and both mutually misrepresent each other to the court of Great Britain. Military measures demand secrecy and dispatch; but while the colonies remain divided, and nothing can be transacted but with their universal assent, it is impossible to maintain the one or proceed with the other. Without a general constitution for warlike operations, we can neither plan nor execute. We have a common interest, and must have a common council; *one head* and *one purse*. [An extract from a letter supposed to have been written by Gov. Livingston of New York, and his friends Messrs. W. Smith and Scott, 1756.]—*Massachusetts Hist. Society Col., series I, vol. VII, pp. 161-62.*

Mr. Nelson's memorial about the state of the northern colonies in America:

24 Sept: 1696.

Fifthly I am now to make another remark upon the principall, and greatest defect and mistake, in which we have been, and are yet under, I meane the number and independency of so many small Governments, whereby our strength is not only divided and weakened, but by reason of their severall interests, are become and doe in a manner esteeme each as foreigners the one unto the other, soe that whatever mischiefs doth happen in one part, the rest by the reason of this disunion remaine unconcerned and our strength thereby weakened; whereas were the Colonies of New England,

Hampshire, Road Island, Conecticot, New York joined in one, we then should be near to [ten?] or 15 for one of those of the French in Canada, and might reasonably propose . . . to make an entire conquest of that place. . .
—*New York Colonial Records, vol. IV, p. 209.*

MR. PENN'S PLAN OF UNION. [1698].

A Briefe and Plaine Scheam how the English Colonies in the North parts of America, viz: Boston, Connecticut, Road Island New York New Jerseys, Pensilvania, Maryland, Virginia and Carolina may be made more usefull to the Crowne, and to one anothers peace and safty with an universall concurrence.

1st. That the Severall colonies before mentioned do meet once a year, and oftener if need be, during the war, and at least once in two years in times of peace, by their stated and appointed deputies, to debate and resolve . . . [on measures for public good.]

2. That in order to it two persons well qualified for sence sobriety and substance be appointed by each Province, as their Representatives . . [in Congress].

3. That the Kings Commissioner for that purpose specially appointed shall have the Chaire and preside in the said Congresse.

4. [Central meeting place.]

5. [Suggests governor of New York as King's Commissioner.]

6. That their business shall be to hear and adjust all matters of Complaint or difference between Province and Province. As 1st where persons quit their own Province and goe to another, that they may avoid their just debts . . ., 2d where offenders fly justice, . . ., 3dly to prevent or cure injuries in point of commerce, 4th, to consider of ways and means to support the union and safety of these Provinces against the publick enemies In which Congresse the Quotas of men and charges will be much easier, and more equally sett, than it is possible for any establishment made here to do; for the Provinces, knowing their own condition and one anothers, can debate that matter with more freedome, and satisfaction and better adjust and ballance their affairs in all respects for their common safty.

7ly That in times of war the Kings High Commissionr shall be generall or Chief Commander .—*New York Colonial Documents, vol. IV, p. 296.*

From the scheme of Gov. Livingston, recommended to the Lords of Trade, May 13, 1701:

> To settle the American Governments to the greatest possible advantage, it will be necessary to reduce the number of them; in some places to unite and consolidate; in others to separate and transfer; and in general to divide by natural boundaries instead of imaginary lines. If there should be but one form of government established for the North-American provinces, it would greatly facilitate the reformation of them. . . . . A nobility appointed by the king for life and made independent, would probably give strength and stability to American governments as effectually as hereditary nobility does to that of Great Britain.—*Cited in Frothingham, p. 117.*

Shirley says in a letter dated Oct. 21, 1754, to Governor Morris, newly appointed governor of Pennsylvania:

> The best advice I can give you is to lose no time for promoting the plan of a union of the colonies for their mutual defence, to be concerted at home, and established by act of Parliament as soon as possible . I am laboring this point *totis viribis.—Ibid, p. 146.*

Daniel Coxe, 1722, proposed that all the British colonies be

> united under a legal, regular, and firm establishment, over which a lieutenant or supreme governor should be constituted and appointed to preside on the spot, to whom the governors of each colony should be subordinate; . . . that two deputies should be annually elected by the council and assembly of each province, who are to be in the nature of a great council or general convention of the states of the colonies [to fix on quotas of men and money which] should be levied and raised by its own assembly in such manner as they should judge most easy and convenient.—*Cited by Frothingham, p. 113.*

About 1725, when a proposal had been made by the Massachusetts assembly for a convention of all the colonies, it was pronounced by the Board of Trade as "a mutinous proposal."—*Hutchinson's History of Mass.*, vol. III, p. 119.

The following extracts give us an insight into the conditions from the standpoint of the colonial governors:

Reasons why this great undertaking of building of New Forts &c extending the English settlements into the Indian country is not effected as begun by this Province alone.

6thly. We have late experience how ineffectual Her Majesty's circular letters in the late war did prove, appointing the several Governors to send Commissioners to New York to agree upon certain quotas of men, and for a supply of money, and tho' the Governors of Virginia and Maryland did prevail with their people to assist us with some money, yet could not prevail with them to send any men; some of the commissioners came others came not; those that came refused to act without the rest, and gave reason enough to believe they were fond of the opportunity of that colour, by various excuses, doubts, fears and jealousies; so parted doing nothing.—*New York Colonial Documents, vol. IV, 873.*

To carry on this design of extending the Christian settlements and English forts into the Indian country for the security of all His Majesty's Plantations on this North Continent of America;—

I humbly begg leave to propose that it is best to be done in time of peace with France. 1st That one form of government be establish'd in all the neighbouring colonies on this main continent.

That they be divided into three distinct governments—to-wit.

That Virginia and Maryland be annexed to South and North Carolina.

That some part of Connecticut, New York, East and West Jersey, Pennsylvania and New Castle be added together.

And that to Massachusetts be added New Hampshire and Rhoad Island and the rest of Connecticut.—*Ibid, p. 874.*

The degree of union is well illustrated by the following extract from a letter of Gov. Fletcher:

Our neighbours on the Right and left sitt at ease, they govern by theire own Fancies, Connecticutt full of people keep up a Comonwealth Power, oppress the better sort who dissent from them but will not send a man or sixpence to our relief.

And from that Collony I could march up men dry foot to Repell our Enemies, from hence we have a voyage of fifty leagues to Albany, In my absence the Councill here writ to all the neighbouring Collonies for men or money, the Republick of Connecticutt quarrell att the Superscription of the Councills letter for want of theire proper Title.—*Ibid.*

From Pensilvania they say they have nothing to send us but theire good wishes. East Jersey has sent us £248 and promiss to make itt £400 those remoter Collonies I have not yet heard from. .... Nothing in my sight but an addition of Connecticutt and some other Colonys can support us by paying equall duties to the Crown, the Acts of Navigation are wholy violated by these out lyers. ... I send this to Boston in hopes of a passage from thence if Sr William Phips do not intecept it.—*New York Colonial Documents, vol. IV, p. 13.*

The governor of New York writes as follows of the conditions in America:

Notwithstanding their Majst Lett^{rs} Mandatorie to the several governments to assist this Province little or no assistance had been given or can be hoped for through the remoteness of some Governments and Excuses and delays of others.

That Pensilvania being most Quakers will give no men or money for warr unless they were joined to the Government of New York, by which that Province may be able to outvote them.

That this Province lying under heavy Taxes and Pressures, most of the young men and those that can in any way remove, depart this Province to the neighbouring Government where they are wholly free from Tax or any other Contrybution towards the Common Security.—*Ibid, p. 53.*

A NEW STAGE—THE ALBANY CONGRESS—INSTRUCTIONS TO COMMISSIONERS.

William Shirley, Esq. Captain General and Governor in Chief in and over his Majesty's Province of Massachusetts Bay in New England,

To Samuel Welles, John Chandler, Thomas Hutchinson, Oliver Partridge, and John Worthington Esq'rs Greeting. Whereas, in pursuance of letters from the right honorable the Lords Commissioners for Trade and the Plantations, ... a General Convention of Commissioners for their respective Governments is appointed to be held at the city of **Albany** in the month of June next [1754] for holding an interview with the Indians of the Five Nations and making them presents on the part of said Governments usual upon such occasions, in order to confirm and establish their ancient attachment to his Majesty and their constant friendship to his Majesty's subjects on this continent; and whereas the Great and General Court or assembly of the Province of Massachusetts Bay aforesaid, have elected and appointed you to represent and appear for said Province at the Convention aforesaid for the purposes abovementioned; as also for entering into articles of Union and Confederation with the aforesaid Governments for the general defence of his Majesty's subjects and interests in North America, as well in time of peace as of war:—

Now I do, by these presents, empower and commissionate you, the said Samuel Wells, John Chandler, Thomas Hutchinson, Oliver Partridge, and John Worthington, as Commissioners (or any three of you) to appear for and represent the Province of Massachusetts Bay aforesaid.

Given under my hand and the public seal of the Province of Massachusetts Bay aforesaid, the nineteenth day of April, 1754, in the twenty seventh year of his Majesty's reign.

W. SHIRLEY.

By his Excellency's command:
J. WILLARD, *Secretary.*
A true copy.

Attest: SAMUEL WELLER
JOHN CHANDLER.
OL'R PARTRIDGE.
JOHN WORTHINGTON.

Similar instructions were given to the commissioners from the other provinces.—*Massachusetts Historical Collections,* vol. V, 3d series, p. 9.

It was proposed by the Governor, that to avoid all disputes about the precedency of the colonies, they should be named in the minutes according to their situation from north to south; which was agreed to.—*Ibid, p. 26.*

A motion was made that the Commissioners deliver their opinion whether a Union of all the Colonies is not at present absolutely necessary to their security and defence. The question was accordingly put, and it was decided in the affirmative unanimously. . . . Which proposal the Board determined to proceed upon after they had considered some method of effecting the Union between the Colonies.—*Ibid. pp. 27-28.*

After debates held on the plan of a Union, it was moved if the Board should proceed to form the plan of a Union of the Colonies, [it ought] to be established by an Act of Parliament.—*Ibid, p. 39.*

That the said Colonies being in a divided disunited, state, there has never been any joint exertion of their force or counsels to repel or defeat the measures of the French, and particular Colonies are unable and unwilling to maintain the cause of the whole.—*Ibid, p. 67.*

It is proposed that humble application be made for an Act of parliament of Great Britain, by virtue of which one general government may be formed in America, including all the said colonies, within and under which government each colony may retain its present constitution, except in the particulars wherein a change may be directed by the said Act, as hereinafter follows. . . .

That the said general government be administered by a President-General, to be appointed and supported by the Crown; and a Grand Council, to be chosen by the representatives of the people of the several Colonies met in their respective Assemblies.

That the House of Representatives [of each colony] may and shall choose members for the Grand Council, in the following proportion, that is to say,

Massachusetts	7	Maryland	4
New Hampshire	2	Virginia	7
Connecticut	5	North Carolina	4
Rhode Island	2	South Carolina	4
New York	4		
New Jersey	3		48
Pennsylvania	6		

. . That there shall be a new election of members of the Grand Council every three years. . . .

That after the first three years, when the proportion of money arising out of each colony to the general treasury can be known, the number of members to be chosen for each colony shall from time to time . . . , be regulated by that proportion, yet so as that the number to be chosen by any one province be not more than seven, nor less than two.

. . .

That the assent of the President-General be requisite to

all acts of the Grand Council, and that it be his office and duty to cause them to be carried into execution. . . .

That they raise and pay soldiers and build forts for the defence of any of the colonies, and equip vessels of force to guard the coasts and protect the trade on the ocean, lakes or great rivers; but they shall not impress men in any colony, without the consent of the Legislature.

That for these purposes they have power to make laws, and lay and levy such general duties, imposts or taxes, as to them shall appear most equal and just (considering the ability and other circumstances of the inhabitants in the several colonies), and such as may be collected with the least inconvenience to the people; rather discouraging luxury, than loading industry with unnecessary burdens.

. . . That laws made by them for the purposes aforesaid shall not be repugnant, but, as near as may be, agreeable to the laws of England, and shall be transmitted to the King in Council for approbation, as soon as may be after their passing, and if not disapproved within three years after presentation, to remain in force. . . .

And all civil officers are to be nominated by the Grand Council, and to receive the President-General's approbation before they officiate.—*Ib., pp. 70-73.*

Franklin, in 1789, speaks of the results of the rejection of the Albany plan of union of 1754 as follows:

On reflection, it now seems probable that, if the foregoing plan, or something like it had been adopted and carried into execution, the subsequent separation of the colonies from the Mother-country might not so soon have happened, nor the mischiefs suffered on both sides have occurred, perhaps, during another century. For the colonies, if so united, would have really been, as they then thought themselves, sufficient to their own defence,—and being trusted with it, as by the plan, an army from Britain for that purpose, would have been unnecessary. The pretenses for framing the Stamp Act would then not have existed, nor the other projects for drawing a revenue from America to Britain by acts of parliament, which were the cause of the breach, and attended with such terrible expense of blood and treasure, so that the different parts of the empire might still have remained in peace and union. But the fate of this plan was singular. After many days' thorough discussion of all its ars, in Congress, it was unanimously agreed to, and copies ordered to be sent to the assembly of each province for concurrence, and one to the ministry in England for approbation of the crown.

The crown disapproved it, as having too much weight in the democratic part of the constitution, and every assembly as having allowed too much to prerogative; so it was totally rejected.—*Cited in Frothingham, p. 149.*

Nothing can exceed the jealousy and emulation which they possess in regard to each other. The inhabitants of Pennsylvania and New York have an inexhaustible source of animosity in their jealousy for the trade of the Jerseys. Massachusetts Bay and Rhode Island are not less interested in that of Connecticut . . were they left to themselves, there would soon be a civil war from one end of the continent to the other.—*Ib., p. 152.*

The circular to the various colonies, prepared by the legislature of Massachusetts, calling for a congress of the colonies, dated July 8, 1765, reads as follows:

SIR,—The House of Representatives of this province, in the present session of General Court, have unanimously agreed to propose a meeting . . . of committees from the houses of representatives or burgesses of the several British colonies on this continent, [give reasons] and to consider of a general and united . . . representation of their condition. . . —*Niles, Principles and Acts of the American Revolution, p. 156.*

In organizing the Congress Oct 7, 1765, it was decided that the committee of each colony shall have one voice (vote) only in determining any question that shall rise in the congress.—*Ib., 162.*

Wednesday, Oct. 9th, 1765, A. M.— . . . The congress resumed the consideration of the rights and privileges of the British American colonists, &c. . . —*Ib., 162.*

Thursday, Oct. 24, 1765, A. M.— . . . The Congress took into consideration the manner in which their several petitions should be preferred and solicited in Great Britain, and thereupon came to the following determination, viz:

It is recommended by the Congress to the several colonies to appoint special agents for soliciting relief from their present grievances, and to unite their utmost interests and endeavors for that purpose.—*Ib., 163.*

One stanza of a "song sung at Boston, in New England," 1765, entitled "Advice from the Country," is of interest in this connection:

> With us of the woods
> Lay aside your fine goods,
> Contentment depends not on fine clothes
> We hear, smell and see,
> Taste and feel with high glee,
> And in winter have huts for repose.

In 1766 an article appears signed "A British American."—*Frothingham*, 194.

Sam. Adams, Sept. 16, 1771, writes in the "Boston Gazette":

I have often thought that in this time of common distress, it would be the wisdom of the colonists more frequently to correspond with and to be more attentive to the particular circumstances of each other. . . . The colonists form one political body of which each is a member. . . . The liberties of the whole are invaded ; it is therefore the interest of the whole to support each individual with all their weight and influence.—*Frothingham, p. 263.*

In the House of Burgesses in Virginia, March, 1773.

And whereas the affairs of the colony are frequently connected with those of Great Britain, as well as the neighboring colonies . . . therefore . . . *Be it resolved*, that a standing committee of [11 including Patrick Henry and Thomas Jefferson] be appointed . . . whose business it shall be to obtain [information concerning acts of British government] and to keep up and maintain a correspondence . . . with her sister colonies. . . . *Resolved*, that the speaker of this House do transmit to the speakers of the different assemblies copies of the said resolutions . . . and request them to appoint some person or persons . . . to communicate from time to time with the said committee. —*Cited in Frothingham, pp. 280-81.*

This is no time for ceremony. The question before the House is one of awful moment to this country. For my own part I consider it as nothing less than a question of freedom or slavery; and in proportion to the magnitude of the subject ought to be the freedom of the debate. It is only in this way that we can hope to arrive at truth, and fulfil the great responsibility which we hold to God and our country. Should I keep back my opinions at such a time,

DEVELOPMENT OF UNION AMONG COLONIES. 45

through fear of giving offense, I should consider myself as guilty of treason toward my country . . .

They tell us, sir, that we are weak; unable to cope with so formidable an adversary. . . . Sir, we are not weak, if we make a proper use of the means which the God of nature hath placed in our power. Three millions of people, armed in the holy cause of liberty, and in such a country as we possess, are invincible by any force which one enemy can send against us.

Patrick Henry, March 28, 1775, in Virginia Convention.—*Cited in American Orations, p. 133.*

QUESTIONS.

1. Why were Mr. Coddington and Mr. Brereton not to be communicated with by the governor of Massachusetts? 2. What does it prove in regard to union? 3. What colony made the first movement toward confederation?)4. Name the provinces in New England, 1640. 5. Who were magistrates? 6. Who were deputies? 7. Name reasons for union in 1643. 8. Who was Bradford? 9. Who was Winthrop? 10. Did the colonies have the right to form the confederation? 11. Do you find any evidences of jealousy among the colonies? 12. What were the terms of union? 13. Were they just? 14. What qualification for being a "commissioner"? 15. What provisions in our present constitution can you find in the confederacy of 1643? 16. Did the English government approve of the confederacy? 17. What claims did the colonists make in regard to the benefits of the confederation? 18. Why did the English "commissions" dislike the use of the words state, commonwealth, etc., by the colonists? 19. Were the English "commissions" and the colonists on good terms? Why? 20. Was Jacob Leisler for union? 21. How did the Indian feel about unity? 22. What did Governor Treat mean by the "ancient confederation"? 23. Under what name do you find Massachusetts sometimes spoken of? 24. Was Jacob Leisler an educated man? 25. Name the various times when there was a union more or less perfect. 26. Which were most numerous in America, the English or the French? 27. Why did the French get possession of so large a part of America, about 1750? 28. Name the reasons given by Gov. Livingston. 29. What remedy was proposed for the weakness of the English? 30. Can you see that union was wished for different purposes? 31. Why did the English wish to unite the colonies? 32. Why did the colonies desire to form a union? 33. Name the means the party of the "prerogative," the English party, proposed to bring about unity. 34. Do you approve of Mr. Penn's plan of union? 35. Which the better, his, or that of Governor Livingston, 1701? 36. Name the various persons who proposed plans of union. 37. Who were the greatest among them? 38. How did the Board of Trade like conventions? 39. Why did Governor

Fletcher not expect any help from Pennsylvania? 40. Trace the steps that led to the Albany congress. 41. Why were the colonies named in order from north to south? 42. How are they ordinarily named now? 43. Who authorized the union? 44. Name the points in the plan of Franklin for a union, 1754. 45. Why were these articles of confederation rejected by the colonies? by England? 46. Compare this plan with that of 1643. 47. Which the better? 48. Importance of the word American as used about 1766. 49. Why did the colonies desire to unite about 1765? 50. Write all you can on the significance of the phrase "A British-American." 51. What were the committees of correspondence? 52. In what states was the idea of having them conceived? 53. How did Patrick Henry regard union? 54. What kind of union was possible? 55. Write an essay tracing the growth of the idea of union. 56. How is the poetry connected with the topic of union?

American History Studies

No. 3   NOVEMBER, 1897.

CAUSES OF THE

AMERICAN REVOLUTION.

SELECTIONS MADE FROM THE SOURCES

BY

H. W. CALDWELL,

UNIVERSITY OF NEBRASKA.

J. H. MILLER, Publisher,
LINCOLN, NEBRASKA.

Yearly Subscription, 40 cents.   Single Copy, 5 cents.

PUBLISHED MONTHLY, EXCEPT JULY AND AUGUST.

Entered as second-class matter at the Post Office, Lincoln, Nebraska, U. S. A.

AMERICAN HISTORY STUDIES.

CAUSES OF AMERICAN REVOLUTION.

IN the last study we traced some of the movements looking to a union of the colonies. An attempt was made to show that two forces were at work, one tending to emphasize the importance of the colony, and the other the value and necessity of union. In the causes of the American Revolution we shall find many factors which intensified the spirit of union. In fact, the necessity of union in order to resist the plans of the English king and ministry was in itself a great educative force in this movement. The right of local self-government was perhaps the most fundamental issue. The colonies were accustomed to make their own laws, and to live their own life, hence, when the acts of the king and parliament in the years following 1760, seemed to endanger these privileges, resistance appeared and increased till independence was established.

It must be seen clearly, if we are to understand this movement at all, that a *spirit* existed in America different from that in England. The colonists already, as early as 1760, looked at all social, political, and even religious questions out of different eyes than their fellow citizens on the other side of the water. This *spirit* was the product of past forces in their colonial life. In short, it must be noticed that *a new people* was in process of formation. Hence, if any question arose which necessitated the yielding of one view or the other a conflict was sure to occur. The literature of the period, 1760 to 1776, is very abundant, both in American and in English publications. The debates in parliament furnish the views of English statesmen. The letters that were sent from the English cabinet to governors and other officials in America give us the spirit that animated the English government of the time. The instructions that were sent by the colonial assemblies to their agents in England, the resolutions of the Stamp Act Congress, and of the first and second Continental Congresses, together with the letters and writings of statesmen of the time, preserve a very vivid picture of the views of the Americans. It is felt that in the following extracts the views of England and of the "Tories" are not adequately set forth; the reason, the press of other duties which made the time at my command unequal to the necessities of the occasion.

For those who can invest a few dollars in the very best body of sources which has yet appeared, I wish to speak of Prof. Hart's "American History as Told by Contemporaries." The first volume is out, and the second, which brings the history down to 1783, is announced for this month. There are to be four volumes, published by Macmillan & Co., at $2.00 per volume, or $7.00 for the set.

The Acts of Navigation and of Trade of 1660, 1664, and 1672 should be noted as factors in the formation of an American spirit hostile to English conceptions.

Act of Navigation, 1660.

For the increase of shipping and encouragement of the navigation of this nation . . . be it enacted, that . . . no goods or commodities, whatsoever, shall be imported into, or exported out of, any lands, islands . . . to his Majesty belonging . . . in Asia, Africa or America, in any other ships or vessels . . . but in such ships or vessels, as do truly . . .

belong to the people of England . . . or are of the build of, and belonging to, any of the said islands . .

Section 18. And it is further enacted . . . that from and after the first day of April, which shall be in the year of our Lord 1661, no sugars, tobacco, cotton, wool, indigoes, ginger, fusticks or other dyeing wood of the growth . . . of an English plantation in America, Asia or Africa shall be shipped, carried . . . to any land . . . other than to such English plantations as do belong to his Majesty . . . or to the kingdom of England. . . . —*Rot. Parl. 12 C. II.*, *p. 2 nu. 6. 5 Statutes of the Realm, 246. Cited in Scott Development of Constitutional Liberty, pp. 314-16.*

Statute 15 Car. II., c. 7—A. D. 1663.

Section fifth. And in regard [to] his Majesty's plantations beyond the seas [which] are inhabited and peopled by his subjects of this his kingdom of England, for . . . keeping them in a firmer dependence upon it, and rendering them yet more beneficial and advantageous unto it, in the further . . . increase of English shipping and seamen, vent of English wool and other manufactures . . .

Section sixth. Be it enacted etc., that no commodity of the growth, production, or manufacture of Europe, shall be imported into any land, island . . . colony or place . . . to his Majesty belonging . . . in Asia, Africa, or America, . . . but which shall be *bona fide*, and without fraud, laden and shipped in England, . . . and in English-built shipping, etc. . . . —*Cited in Scott, Appendix, pp. 316-17.*

Stat. 25 Car. II., c. 7—A. D. 1672.

Section fifth. And whereas, by one Act passed in this present Parliament, . . . it is permitted to ship, carry, convey, and transport sugar, tobacco, cotton, wool, indigo, ginger, fustick, and all other dyeing wood . . from the place of their growth . . . to any other of your Majesty's plantations in those parts, and that without paying of customs for the same, [act here recites that this privilege has been abused by exporting these articles to *other* countries, therefore] for the prevention thereof . . . be it enacted that . . . if any ship or vessel which by law may trade in any of your Majesty's plantations shall . . . take on board any of the aforesaid commodities, [a bond shall be given] to bring the same to England . . . and to no other place [except, of course, to another colony.]

QUESTIONS.

1. In what ships must all trade with England be carried on? 2. Where must all sugar, etc., be sent to be sold? 3. Why was the statute of 1763 passed? 4. If the colonies wished to buy any goods of Portugal, where must they first take them? 5. For what object did colonies exist? 6. What does 15 Car. II., c. 7 mean? 7. What effect did the law of 1672 have on colonial trade in sugars, etc.?

The town of Boston, as early as May 24, 1764, in instructions given to its delegates in the General Assembly of Massachusetts, gives us some indication of the spirit which was already abroad in regard to colonial rights. These instructions were drafted by Samuel Adams. The whole series may be found in "American Patriotism."

Our trade has for a long time labored under great discouragements, and it is with the deepest concern that we see such further difficulties coming upon us as will reduce it to the lowest ebb, if not totally obstruct and ruin it. . . .

There is now no room for further delay; we therefore expect that you will use your earliest endeavors in the General Assembly that such methods may be taken as will effectually prevent these proceedings against us. . . .

[We fear] that these unexpected proceedings may be preparatory to new taxations upon us; for if our trade may be taxed, why not our lands? . . . This we apprehend annihilates our charter right to govern and tax ourselves. It strikes at our British privileges, which, as we have never forfeited them, we hold in common with our fellow subjects who are natives of Britain. If taxes are laid upon us in any shape without our having a legal representation where they are laid, are we not reduced from the character of free subjects to the miserable state of tributary slaves?—*American Patriotism, p. 2 f.*

October 19, 1765, the Convention of Delegates from nine of the colonies—the Stamp Act

Congress—formulates the principles of the American people in these words:

The members of this Congress, sincerely devoted, with the warmest sentiments of affection and duty, to his Majesty's person and government, inviolably attached to the present happy establishment of the Protestant succession; . . . having considered as maturely as time will permit, the circumstances of the said colonies, esteem it our indispensable duty to make the following declarations of our humble opinion respecting the most essential rights and liberties of the colonists and of the grievances under which they labor by reason of the several late acts of Parliament:

1. That his Majesty's subjects, in these colonies, owe the same allegiance to the crown of Great Britain, that is owing from his subjects born within the realm; and all due subordination to that august body, the Parliament of Great Britain.

2. That his Majesty's liege subjects, in these colonies, are entitled to all the inherent rights and liberties of his natural-born subjects within the kingdom of Great Britain.

3. That it is inseparably essential to the freedom of a people, and the undoubted right of Englishmen, that no taxes be imposed on them but with their own consent, given personally, or by their representatives.

4. That the people of these colonies are not, and from their local circumstances cannot be, represented in the House of Commons in Great Britain.

5. That the only representatives of the people of these colonies, are persons chosen therein by themselves; and that no taxes ever have been, or can be constitutionally imposed on them, but by their respective legislatures.

6. That all supplies to the crown being the free gifts of the people, it is unreasonable and inconsistent with the principles and spirit of the British constitution, for the people of Great Britain to grant to his Majesty, the property of the colonists.

8. That the late act of Parliament entitled, "An act for granting and applying certain stamp duties, and other duties in the British colonies and plantations in America, etc.," by imposing taxes on the inhabitants of these colonies, and the said act, and several other

acts, by extending the jurisdiction of the courts of admiralty beyond its ancient limits, have a manifest tendency to subvert the rights and liberties of the colonists. . . . —*Niles' "Principles and Acts of the Revolution," under New York.*

The Resolves of the House of Burgesses of Virginia, passed May 16, 1769, may also be cited to show the constitutional doctrines set forth some four years afterwards by that colony, which later, when a state, became known as the Mother of Presidents.

Resolved, *Nemine contradicente,* That the sole right of imposing taxes on the inhabitants of this, his Majesty's colony and Dominion of Virginia, is now, and hath been, legally and constitutionally vested in the House of Burgesses, lawfully convened, according to the ancient and established practice, with the consent of the council, and of his Majesty, the King of Great Britain, or his Governor for the time being.

Resolved, *Nemine contradicente,* That it is the undoubted privilege of the inhabitants of this colony to petition their Sovereign for redress of grievances; and that it is lawful . . . to procure the concurrence of His Majesty's other colonies, . . . praying the royal interposition in favor of the violated rights of America.

Resolved, *Nemine contradicente,* That all trials for treason, . . . or for any felony or crime whatsoever, committed . . . in said colony . . . ought of right to be had, and conducted in and before His Majesty's courts, held within his said colony, . . . ; and that the seizing . . . and sending such person . . . beyond the sea to be tried, is highly derogatory of the rights of British subjects, . . . —*Cited in Channing, The United States of Ameripa, p. 300.*

Patrick Henry formulates their doctrines in these stirring sentences, May 29, 1765:

WHEREAS, The Honorable House of Commons, in England, have of late drawn into question how far the General Assembly of this colony hath power to enact laws for laying of taxes . . . ; for settling and ascertaining the same to all future times, the House of

Burgesses of this present General Assembly have come to the following resolves:—

Resolved, That the first . . . settlers of . . . Virginia, brought with them and transmitted to their posterity, . . . all the privileges and immunities that have at any time been held, enjoyed, and possessed by the people of Great Britain.

Resolved, That his Majesty's liege people of this his ancient colony have enjoyed the right of being thus governed by their own Assembly in the article of taxes and internal police; [the same never yielded up; also the same recognized by king and people of Great Britain.]

Resolved, Therefore, that the General Assembly of this colony, together with his Majesty or his substitutes, have in their representative capacity, the only exclusive right and power to lay taxes and imposts upon the people of this colony; and that every attempt to vest such power in any other person or persons whatsoever than the General Assembly aforesaid, is illegal, unconstitutional, and unjust, and has a manifest tendency to destroy British as well as American liberty.

Resolved, That . . . the inhabitants of this colony, are not bound to yield obedience to any law . . . designed to impose any taxation whatsoever upon them, other than the laws . . . of the General Assembly. . . .

Resolved, That any person who shall . . . assert . . . . that any person, . . . other than the General Assembly . . . have any right or power to . . . lay any taxation on the people here, shall be deemed an enemy to his Majesty's colony.—*Cited in Channing, pp. 51-52.*

Examination of Dr. Franklin before the English House of Commons, in February, 1766, relative to the repeal of the American Stamp Act:

Q. What is your name, and place of abode?
A. Franklin, of Philadelphia.
Q. Do the Americans pay any considerable taxes among themselves?
A. Certainly many, and very heavy taxes.

. . . .

Q. Are not the colonies, from their circumstances, very able to pay the stamp duty?

CAUSES OF AMERICAN REVOLUTION. 55

A. In my opinion there is not gold or silver enough in the colonies to pay the stamp duty for one year.

. . . .

Q. Do not you think the people of America would submit to pay the stamp duty, if it was moderated?

A. No, never, unless compelled by force of arms.

. . . .

Q. What was the temper of America towards Great Britain *before the year 1763?*

A. The best in the world. They submitted willingly to the government of the crown, and paid, in their courts, obedience to acts of parliament. . . . Natives of Britain were always treated with a particular regard; to be an *Old England-man* was, of itself, a character of some respect, and gave a kind of rank among us.

Q. And what is their temper now?

A. O, very much altered.

Q. Did you ever hear the authority of parliament to make laws for America questioned till lately?

A. The authority of parliament was allowed to be valid in all laws, except such as should lay internal taxes. It was never disputed in laying duties to regulate commerce.

. . . .

Q. And have they not still the same respect for parliament?

A. No, it is greatly lessened.

Q. To what cause is that owing?

A. To a concurrence of causes: the restraints lately laid on their trade, . . . the prohibition of their making paper-money among themselves, and then demanding a new and heavy tax by stamps, taking away, at the same time trials by juries, and refusing to receive and hear their humble petitions.

. . . .

Q. Was it an opinion in America before 1763, that the parliament had no right to lay taxes and duties there?

A. I never heard any objection to the right of laying duties to regulate commerce, but a right to lay internal taxes was never supposed to be in parliament, as we are not represented there.

. . . .

Q. Suppose an act of internal regulations connected with a tax, how would they receive it?

A. I think it would be objected to.

Q. Then no regulation with a tax would be submitted to?

A. Their opinion is, that when aids to the crown are wanted, they are to be asked of the various assemblies, according to the old established usage; who will, as they always have done, grant them freely. And that their money ought not to be given away, without their consent, by persons at a distance, unacquainted with their circumstances and abilities. The granting aids to the crown is the only means they have of recommending themselves to their sovereign; and they think it extremely hard and unjust, that a body of men, in which they have no representatives, should make a merit to itself of giving and granting what is not its own, but theirs; and deprive them of a right they esteem of the utmost value and importance, as it is the security of all their other rights.

. . . .

Q. Are they (the colonists) acquainted with the declaration of rights? And do they know that, by that statute, money is not to be raised on the subject but by consent of parliament?

A. They are very well acquainted with it.

Q. How then can they think they have a right to levy money for the crown? . . .

A. They understand that clause to relate to subjects only within the realm; that no money can be levied on them (i. e. those within the realm) for the crown, but by consent of parliament. The *colonies* are not supposed to be within the realm; they have assemblies of their own, which are their parliaments, and they are, in that respect, in the same situation as Ireland. . . . They think the parliament of Great Britain can not properly give that consent, till it has representatives from America; for the petition of right expressly says, it is to be by *common consent in parliament;* and the people of America have no representatives in parliament to make a part of that common consent.

. . . .

A. They find in the great charters, and the petition and declaration of rights, that one of the privileges of English subjects is, that they are not to be taxed but by their *common consent;* they have therefore relied upon it, . . . that parliament never would, nor could, . . . assume a right of taxing them, *till* it had qualified itself to exercise such a right, by admitting representatives from the people to be taxed, who ought to make a part of the common consent.

. . . .

Q. What used to be the pride of the Americans?
A. To indulge in the fashions and manufactures of Great Britain.
Q. What is now their pride?
A. To wear their old clothes over again, till they can make new ones.—*Franklin, Works, IV, p. 709 f.*

Perhaps there is no document that gives us a deeper and keener insight into the thought of the times than Franklin's "Causes of American Discontent," written in 1768. The following quotations will indicate the scope of his arguments. It will be noticed that he writes as an Englishman.

From the time that the colonies were first considered as capable of granting aids to the crown, . . . it is said that the constant mode . . . was by requisitions made from the crown, . . . to the several asemblies, . . .

Had this happy method . . . been continued . . . there is no doubt but all the money that could reasonably be expected to be raised from them in any manner might have been obtained without the least . . . breach of the harmony of affections . . . between the two countries.

[They believed that] whatever money was to be raised from the people in the colonies must first be granted by their assemblies, as the money to be raised in Britain is first to be granted by the House of Commons; . . .

[Another act was passed] to oblige the several Assemblies to provide quarters for the soldiers, furnishing them with fireing (fuel), bedding, candles, small beer or rum, etc.

[Later, 1767, another person, Townshend] projected the levying more money from America, by new duties on various articles of our own manufacture, as glass, paper, . . . etc., which were . . . for the payment of salaries of governors, judges and other officers of the crown in America, it being a pretty general opinion here that those officers ought not to depend on the people there for any part of their support.

They say there [in America] as to governors . . . that they are generally strangers to the provinces they are sent to govern. They have no estate . . . or natural relation there to give them an affection for the country; that they come only to make money as fast as they can; are sometimes men of vicious character . . As to judges, they allege that, being appointed from this country, and holding their commissions not during good behavior, as in Britain, but during pleasure, all the weight of interest or influence would be thrown into *one* of the scales, . . . if the salaries are also to be paid out of duties raised upon the people without their consent, . . .

They reflected how lightly the interests of all America had been estimated here, when the interests of a few of the inhabitants of Great Britain happened to have the smallest competition with it. . . . The hatters of England have prevailed to obtain an act in their own favor, restraining that manufacture in America. . . .

In the same manner have a few nail-makers, and a still smaller body of steel-makers . . . prevailed totally to forbid by an act of Parliament the erecting of slitting mills, or steel furnaces, in America.—*Franklin's Works; also in "American Patriotism."*

Stephen Hopkins, of Providence, Rhode Island, sets forth the grievances of the colonies in a very elaborate paper. From it a few extracts are made, which bring out some points not found in the other documents cited:

. . . Whether the colonies will ever be admitted to have representatives in Parliament—whether it be consistent with their distant and dependent state; whether, if it were admitted, it would be to their advantage—are questions we will pass by. . . .

The colonies are at so great a distance from England that the members of Parliament can generally have but little knowledge of their business . . . and interests. . .

For what good reason can possibly be given for making a law to cramp the trade and interests of many of

CAUSES OF AMERICAN REVOLUTION. 59

the colonies, and at the same time lessen . . . the consumption of the British manufactures in them? . . The duty of three pence per gallon on foreign molasses . . . . must operate as an absolute prohibition. This will put a total stop to the exportation of lumber, horses, flour and fish to the French and Dutch sugar-colonies. . . . Putting an end to the importation of foreign molasses . . . puts an end to all the costly distilleries in these colonies and to the rum trade with the coast of Africa, and throws it into the hands of the French. . . .

By the same act of parliament the exportation of all kinds of timber and lumber, the most natural products of these colonies is greatly encumbered. . . .

Enlarging the power and jurisdiction of the courts of vice-admiralty in the colonies, is another part of the same act greatly and justly complained of. Courts of admiralty have long been there in most of the colonies whose authority were circumscribed within moderate territorial jurisdiction. . . .

But now this case is quite altered, and a custom-house officer may make a seizure in Georgia of goods ever so legally imported, and carry the trial to Halifax, . . . and thither the owner must follow him to defend his property; . . .

We are not insensible that when liberty is in danger the liberty of complaining is dangerous; yet a man on a wreck was never denied the liberty of roaring as loud as he could, says Dean Swift. And we believe no good reason can be given why the colonies should not modestly and soberly inquire, what right the Parliament of Great Britain have to tax them.—*Cited in American Patriotism, p. 4 f.*

THE LETTERS FROM A FARMER.

Among the most famous writings of the time, as well as the most influential, were the Letters of a Farmer. These letters were written by John Dickinson, a lawyer of Pennsylvania, in 1768. The sentiment of the man, and the arguments of the time are indicated in the following extracts, taken from different parts of the twelve letters which he wrote and published in the newspapers of the day:

With a good deal of surprise I have observed, that little notice has been taken of an act of parliament, as injurious in its principle to the liberties of these colonies, as the Stamp-Act was; I mean the act for suspending the legislature of New York. . . . If the British parliament has a legal authority to issue an order, that we shall furnish a single article for the troops here, and to compel obedience to that order, they have the same right to issue an order for us to supply those troops with arms, cloths, and to compel obedience to that order also; in short to lay any burdens they please upon us. What is this but taxing us at a certain sum, and leaving to us only the manner of raising it? How is this made more tolerable than the Stamp-Act? . . .

"It is my opinion [quoted from Wm. Pitt] that this kingdom has no right to lay a tax upon the colonies." . . . "The *Americans* are the *sons*, not the *bastards* of England." "Taxation is no part of the governing and legislative power." . . . The taxes are a voluntary gift and grant of the commons alone. In Legislation the three estates of the realm are alike concerned, but the concurrence of the peers and the crown to a tax is only necessary to close with the form of law. The gift and grant is of the commons alone." . . . "The distinction between legislation and taxation is . . . necessary to liberty." The commons of America represented in the assemblies have ever been in possession of the exercise of *this* their constitutional right, of giving and granting their own money. "They would have been slaves if they had not enjoyed it."

The idea of a virtual representation of America in this house, is the most contemptible idea that ever entered the head of man,—it does not deserve a serious refutation. . . .

For Who Are a Free People? Not those, over whom government is reasonably and equitably exercised, but those who live under a government so constitutionally checked and controlled, that proper provision is made against its being otherwise exercised. The late act is founded on the destruction of this constitutional security. If the parliament have a right to lay a duty of Four Shillings and Eight pence on a hundred weight of glass, or a ream of paper, they have a right to lay

, duty of any other sum on either. . . . ; If they have a right to lay a tax of one penny upon us, they have a right to levy a million, for where does their right stop? At any given number of Pence Shillings or Pounds? To attempt to limit their right, after granting it to exist at all, is as contrary to reason—as granting it at all is contrary to justice. . . .. If they have any right to tax us—then whether *our own money*, shall continue in our own pockets or not, depends no longer on *us*, but on them, . . . There is nothing which we can call our own, or to use the words of Mr. Locke—"What property have we in that, which another may, by right, take when he pleases, to himself?" These duties, which will inevitably be levied upon us— which are now upon us—are expressly laid for the sole purpose of *taking money*. This is the true definition of "taxes." They are therefore taxes. This money is to be taken from us. We are therefore taxed. Those who are taxed without their own consent expressed by themselves or their representatives are *slaves*.

We are taxed without our own consent, expressed by ourselves or our representatives. We are therefore *Slaves*.

* * * * * * *

The three most important articles that our assemblies, or any legislature can provide for, are First—the defence of the society; Secondly—the administration of justice; Thirdly—the support of civil government. Nothing can properly regulate the expense of making provisions for these occasions, but the *necessities* of society; its abilities; the conveniency of the modes of levying money in the *manner* in which the laws have been executed; and the conduct of the officers of governments. All which are circumstances, that cannot possibly be properly known, but by society itself; or if they should be known, will not probably be properly considered but by that society. . ... "We have all the rights requisite for our prosperity." The legal authority of Great Britain may indeed lay hard restrictions upon us; but like the spear of Telephus, it will cure as well as wound. Her unkindness will instruct and compel us, to discover, in our industry or frugality, surprising remedies—if our rights continue unviolated; for as long as the products of our labor, and the rewards of our care, can properly be called our own, so long it will be worth our while to be industrious and frugal. But if when we plow—sow—reap—gather—and thresh—we find that we—plow—sow—reap—gather—and thresh for others, whose *Pleasure* is to be the *Sole Limitation* how much they shall take, and how much they shall leave, why should we repeat the unprofitable *toil?* "Horses and oxen are content with that portion of the fruits of their work, which their owners assign them, in order to keep them strong enough to raise successive crops; but even *these beasts* will not submit to draw for their *masters*, until they are *subdued* by *whips* and *goads*." . . .

"If I am an Enthusiast, in anything; it is in my zeal for the perpetual dependence of these colonies on their mother country—a dependence founded on *mutual benefits*, the continuance of which can be secured only by *mutual* affections."

For my part I regard Great Britain as a Bulwark, happily fixed between these colonies and the powerful nations of Europe. It is therefore our *duty*, and our *interest*, to support the strength of *Great Britain.—Life and Writings of J. Dickinson, pp. 308-403.*

Lord Mansfield made a reply to Pitt (Chatham) in regard to the right of the English Parliament to tax the colonies. Something of an idea of his arguments may be seen in the following extracts:

I am extremely sorry that the question has ever become necessary to be agitated, and that there should be a decision upon it. No one in this house will live long enough to see an end put to the mischief which will be the result of the doctrine which has been inculcated; but the arrow is shot, and the wound already given. . . .

. . . There can be no doubt, my Lords, but that the inhabitants of the colonies are as much represented in Parliament, as the greatest part of the people in England are represented; among nine millions of whom there are eight which have no votes in electing members of parliament. Every objection therefore to the dependency of the colonies upon Parliament which arises to it upon the ground of representation goes to the whole present constitution of Great Britain; and I suppose it is not meant to new model *that* too. . . .

A member of Parliament, chosen for any borough, represents not only the constituents and inhabitants of that particular place, but he represents the inhabitants of every other borough in Great-Britain. He represents the city of London and all the other commons of this land, and the inhabitants of all the colonies and dominions of Great-Britain; and is in duty and conscience, bound to take care of their interests.

. . . .

I am far from bearing any ill will to the *Americans;* they are a very good people, and I have long known them, I began life with them, and owe much to them, having been much concerned in the plantation causes before the privy council; and, so I become a good deal acquainted with American affairs and people. I dare say their heat will soon be over, when they come to feel a little the consequences of their opposition to the Legislature. Anarchy always cures itself; but the ferment will continue so much the longer, while hot-headed men there, find that there are persons of weight and character to support and justify them here. . . .

"You may abdicate your right over the colonies. Take care my Lords, how you do so, for such an act will be irrevocable. Proceed, then, my Lords, with spirit and firmness, and when you shall have established your authority, it will then be time to show your lenity.

The Americans, as I said before, are a very good people, and I wish them exceedingly well; but they are heated and inflamed. The noble Lord who spoke before ended with a prayer. I can not end better than by saying to it, Amen; and in the words of Maurice, prince of Orange, concerning the Hollanders, "God bless this industrious, frugal, and well-meaning, but easily deluded people."—*Goodrich, British Eloquence, p. 148 f.*

The following arguments are taken from the protest that was entered in the Lords' journal by some of the members of that house against the proposed repeal of the Stamp Act:

This house has most solemnly asserted and declared, first,—'That the King's majesty, by and with the advise and consent of the Lords spiritual and temporal, and commons of Great Britain, in Parliament assembled, had, hath, and of right ought to have, full power and authority to make laws and statutes of sufficient force and validity to bind the colonies and people of America, subject to the crown of Gt. Britain in all cases whatsoever.' Secondly, 'That tumults and insurrections of the most dangerous nature have been raised and carried on in several of the North-American colonies, in open defiance of the power and dignity of his Majesty's Government, and in manifest violation of the laws and legislative authority of this Kingdom.' Thirdly, 'That the said tumults and insurrections have been encouraged and inflamed, by sundry votes and resolutions passed in several of the assemblies of the said provinces, derogatory to the honour of his Majesty's Government, and destructive of the legal and constitutional dependency of said colonies, on the Imperial Crown and Parliament of Great-Britain.'

. . . .

"2dly, Because the laws, which this bill now proposes to repeal, was passed in the other house with very little opposition and in this without one dissentient voice, during the last session of Parliament, which we presume, if it had been wholly, and fundamentally wrong, could not possibly have happened;"

. . . .

4thly, Because it appears to us, that a most essential branch of that authority, the power of taxation, cannot be properly, equitably, or impartially exercised, if it does not extend itself to all the Members of the State, in proportion to their respective abilities, but suffers a part to be exempt from a due share of those burdens which the public exigencies require to be imposed upon the whole; a partiality, which is directly repugnant to the trust reposed by the people in every legislature, and destructive of that confidence on which all Government is founded.

. . . .

6thly, Because not only the right but the expediency and necessity of the supreme Legislature's exerting its authority to lay a general tax on our American colonies, whenever the wants of the public make it fitting and reasonable that all the provinces should contribute, in a proper proportion, to the defence of the whole, appear to us undeniable. . . .

7thly. Because the reasons assigned in the public resolutions of the provincial Assemblies, in the North American colonies, for their disobeying the Stamp-Act, viz., "That they are not represented in the parliament of Gt.-Britain," extends to all other laws of what nature soever, which that Parliament has enacted, or shall enact, to bind them in times to come, and must (if admitted) let them absolutely free from any obedience to the power of the British Legislature. . . .

8thly. Because the appearance of weakness and timidity in the Government and Parliament of this kingdom, which a concession of this nature may too probably carry with it, has a manifest tendency to draw on farther insults, and, by lessening the respect of his Majesty's subjects to the dignity of his crown, and authority of his laws, throw the whole British empire into a miserable state of confusion and anarchy, with which it seems, by many symptoms, to be dangerously threatened.—*Parliamentary Debates, 1761-1768, p. 368 f.*

From the Declaration of Rights of the Continental Congress at Philadelphia, in 1774:

Whereupon the deputies so appointed being now assembled, in a full and free representation of these colonies, taking into their most serious consideration, the best means of attaining the ends aforesaid, do, in the first place, as Englishmen, their ancestors, in like cases have usually done, for effecting and vindicating their rights and liberties, *Declare,—*

That the inhabitants of the English colonies in North America, by the immutable laws of nature, the principles of the English constitution, and the several charters or compacts, have the following *Rights:—*

Resolved, N. C. D. 1. That they are entitled to life, liberty, and property, and that they have never ceded to any sovereign power whatever, a right to dispose of either without their consent.

Resolved, N. C. D. 2. That our ancestors, who first settled these colonies, were at the time of their emigration from the mother country, entitled to all the rights, liberties, and immunities, of full and natural-born subjects, within the realm of England.

Resolved, N. C. D. 3. That by such emigration, they by no means forfeited, surrendered, or lost, any of those rights, but that they were, and their descendants now are entitled to the exercise and enjoyment of all such of them, as their local and other circumstances enable them to exercise and enjoy.

Resolved, 4. That the foundation of English liberty, and of all free government, is a right in the people to participate in their legislative council; and as the English colonists are not represented, and from their local and other circumstances, cannot properly be, in the British Parliament, they are entitled to a free and exclusive power of legislation in their several provincial legislatures, where their right of representation can alone be preserved, in all cases of taxation and internal polity, subject only to the negative of their sovereign, in such manner as has been heretofore used and accustomed.—*Preston, Documents Illustrative of American History.*

The hiring of the Hessians and other German troops brought on a long debate in the Commons, from which the following extracts are made:

Mr. Fox: I have always said that the war carried on against the Americans is unjust, that it is not practicable. I say, that the means made use of are by no means such as will obtain the end. I shall confine myself singly to this ground, and shew this bill, like every other measure, proves the want of policy, the folly and madness of the present set of ministers. I was in great hopes, that they had seen their error, and had given over their endeavor to coerce, and to carry on war against America, by means of Acts of Parliament. In order to induce Americans to submit to your legislature, you pass laws against them, cruel and tyrannical in the extreme. If they complain of one law, your answer to their complaint is to pass another more rigorous and severe than the former; but they are in rebellion, you say; if they are, treat them as rebels are wont to be treated.

I have ever understood it as a first principle, that in rebellion you punish the individuals, but spare the country; in a war against the enemy, you spare individuals, and lay waste the country.

This last has been invariably your conduct against America. I suggested this to you when the Boston port bill passed. I advised you to find out the offending persons and to punish them; but what did you do instead of this? You laid the whole town of Boston under terrible contribution, punishing the innocent with the guilty. You answer, that you could not come at the guilty. This very answer shews how unfit, and how unable you are, to govern America.

. . . .

MR. DEMPSTER said, he was sorry to see such a disposition in administration to stifle and squash all enquiry. . . . He then turned, and took a short view of the Quebec bill, and concluded, by solemnly averring, that in his opinion, no Turkish emperor ever sent a more arbitrary and oppressive mandate, by a favorite bashaw, to a distant province, than that bill was with the instructions to the governor, which accompanied it.

. . . .

MR. D. HARTLEY: In the course of our debates upon American measures, I frequently hear the terms of rebellion and rebels made use of, which I shall never adopt; not only because I would avoid every term of acrimony which might increase the ill-blood between us and our fellow-subjects in America, but likewise thinking as I do, that the ministry of this country have been in every stage the aggressors: I never will, as a Whig of revolutionary principles, confound terms so fundamentally the reverse to each other, as defensive resistance in the support of constitutional rights, with unprovoked and active treason. The colonies have been condemned unheard. I wish to enter my protest once for all, that I shall always think that our American fellow-subjects have been driven to resistance in their own defence, and in support of those very claims which we ourselves have successfully taken up arms in former times, to secure us from the violence and tyrannical pretensions of the House of Stuart. These rights are the giving and granting freely our own property, and the security of charters.

HONORABLE JAMES LETTRELL: The Americans have never sought nor desire to be independent of England. They thought ministry misinformed, therefore they requested to be heard, and however artfully they may have been deprived of that privilege before this House, I do respect it as the grand judicial inquest of the nation, which must be too high . . . to condemn an individual without a hearing, much less three millions of subjects. Yet 'tis said that Parliament declared this war against America; let who will have done it, I have seen enough of that country to think it my duty to endeavor to express, how much I am adverse to so iniquitious, so impolitic a persecution. . . . Sir, I comprehend that ministry now apply to Parliament for seventeen thousand Germans to send to America, Good God, for what end? To enslave a hundred and fifty thousand of their own countrymen, many of whom fled from tyrants to seek our protection.

MR. ALDERMAN BULL: I cannot, Sir, . . . forbear to express my astonishment . . . that . . . so many gentlemen should have been prevailed upon . . to approve and sanctify those cruel and arbitrary measures . . . by an unfeeling, an unrelenting administration, who have dared to abuse the throne by their wicked and sanguinary councils, and whose whole conduct has proved them entirely destitute of every principle of justice, humanity, and the religion of their country. . . . Sir, is it certain, is it probable that the exertions of ministerial tyranny and revenge will be much longer permitted? . . . Or can it be expected that the people of this country, reduced by thousands to beggary and want, will remain idle spectators till the sword is at their breasts, or dragoons at their doors? . . .

The war which you are now waging is an unjust one, it is founded in oppression, and its end will be distress and disgrace. . . . I shall not now trouble the House further, than to declare my abhorrence of all the measures which have been adopted against America; measures equally inimical to the principles of commerce, to the spirit of the constitution, and to the honor, to the faith, and the true dignity of the British nation.—*Parliamentary Debates, 1775-'76, pp. 20-106.*

QUESTIONS.

1. In what ways were the Navigation acts connected with the American Revolution? 2. What industries were encouraged in America? 3. What ones discouraged? 4. Why do the people of Boston say their trade has been bad for a long time, in 1764? 5. What reasons are given in 1764 against taxation by British parliament? 6. What reasons assigned for opposing? 7. Would they have been willing to be taxed, if they had had representatives in Parliament? 8. What were

courts of Admiralty? 9. How were their powers extended? 10. Were there any new reasons given in 1765 that you do not find in 1764? 11. Why do the Virginians in 1769 speak of right of petition? 12. What new reasons of discontent mentioned in 1769? 13. Compare arguments of P. Henry with those of S. Adams. 14. Why does Franklin object to the Stamp Act? 15. How did the Americans feel towards the English as set forth by Franklin? 16. Did he distinguish between internal and external taxation? 17. Did the colonies in later years, 1768-'76? 18. What privileges did he claim for the colonies? 19. What foundation for these claims? 20. What force in the arguments of Mr. Pownall? 21. Would we reason now much in the same way? 22. Is Franklin's answer satisfactory? 23. Summarize the arguments of Franklin in Causes of American Discontent. 24. How does Stephen Hopkins' argument differ from the others? 25. What new points does he suggest? 26. Are the Farmer's letters convincing? 27. Is it true that any authority which may be abused ought not to be granted? 28. What are the arguments of Mansfield in regard to right of Parliament to tax? 29. Does present doctrine follow his view or that of Dickinson and Chatham? 30. Were all the American arguments based on idea of nationality or state sovereignty? 31. How did the colonists regard the English Constitution, as written or unwritten? 32. How did they differ in regard to meaning of representation? 33. Did the Lords' protest set forth any good grounds for their position? 34. Compare ideas of Stamp Act Congress with ideas and arguments of Congress of 1774. 35. What points does John Rutledge emphasize? 36. Why were not the colonies virtually represented when they had such friends in Parliament as are cited from Parliamentary Debates? 37. Was there danger of over-taxation with such men there? 38. Would not agitation alone in time have secured redress? 39. How far was the war caused by improper men in English cabinet? 40. Judged by the Declaration of Independence, who caused the war? 41. Can you find proof that all the charges contained in the Declaration of Independence were well founded?

American History Studies

No. 4.   DECEMBER, 1897.

STEPS IN THE FORMATION

OF THE

UNITED STATES CONSTITUTION.

SELECTIONS MADE FROM THE SOURCES

BY

H. W. CALDWELL,

UNIVERSITY OF NEBRASKA.

J. H. MILLER, Publisher,

LINCOLN, NEBRASKA.

Yearly Subscription, 40 cents.   Single Copy, 5 cents.

PUBLISHED MONTHLY, EXCEPT JULY AND AUGUST.

Entered as second-class matter at the Post Office, Lincoln, Nebraska, U. S. A.

AMERICAN HISTORY STUDIES.

STEPS IN THE FORMATION OF THE UNITED STATES CONSTITUTION.

IN the first place it must be noticed that our constitution is a growth and not a creation of any one moment in our history. Its elements may be traced back to the days when our Teutonic ancestors were yet in the swamps and forests of Germany. On American soil several stages in its growth may be marked. In the New England confederacy, in the Albany plan of union of 1754, in the various plans proposed about 1774 and 1775, in the Articles of Confederation of 1781, we see successive movements, all essential parts of the ultimate result obtained in the convention of 1787. Along another line of development we may also trace the growth of the forces which became factors in this result. The charters granted by the crown to Virginia, to Massachusetts, to Rhode Island, to Connecticut, and to other colonies, the charters granted by the proprietors to Maryland, to Pennsylvania, etc., furnished many elements for the final structure. The principles of the common law, and the English constitution itself directly, were not without great influence. Anything like a complete study, therefore, of the genesis of our constitution would necessitate an elaborate collection of the material contained in the foregoing suggestions. Our aim will be rather to trace the causes which were the immediate occasion for the constitutional convention, and to note the more important steps in the years which Mr. Fiske has so well called "The Critical Period." Also in studying the formation of the constitution it must ever be kept in mind that there were still in existence the two forces we have noticed at work in the colonial period, the one tending to union, and the other to localism. They operated at this time both as factors in determining whether there should be a new constitution at all, and also in influencing the nature of the union that should be formed. The question of the location of sovereignty was at issue. Did it rest in the state, or in the union? Should it be placed in the people as a whole, or should it be left in the hands of the local powers? The compromises in the constitution must be traced to their causes if we are to have a full understanding of the forces which were at work at the time. Sectionalism may be seen in many incidents occurring during these years, and especially in the debates in the constitutional and ratifying conventions. Slavery as a question of a distracting import crops out in many places. It was not yet at all an overshadowing issue, but it made itself felt. Class interests and class feelings are not absent. Creditor and debtor, city and country, coast region and interior, are all factors in determining the final form of the struggle and its result.

In connection with the quotations from the documentary records, extracts have been made from the writings of a few of the great statesmen of the time. It was the intention to have presented the views of a greater number of the statesmen of that day, but the usual plea has to be made that it takes a great amount of time to go through hundreds of pages of matter to find out the quotable material, and the time was not at hand. It is believed, however, that the extracts made are directly to the point, and will present the ideas of the day very sharply and vividly.

Thomas Paine, in 1780, in "Public Good," an article arguing that the western territory should belong to the United States collectively, instead of to Virginia and other states individually, concludes with these remarkable words:

> I shall in this place take the opportunity of renewing a hint which I formerly threw out in the Pamphlet "Common Sense," and which the States will, sooner or later, see the convenience, if not the necessity, of adopting; which is, that of electing a continental convention, for the purpose of forming a continental constitution, describing and defining the powers and authority of Congress.—*Paine's Writings (Conway), vol. II, p. 66.*

Washington's letters at least as early as 1780 show that he saw the necessity of a stronger bond of union among the states than the one which existed. Among other letters we find one to Hamilton, 4 March, 1783.

> The States cannot surely be so devoid of common sense, common honesty, and common policy, as to refuse their aid on a full, clear, and candid representation of facts from Congress. . . . To me who know nothing of the business before Congress, nor of the arcana, it appears that such a measure would tend to promote the public weal; for it is clearly my opinion, unless Congress have powers competent to all general purposes, that the distresses we have encountered, the expense we have occurred, and the blood we have spilt, will avail us nothing.—*Washington, Works, vol. VIII, p. 391.*

On March 31, 1783, he writes again to Hamilton in these words:

> My wish to see the union of these States established upon liberal and permanent principles, and inclination to contribute my mite in pointing out the defects of the present constitution, are equally great. . . . No man in the United States is or can be more deeply impressed with a necessity of a reform in our present

confederation than myself. No man perhaps has felt the bad effects of it more sensibly; for to the defects thereof, and want of power in Congress, may justly be ascribed the prolongation of the war, . . .—*Washington, Works, vol. VIII, p. 410.*

To Lafayette he writes:

To avert these evils, to form a new constitution . . is a duty incumbent on every man . . .

In Washington's Circular Letter to the Governors, 8 June, 1783, he sets forth his hopes and his fears again in eloquent words:

Such is our situation, and such are our prospects; but, notwithstanding . . . happiness is ours, if we have a disposition to seize the occasion and make it our own; yet it appears to me there is an option still left to the United States of America, that . . . it depends upon their conduct, whether they will be respectable and prosperous, or contemptible and miserable, as a nation. This is the time of their political probation; this is the moment when the eyes of the whole world are turned upon them; this is the moment to establish or ruin their national character forever; this is the favorable moment to give such a tone to our federal government as will enable it to answer the ends of its institution, or this may be the ill-fated moment for relaxing the powers of the Union, annihilating the cement of the confederation, and exposing us to become the sport of European politics, which may play one State against another . . . For, according to the system of policy the States shall adopt at this moment, they will stand or fall; and by their confirmation or lapse it is yet to be decided whether the revolution must ultimately be considered a blessing or a curse: a blessing or a curse, not to the present age alone, for with our fate will the destiny of unborn millions be involved, . . .

There are four things which . . . are essential . . . to the existence of the United States, as an independent power.

First. An indissoluble union of the States under one federal head.

Second. A sacred regard to public justice.

Third. The adoption of a proper peace establishment; and,

Fourth. The prevalence of that pacific and friendly disposition among the people of the United States which will induce them to forget their local prejudices and policies; . . . —*Washington, Works, vol. VIII, p. 441-'43; also in "Old South Leaflets."*

The following additional extracts from Washington's letters show his opinions in regard to the conditions of the times, and the necessity for a stronger government.

Notwithstanding the jealous and contracted temper, which seems to prevail in some of the States, yet I cannot but hope and believe, that the good sense of the people will ultimately get the better of their prejudices; and that order and sound policy, though they do not come so often as one would wish, will be produced from the present unsettled and deranged state of public affairs. Indeed, I am happy to observe that the political disposition is actually ameliorating every day. Several of the States have manifested an inclination to invest Congress with more ample powers. . . . —*To Jonathan Trumbull, Jr., Jan. 5, 1784.*

That the prospect before us is . . . fair, none can deny. [But] the disinclination of the individual States to yield competent powers to Congress for the federal government, their unreasonable jealousy of that body and of one another, and the disposition, which seems to pervade each, of being all-wise and all-powerful within itself, will, if there is not a change in the system, be our downfall as a nation, . . . and I think we have opposed Great Britain, and have arrived at the present state of peace and independency, to very little purpose, if we cannot conquer our own prejudices. . . . But I have many [fears] and powerful ones indeed, which predict the worst consequences, from a half-starved, limping government, that appears to be always moving upon crutches, and tottering at every step. . . My political creed, therefore, is, to be wise in the choice of delegates, . . give them competent powers for all federal purposes, support them in the due exercise thereof, . . . —*To Benjamin Harrison, 18 January, 1784.*

We are either a united people under one head and for federal purposes, or we are thirteen independent sovereignties, eternally counteracting each other. If the former, whatever such a majority of the States, as the constitution points out, conceives to be for the benefit of the whole, should . . . be submitted to by the minority. . . . I confess to you candidly, that I can foresee no evil greater than disunion: . . . As you have asked the question, I answer, I do not know that we can enter upon a war of imposts with Great Britain, or any other foreign power; but we are certain, that this war has been waged against us by the former; professedly upon a belief that we never could unite in opposition to it; and I believe there is no way of putting an end to [it] . . . but to convince them of the contrary. . . .

To sum up the whole, I foresee . . . the many advantages which will arise from giving powers of this kind to Congress . . . without any evil save that which may proceed from inattention, or want of wisdom in the formation of the act; while without them, we stand in a ridiculous view in the eyes of the nations of the world, with whom we are attempting to enter into commercial treaties, without the means of carrying them into effect; who must see and feel that the Union or the States individually are sovereigns, as best suits their purposes; in a word that we are one nation to-day and thirteen to-morrow.—*To James McHenry, 22 August, 1785.*

The war . . . has terminated most advantageously for America, and a fair field is presented to our view; but I confess to you freely, dear Sir, that I do not think we possess wisdom or justice enough to cultivate it properly. Illiberality, jealousy, and local policy mix too much in all our public councils for the good government of the Union. In a word, the confederation appears to me to be little more than a shadow without substance, and Congress a nugatory body, . . —*To James Warren, 7 October, 1785.*

My sentiments with respect to the federal government are well known. Publicly and privately have they been communicated without reserve; but my opinion is, that there is more wickedness than ignorance in the conduct of the States, or, in other words, in the conduct of those who have too much influence in the government of them; and until the curtain is withdrawn, and the private views and selfish principles, upon which these men act, are exposed to public notice, I have little hope of amendment without another convention.—*To Henry Lee, 5 April, 1786.*

I coincide perfectly with you . . . that there are errors in our national government which call for correction; . . . but I shall find myself happily mistaken if the remedies are at hand. We are certainly in a delicate situation; but my fear is that the people are not yet sufficiently *misled* to retract from error. To be plainer, I think there is more wickedness than ignorance mixed in our councils. . . . That it is necessary to revise and amend the articles of confederation, I entertain no doubt; but what may be the consequences of such an attempt is doubtful. . . .

I think often of our situation, and view it with concern. From the high ground we stood upon, from the plain path which invited our footsteps, to be so fallen, so lost, is really mortifying. But virtue, I fear, has in a great degree taken its departure from our land, and the want of a disposition to do justice is the source of the national embarrassments; . . .—*To John Jay, 18 May, 1786.*

Is it not among the most unaccountable things in nature, that the representatives of a great country should generally be so thin as not to be able to execute the functions of government. To what is this to be ascribed? . . . Be the causes what they may, it is shameful and disgusting. In a word, it hurts us. Our character as a nation is dwindling; and what it must come to, . . . our enemies have foretold; for in truth we seem either not capable, or not willing to take care of ourselves. . . .

It was impolitic and unfortunate if not unjust in these States to pass laws, which by fair construction might be considered as infractions of the treaty of peace. It is good policy at all times to place one's adversary in the wrong. Had we observed good faith, and the western posts had then been withheld from us by Great Britain, we might have appealed to God and man for justice; . . . But now we cannot do this . . .—*To William Grayson, 26 July, 1786.*

The greater part of the Union seems to be convinced of the necessity of federal measures, and of investing

Congress with the power of regulating the commerce of the whole.—*To de la Luzerne, 1 August, 1786.*

What astonishing changes a few years are capable of producing. I am told that even respectable characters speak of a monarchical form of government without horror. From thinking proceeds speaking; thence to acting is often but a single step. But how irrevocable and tremendous! What a triumph for our enemies to verify their predictions! What a triumph for the advocates of despotism to find that we are incapable of governing ourselves, and that systems founded on the basis of equal liberty are merely ideal and fallacious!—*To John Jay, 1 August, 1786.*

You talk, my good Sir, of employing influence to appease the present tumults in Massachusetts. I know not where that influence is to be found, or, if attainable, that it would be a proper remedy for the disorders. *Influence* is not *government*. Let us have a government by which our lives, liberties, and properties will be secured, or let us know the worst at once.—*To Henry Lee, in Congress, 31 October, 1786.*

Fain would I hope, that the great and most important of all subjects, the *federal government*, may be considered with that calm and deliberate attention, which the magnitude of it so critically and loudly calls for. Let prejudices, unreasonable jealousies, and local interests yield to reason and liberality. . . .

[In] a letter . . . from General Knox, . . . among other things he says, "Their creeds, that the property of the United States has been protected from the confiscation of Britain by the joint exertions of *all*, and therefore ought to be the *common property of all*," . They are determined to annihilate all debts, public and private, and have agrarian laws, . . .—*To James Madison, 5 November, 1786.*

By a late act, it seems very desirous of a general convention to revise and amend the federal constitution. *Apropos:* what prevented the eastern States from attending the September meeting at Annapolis? Of all the States in the Union it should seem, that a measure of this sort, distracted as they were with internal commotions and experiencing the want of energy in the government, would have been most pleasing to them.—*To Henry Knox, 26 December, 1786.*

I am indirectly and delicately pressed to attend this

convention [Philadelphia, 1787]. Several reasons are opposed to it in my mind . . . [Partly personal.] A thought has lately run through my mind, however, which is accompanied with embarrassment. It is whether my non-attendance in the convention will not be considered as a dereliction of republicanism. [Some friends advised him to attend, others the contrary. It was about three months after appointment before he decided to accept.]—*To Henry Knox, 8 March, 1787.*

Every attempt to amend the constitution at this time is in my opinion idle and vain. If there are characters, who prefer disunion, or separate confederacies, to the general government, which is offered to them, their opposition may, for aught I know, proceed from principle; but, as nothing, according to my conception of the matter, is more to be deprecated than a disunion or these distinct confederations, as far as my voice can go it shall be offered in favor of the latter.—*To David Stuart, 30 November, 1787.*

Should it [the constitution] be adopted, and I think it will be, America will lift up her head again, and in a few years become respectable among the nations. It is a flattering . . . . reflection that our rising republics have the good wishes of all the philosophers, patriots, and virtuous men in all nations; and that they look upon them as a kind of asylum for mankind. God grant that we may not disappoint their honest expectations by our folly or perverseness.—*To the Marquis de Chastellux, 25 April, 1788.*

The above extracts are all taken from Spark's Writings of Washington, vol. IX, pp. 5, 12-13, 121-24, 140, 156, 166, 178-80, 183, 189, 204-206, 226, 238, 284, 297.

Part of the extracts from Jefferson's writings are taken from the edition of his work of 1830, and part from the new edition by Ford, published in 1895.

I remain in hopes of great and good effects from the decisions of the Assembly [Constitutional Convention] over which you are presiding. To make our States one as to all foreign concerns, preserve them several as to all merely domestic, to give to the federal head some peaceable mode of enforcing its just authority, to organize that head into legislative, executive, and judiciary departments, are great desiderata in our federal constitution.—*Jefferson to Washington, Works of Jefferson (ed. 1830), vol. II, p. 222.*

I find by the public papers that your Commercial Convention failed in point of representation. If it should produce a full meeting in May and a broader reformation, it will still be well. To make us one nation as to foreign concerns, and keep us distinct in Domestic ones, gives the outline of the proper division of power between the general and particular governments. But to enable the Federal head to exercise the power given it, to best advantage, it should be organized, as the particular ones are, into Legislative, Executive, and Judiciary. The 1st and last are already separated. The 2d should also be. When last with Congress I often proposed to members to do this by making of the Committee of the states, an Executive committee during the recess of Congress and during its sessions to appoint a Committee to receive and dispatch all executive business, so that Congress itself should meddle only with what should be legislative.—*Jefferson to Madison, Dec. 16, 1786, Works, vol. IV, p. 331.*

The negative proposed to be given them [Congress] on all the acts of the several legislatures is now for the first time suggested to my mind. *Prima facie* I do not like it. It fails in the essential character that the hole and the patch should be commensurate. But this proposes to mend a small hole by covering the whole garment. . . . Would not an appeal from the State Judicatures to a federal court in all cases where the act of Confederation controlled the question, be as effectual a remedy, and exactly commensurate to the defect? . . . An appeal to a federal court sets all to rights.' It will be said that this court may encroach on the jurisdiction of the state courts. It may. But there will be a power, to-wit, Congress, to watch and restrain them. But place the same authority in Congress itself, and there will be no power above them to perform the same office. . . .—*Jefferson to Madison, June 20, 1787, Works, vol. IV, pp. 390-91.*

Our new constitution is powerfully attacked in the newspapers. The objections are that it would be to form the 13 states into one: that proposing to melt all down into one general government they have fenced the people by no declaration of rights, they have not renounced the power of keeping a standing army, they have not secured the liberty of the press, they have reserved the power of abolishing trial by jury in civil cases, . . . they have abandoned rotation in office; and particularly their president may be re-elected from 4 years to 4 years for life, so as to render him a king for life like a king of Poland, and have not given him either the check or aid of a council. . . . You will see that these objections are serious, and some of them not without foundation.—*To William Carmichael, Paris, Dec. 15, 1787, Jefferson's Works (1895 ed.), vol. IV, p. 470.*

. . . I like much the general idea of framing a government which should go on of itself peacefully, without needing continual recurrence to the state legislatures. I like the organization of the government into Legislative, Judiciary and Executive. I like the power given the Legislature to levy taxes, . . . I am captivated by the compromise of the opposite claims of the great and little states, of the latter to equal and the former to proportional influence. I am much pleased too with the substitution of the method of voting by persons, instead of voting by states; and I like the negative given to the Executive . . . There are other good things of less moment. I will now add what I do not like. First the omission of a bill of rights providing clearly and without the aid of sophisms for freedom of religion, freedom of the press, protection against standing armies, restriction against monopolies, the eternal and unremitting force of the habeas corpus laws, and trials by jury in all matters of fact triable by the laws of the land and not by the law of nations. . . . Let me add that a bill of rights is what the people are entitled to against every government on earth, general or particular, and just what no just government should refuse, or rest on inferences. The second feature I dislike, . . . is the abandonment in every instance of the necessity of rotation in office, and most particularly in the case of the President. [Here a prediction follows which has not been fulfilled.] . . . I do not pretend to decide what would be the best method of procuring the establishment of the manifold good things in this constitution, and of getting rid of the bad. . . . I own I am not a friend to a very energetic government. It is always oppressive. The late rebellion in Massachusetts has given more alarm than I think it should have done. . . . After all, it is my principle that the will of the majority should always prevail. If they approve the proposed convention in all its parts, I shall concur in it cheerfully, in hopes that they will amend it whenever they shall find it work wrong. I think our governments will remain virtuous for many centuries; as long as they are chiefly agricultural; and this will be as long as there shall be vacant lands in any part of America. When they get piled upon one another in large cities, as in Europe, they will become corrupt as in Europe. . . .—*To James Madison, Paris, Dec. 20, 1787, Ib., 474-76.*

PUBLIC ACTION.

The powers of the delegates to the first Continental Congress of 1774 will indicate the purpose for which these delegates came together. The instructions to the Virginia and Maryland delegates illustrate the spirit of all.

VIRGINIA: To consider of the most proper and effectual manner of so operating on the Commercial convention of the Colonies with the Mother country, as to procure redress for the much-injured Province of Massachusetts Bay, to secure British America from the ravage and ruin of arbitrary taxes, and speedily to procure the return of that harmony and union so beneficial to the whole Empire, and so ardently desired by all British America.

MARYLAND: To attend a General Congress to assist one general plan of conduct operating on the Commercial connection of the Colonies with the mother country, for the relief of Boston and the preservation of American Liberty.

The Congress of 1774 passed the following resolutions in regard to the vote of the various delegations present:

Resolved, That, in determining questions in this Congress, each colony or province shall have one vote; the Congress not being possessed of, or at present able to procure, proper materials for ascertaining the importance of each colony.—*Journal of Congress, vol. I, p. 7.*

On October 20, 1774, this Congress passed the Non-importation agreement. It has sometimes been called the beginning of the government of the United States.

[Name grievances, then say] To obtain redress of these grievances, . . . we are of opinion, that a non-importation, non-consumption, and non-exportation agreement, faithfully adhered to, will prove the most speedy, effectual, and peaceable measure: [terms follow] . . .

Sec. 11. That a committee be chosen in every county, city and town by those who are qualified to vote for representatives in the legislature whose business it shall be attentively to observe the conduct of all persons touching this association; and when it shall be made to appear . . . that any person . . . has violated this association that [his name be] published in the gazette; to the end that all such foes to the rights of British-America may be publicly known, and universally contemned as the enemies of American liberty; and thenceforth we respectively will break off all dealings with him or her.

Sec. 12. That the committee of correspondence, in the respective colonies, do frequently inspect the entries of their custom-houses, and inform each other, . . . of the true state thereof, . . .

Sec. 14. And we do further agree and resolve, that we will have no trade . . . or dealings . . . with any colony or province in North America, which shall not accede to or which hereafter shall violate this association, but will hold them as unworthy of the rights of freemen, and as inimical to the liberties of their country.

And we do solemnly bind ourselves and our constituents, . . . to adhere to this association, until [redress of grievances obtained].—*Journal of Congress, vol. I, pp. 23-25.*

The Congress of 1775 met for the same purpose, but soon had to begin to act as a revolutionary body, and carried on the government and the war till 1781, when the articles of confederation were adopted.

ARTICLES OF CONFEDERATION

Articles of Confederation and Perpetual Union between the states of New Hampshire, Massachusetts Bay . . .

Article I. The style of this Confederacy shall be "The United States of America."

Article II. Each State retains its sovereignty, freedom and independence, and every Power, Jurisdiction and right which is not . . expressly delegated. . .

Article III. The said States hereby severally enter into a firm league of friendship with each other, . . binding themselves to assist each other against all force offered to, or made upon them, . . .

Even before the Articles of Confederation were ratified by the last state, Maryland, a proposal had been made in Congress, on February 3, 1781, to submit the following amendment to the states for their action. It failed of adoption:

Resolved, That it be recommended to the several States, . . . that they vest a power in Congress to levy, for the use of the United States, a duty of five per cent *ad valorum*, . . . at the time and place of importation, upon all goods, . . . of foreign growth or manufacture, . . .

That the moneys arising from said duties be appropriated to the discharge of the principal and interest of the debts already contracted . . .—*Elliot's Debates, vol. I, p. 92.*

On April 18, 1783, a second attempt to secure an amendment was made, which also failed of final adoption.

Resolved, by nine States, that it be recommended to the several States as indispensably necessary to the restoration of public credit, . . . to invest the United States in Congress assembled, with the power to levy, for the use of the United States, the following duties upon goods imported into the said States from

any foreign port, &c. . . . [List of articles.]—
Elliot's Debates, vol. I, p. 93.

On the 30th of April, 1784, Congress recommended for a third time an amendment to the articles, which was finally defeated by the action of New York, in the winter of 1786-87. The reasons for the proposed amendment read in part as follows, and are very important as showing one of the direct causes that led to the calling of the Constitutional Convention:

> The trust reposed in Congress renders it their duty to be attentive to the conduct of foreign nations, and to prevent or restrain, . . . all such proceedings as might prove injurious to the United States. The situation of Commerce at this time claims the attention of the several states, and few objects of greater importance can present themselves to their notice . . [reasons given].
> Already has Great-Britain adopted regulations destructive of our commerce with her West-India island. There was reason to expect that measures so unequal and so little calculated to promote mercantile intercourse, would not be persevered in by an enlightened nation. . . . It would be the duty of Congress, as it is their wish, to meet the attempts of Great-Britain with similar restrictions on her commerce; but their powers on this head are not explicit, and the propositions made by the legislatures of the several states render it necessary to take the general sense of the nation on this subject.
> Unless the United States in Congress assembled, shall be vested with powers competent to the protection of commerce, they can never command reciprocal advantages in trade; and without these, our foreign commerce must decline, and eventually be annihilated. Hence it is necessary that . . . foreign commerce, not founded on principles of equality, may be restrained, . . . to secure such terms they have
> *Resolved,* That it be . . . recommended to the legislatures of the several states, to vest the United States, in Congress assembled, for the term of fifteen years, with power to prohibit any goods . . . from being imported into or exported from any of the

states, in vessels belonging to . . . the subjects of any foreign power with whom these states shall not have formed treaties of commerce.

Resolved, That it be . . . recommended, . . . to vest the United States, in Congress assembled, for the term of 15 years, with the power of prohibiting the subjects of any foreign state . . . unless authorized by treaty, from importing into the United States any goods . . . which are not the product . . . of the dominions of the sovereign whose subjects they are.

After the failure of these various attempts to amend the Articles of Confederation, the friends of greater power in the Union turned to the calling of a convention for taking the question into consideration. Virginia was the first state to act, and on January 21, 1786, its legislature passed the following resolution:

Resolved, that Edmund Randolph, James Madison, . . . be appointed commissioners, who or any five of whom, shall meet such commissioners as may be appointed by other States in the Union, . . . to take into consideration the trade of the United States; to examine the relative situation of the trade of the said States, . . . and to report to the several States such an act relative to this great object as when unanimously ratified by them, will enable the United States in Congress assembled, to provide for the same . . . [Notice of action sent to other states.]—*Elliot's Debates, vol. I, p. 115.*

Commissioners from four other states, New York, New Jersey, Pennsylvania, and Delaware, met with those from Virginia, and sent out a letter to the other states and to Congress asking that a convention be held on the second Monday of the following May. The interesting paragraphs in their resolutions for us read as follows:

To the Honorable the Legislatures of Virginia, etc., . . . the Commissioners from the said States, . . . humbly beg leave to report: . . . That the State of

New Jersey had enlarged the object of their appointment, empowering their commissioners, "to consider how far an uniform system in their commercial regulations, and *other important matters*, might be necessary to the common interest and permanent harmony of the several States": . . . [Your commissioners believe this] was an improvement on the original plan, and will deserve to be incorporated into that of a future Convention, . . .

Under this impression, your Commissioners, . . . beg leave to suggest their unanimous conviction that [Commissioners should meet] at Philadelphia on the second Monday in May next, to take into consideration the situation of the United States; to devise such further provisions as shall appear to them necessary to render the constitution of the Federal Government adequate to the exigencies of the Union; and to report such an act for that purpose, to the United States in Congress assembled, as, when agreed to by them, and afterwards confirmed by the Legislatures of every State, will effectually provide for the same.—*Madison's Journal of the Constitutional Convention, pp. 38-40. (Albert, Scott & Co. edition.)*

Congress took this resolution of the Annapolis convention into consideration, and finally passed, on February 21, 1787, the following:

Resolved, That in the opinion of Congress, it is expedient that, on the second Monday in May next, a Convention of Delegates, who shall have been appointed by the several States, be held at Philadelphia for the sole and express purpose of revising the Article of Confederation, and reporting to Congress and the several legislatures, such alterations and provisions therein as shall, when agreed to in Congress, and confirmed by the States, render the federal Constitution adequate to the exigencies of Government, and the preservation of the Union.—*Journal of Congress, vol. IV, p. —.*

The legislatures of all the states, except Rhode Island, acted in conformity to this resolution, and sent delegates to Philadelphia. They met and organized on May 25, and adjourned on September 17, 1787. The present constitution is the result of their labors. The powers granted by the various state legislatures to their delegates may be seen from the following extracts:

GEORGIA. Be it ordained, by the Representatives of the State of Georgia, . . . that William Few, Abraham Baldwin . . . be, . . . appointed Commissioners, who . . . are authorized . . . to meet such deputies as may be appointed and authorized, by other States . . . and to join with them in devising and discussing all such alterations and further provisions as may be necessary to render the Federal Constitution adequate to the exigencies of the Union, and in reporting such an act for that purpose to the United States in Congress assembled, as, when agreed to by them, and duly confirmed by the several States, will effectually provide for the same. . . .—*Elliot, Debates, vol. I, pp. 126-138.*

MASSACHUSETTS. *Whereas,* Congress did, on the 21st day of February, 1787, Resolve, That, . . . a Convention of Delegates, . . . be held at Philadelphia, for the *sole and express purpose* of revising the Articles of Confederation . . . [rest of resolution quoted]. Now, therefore, etc. [Francis Dana, Elbridge Gerry, Nathaniel Gorham, Rufus King, and Caleb Strong commissioned as delegates.]

CONNECTICUT. *Whereas,* The Congress of the United States, . . . have recommended that, . . . a convention . . . be held at Philadelphia, for the *sole and express purpose* of revising the Articles of Confederation; [names of delegates follow].

NEW YORK. *Resolved,* that Hon. Robert Yates, John Lansing, Jr., and Alexander Hamilton, Esqs. be . . . appointed delegates . . . to meet such delegates . . . at Philadelphia, for the sole and express purpose of revising the Articles of Confederation . . . [etc. as in Georgia].

NEW JERSEY. The Council and Assembly . . . have appointed you [names follow here] to meet such Commissioners . . . as may be appointed by the other States in the Union, . . . for the *purpose* of taking into consideration, the state of the Union, as to *trade and other important* objects, and of devising such other provisions as shall appear to be necessary to render the Constitution of the Federal Government adequate to the exigencies thereof.

PENNSYLVANIA. Be it enacted . . . that [names members] are hereby constituted and appointed Deputies from this State . . . to meet such Deputies as may be appointed . . . by other States . . . and join with them in devising, deliberating on, and discussing, all such *alterations* and *further provisions* as may be necessary to render the Federal Constitution fully adequate to the exigencies of the Union, . . .

DELAWARE. [Almost the same as Pennsylvania.]

MARYLAND. [Almost same wording as Pennsylvania.]

VIRGINIA. [Same wording as Pennsylvania.]

NORTH CAROLINA. For the purpose of revising the Federal Constitution.

SOUTH CAROLINA. By virtue of the power and authority invested by the Legislature of this State, I do hereby commission you [names] to meet such Deputies . . . and to join with [them] in devising and discussing all such alterations, clauses, articles and provisions, as may be thought necessary to render the Federal Constitution entirely adequate to the actual situation and future good government of the Confederated States; . . . [which] when approved and agreed to by them [the United States] and duly ratified and confirmed by the several States, will effectually provide for the exigencies of the Union.

NEW HAMPSHIRE. . . . To remedy the defects of our Federal Union. . . .

THE CONSTITUTIONAL CONVENTION.

Madison's Journal of the Constitutional Convention ought to be in the hands of every teacher who gives instruction in the history and civil government of the United States. No library can be considered complete without it. A few extracts are made which will illustrate some of the great issues discussed in the convention, and the position taken on them by the members of the convention. However, it is not possible to give an adequate idea of the value of this work from any short extracts.

After three days spent in organizing, adopting rules, and determining on plans, the debate began. GOVERNOR RANDOLPH, of Virginia, presented the first plan and opened his speech as follows, as given by Madison:

. . . He observed, that, in revising the Federal system we ought to inquire, first, into the properties which such a government ought to possess; secondly, the defects of the Confederation; thirdly, the danger of our situation; and fourthly, the remedy.

(1.) The character of such a government ought to be secure, first against foreign invasion; secondly against dissensions between members of the Union, or seditions in particular States; thirdly to procure to the several States various blessings of which an isolated situation was incapable; fourthly, it should be able to defend itself against encroachments; and fifthly, to be paramount to the State Constitutions.—*Journal of the Constitutional Convention, p. 59.*

. . . .

Then, after discussing the defects and dangers, he proposed fifteen resolutions as the basis of a remedy. Among these resolutions the following may be cited:

1. Resolved, that the Articles of Confederation ought to be so corrected and enlarged as to accomplish the objects proposed by their institution; namely, "common defense, security of liberty, and general welfare."

3. Resolved, that the National Legislature ought to consist of two branches.

7. Resolved, that a National Executive be instituted; . . . .

9. Resolved, that a National Judiciary be established; . . . —*Ib., pp. 59-62.*

On May 30 MR. RANDOLPH made a motion which led to action that has been much discussed, and concerning which very different opinions have been expressed. He moved that his first proposition, above cited, should be postponed in order to consider the three following:

(1.) That a union of the States merely federal will

not accomplish the objects proposed by the Articles of Confederation, namely . . .

(2.) That no treaty or treaties among the whole or part of the States, as individual sovereignties, would be sufficient.

(3.) That a *national* government ought to be established, consisting of a *supreme* Legislative, Executive and Judiciary.

Consideration of the first and second of the above resolutions was deferred; the third, after some debate, was adopted. In the course of the debate Gen. Pinckney said:

he doubted whether the act of Congress recommending the convention, or the commissions of the Deputies to it, would authorize a discussion of a system founded on different principles from the Federal Constitution.

MR. GOUVERNEUR MORRIS explained the distinction between a *federal* and a *national, supreme* government, the former being a mere compact resting on the good faith of the parties; the latter having a complete and *compulsive* operation.

After the adoption of this resolution, in the discussion of another question, MR. MADISON

observed, that, whatever reason might have existed for the equality of suffrage when the Union was a federal one among sovereign States, it must cease when a national government should be put into the place.

May 31, a debate took place over Mr. Randolph's fourth resolution, *"that the members of the first branch of the National Legislature ought to be elected by the people of the several states,"* which throws much light on the spirit of the time, and of the convention.

MR. SHERMAN opposed the election by the people, insisting that it ought to be by the State Legislatures. The people, he said, immediately should have as little to do as may be about the government. They want information, and are constantly liable to be misled.

MR. GERRY. The evils we experience flow from the excess of democracy. The people do not want virtue, but are the dupes of pretended patriots. . . . He had, he said, been too republican heretofore; he was still, however, republican; but had been taught by experience the danger of the leveling spirit.

MR. MASON. . . . He admitted that we had been too democratic, but was afraid we should incautiously run into the opposite extreme. . . .

MR. WILSON contended strenuously for drawing the most numerous branch of the Legislature immediately from the people. He was for raising the federal pyramid to a considerable altitude, and for that reason wished to give it as broad a basis as possible. No government could long subsist without the confidence of the people. . . .

MR. MADISON considered the popular election of one branch of the National Legislature as essential to every plan of free government. . . .

MR. RANDOLPH. . . . He observed that the general object was to provide a cure for the evils under which the United States labored; that in tracing these evils to their origin, ever man had found it in the turbulence and follies of democracy; that some check therefore was to be sought for against this tendency of our governments; and that a good senate seemed more likely to answer the purpose.—*Ib., pp. 73-81.*

COL. MASON. Under the existing Confederacy, Congress represents the *States*, and not the *people* of the States; their acts operate on the *States*, not on the individuals. The case will be changed in the new plan of government. The people will be represented; they ought therefore to choose the Representatives. . . . —*Ib., p. 116.*

MR. WILSON. . . . He did not see the danger of the States being devoured by the national government. On the contrary, he wished to keep them from devouring the National Government. . . .—*Ib., p. 128.*

One of the most difficult questions before the convention was how to settle the varying interests of the large and the small states. At one time it seems as if the convention would break up over the question. A few expressions taken here and there from the debate may help us to understand the bitterness of feeling.

Mr. Patterson. . . . The convention, he said, was formed in pursuance of an act of Congress; . . . that the amendment of the Confederacy was the object of all the laws and commissions on the subject. . . . The idea of a National Government, as contradistinguished from a federal one, never entered into the mind of any of them. He was strongly attached to the plan of the existing Confederacy, in which the people choose their legislative representatives; and the Legislatures their federal representatives. . . . He alluded to the hint thrown out by Mr. Wilson, of the necessity to which the large States might be reduced, of confederating among themselves. . . . New Jersey will never confederate on the plan before the Committee. She would not be swallowed up. He had rather submit to a monarch, to a despot, than to such a fate. . . .

Mr. Wilson hoped, if the Confederacy should be dissolved, that a *majority*,—nay, a *minority* of the States would unite for their safety.—*Ib., pp. 139-41.*

At this point Mr. Patterson introduced the so-called New Jersey plan, which provided only for amending the Articles of Confederation. The debate was renewed with the following result:

Mr. Wilson. . . . With regard to the *power of the convention*, he conceived himself authorized to *conclude nothing*, but to be at liberty to propose *anything*. . . . With *regard to the sentiments of the people*, he conceived it difficult to know precisely what they are. . . . Why should a National Government be unpopular? . . . Will a citizen of *Delaware* be degraded by becoming a citizen of the *United* States? . . .

Mr. Pinckney. The whole thing comes to this . . Give New Jersey an equal vote, and she will dismiss her scruples, and concur in the National system.—*Ib., pp. 171-174.*

On June 19, by a vote of seven states to three, it was carried to take up Mr. Randolph's plan instead of Mr. Patterson's.

Mr. Wilson. Can we forget for whom we are forming a government? Is it for *men*, or for the imaginary beings called *States?* . . .—*Ib.*, *p. 272.*

DR. FRANKLIN. The diversity of opinions turns on two points. If a proportional representation takes place, the small States contend that their liberties will be in danger. If an equality of votes is to be put in its place, the large States say their money will be in danger. . . .

MR. DAYTON. . . . He considered the system on the table as a novelty, an amphibious monster; and was persuaded that it never would be received by the people.

MR. MARTIN would never confederate, if it could not be done on just principles.

MR. BEDFORD contended, that there was no middle way between a perfect consolidation, and a mere confederacy of the States. The first is out of the question; and in the latter they must continue, if not perfectly, yet equally sovereign. . . . The large States dare not dissolve the confederation. If they do the small States will find a foreign ally, of more honor and good faith, who will take them by the hand, and do them justice. . . .

MR. GERRY. . . . If no compromise should take place, what will be the consequence. A secession he foresaw would take place, for some gentlemen seemed decided on it. . . .—*Ib.*, *p. 297.*

MR. GOUVERNEUR MORRIS regretted the turn of the debate. The States, he found, had many representatives on the floor. Few, he feared, were to be deemed the Representatives of America. He thought the Southern States have, by this Report, more than their share of representation. . . .—*Ib.*, *p. 317.*

On Monday, July 16, the turning point in the convention came. After a very deep and earnest, if not bitter, discussion, a compromise was seen to be practicable, by which the Senate and the House, as we now have them, came into being. It was some days later, however, before the formal terms were agreed upon.

MR. RANDOLPH. . . . He could not but think that we were unprepared to discuss this subject further. It will probably be in vain to come to any final decision with a bare majority on either side. For these reasons he wished the Convention to adjourn, that the large States might consider the steps proper to be taken, in the present solemn crisis of the business; and that the small States might also deliberate on the means of conciliation.

MR. PATTERSON thought that it was high time for the Convention to adjourn; that the rule of secrecy ought to be rescinded; and that our constituents should be consulted. No conciliation could be admissible on the part of the smaller States, on any other ground than than of an equality of votes in the second branch [the Senate]. If Mr. Randolph would reduce to form his motion for an adjournment *sine die*, he would second it with all his heart.

MR. RUTLIDGE could see no need of an adjournment because he could see no chance of a compromise. The little States were fixed, . . . All that the large States, then, had to do was, to decide whether they would yield or not.—*Ib., pp. 358-59.*

There is not space for the proceedings in many of the ratifying conventions. But as the form of words was not greatly different, a few cases will illustrate the spirit, and in the main, the form in all.

DELAWARE. We, the Deputies of the People of the Delaware State, in Convention met, having taken into our serious consideration the Federal Constitution, proposed and agreed upon by the Deputies of the United States, in a General Convention, held at the City of Philadelphia, . . . have approved, assented to, ratified, and confirmed, and by these presents do, . . . for and in behalf of ourselves and our constituents, fully, freely, and entirely approve of, assent to, ratify, and confirm, the said Constitution.—*Elliot's Debates, vol. I, p. 319.*

PENNSYLVANIA. In the name of the people of Pennsylvania. Be it known unto all men that we . . . have assented to and ratified and by these presents do . . . in the name and by the authority of the same people, and for ourselves, assent to and ratify the foregoing Constitution for the United States of America. . . .—*Elliot's Debates, vol. I, p. 319.*

FORMATION OF CONSTITUTION.

QUESTIONS.

1. Who was Thomas Paine? 2. What important part did he play in the American revolution? 3. What the style of his writings? 4. Has he had justice done him by American historians? 5. What view does he take of the western lands? 6. When was "Common Sense" written? 7. What relation did he believe the States ought to sustain to each other? 8. What did he desire a continental convention for? 9. Did time prove him right? 10. Was Washington hopeful of the future in 1783? 11. Did he feel any changes were necessary? 12. Compile from all his letters the reasons he considers the Articles of Confederation defective. 13. Was Washington a hopeful man or not? 14. Did he love his State or the Union the more? 15. Did Washington believe that morally the people were improving or not? 16. What do you think of the four things Washington believed to be essential for our prosperity? 17. Why does he talk so much of local prejudices? 18. What is the important point in Washington's philosophy of government? 19. Where was sovereignty located in Washington's view under the Confederacy? 20. In what way was Great Britain getting the better of us? 21. Does Washington get more or less hopeful as the years pass? 22. Had the treaty with England been kept? 23. Name the doctrine set forth in Knox's letter to Washington, quoted in his letter to Madison. 24. In what section did Washington think there was the greatest need of reform? 25. Give reason Washington assigned for attending the Constitutional Convention. 26. What does it show concerning his character? 27. Look up other reasons.) 28. When do Washington's fears begin to lessen? 29. Do you find any difference in the *tone* of the letters of Washington and Jefferson? 30. What kind of powers does the latter wish given to Congress? 31. Name the various changes he would have made in the Articles of Confederation. 32. What proposal does he object to? 33. Was he right or wrong? 34. What power did he propose to place in the hands of the courts? 35. Name the powers he liked in the new constitution. 36. Name those he objected to. 37. Were his objections well founded? 38. Is he or Washington the more constructive? 39. Name the motive which prompted the meeting of the first Continental Congress. 40. How did they vote? 41. What effect later of this action? 42. When did the enforcing power of the Union begin? 43. What kind of a government formed by the Articles of Confederation? 44. Name the proposed amendments to the Articles of Confederation. 45. Would it have been best to have had them adopted? 46. What question directly led to the Constitutional Convention? 47. Name the conventions held. 48. What was the work

of the Annapolis convention? 49. What did it wish the next one to do? 50. What powers had the delegates to the Constitutional Convention? 51. For what purpose did Congress call the convention? 52. Did the convention act within its granted powers? 53. What important changes proposed in Articles of Confederation by Randolph? 54. What change did he make later in the nature of his resolutions? 55. What does the debate in the convention indicate in regard to the nature of the government under the Articles? 56. Under the Constitution? 57. What marked difference between a national and a federal government? 58. Were the members of the convention believers in democracy? 59. Name those friendly to the idea—those opposed. 60. Explain why so many opposed to the idea. 61. What ideas contending for mastery in the convention? 62. Over what question did the convention come nearest breaking up? 63. Form of ratification of constitution. 64. Who adopted the constitution? 65. Write an essay on the defects of the Articles of Confederation. 66. On the political ideas and spirit of Washington and Jefferson; comparisons. 67. On the growth of the idea of Union. 68. On who stood for the best ideas on the whole in the Constitutional Convention. 69. Were the people then more moral than now? 70. Compare ideas of nationality and localism.

American History Studies

No. 5.   JANUARY, 1898.

INTERPRETATION OF THE CONSTITUTION; NATIONALITY.

SELECTIONS MADE FROM THE SOURCES

BY

H. W. CALDWELL,

UNIVERSITY OF NEBRASKA.

J. H. MILLER, Publisher,

LINCOLN, NEBRASKA.

Yearly Subscription, 40 cents.   Single Copy, 5 cents.

PUBLISHED MONTHLY, EXCEPT JULY AND AUGUST.

Entered as second-class matter at the Post Office, Lincoln, Nebraska, U. S. A.

INTERPRETATION OF THE CONSTITUTION; NATIONALITY.

THE Constitution formed in 1787 has been in process of growth ever since through interpretation and construction. Of course, it has also grown by the addition of fifteen amendments. In time these have been contracted or expanded by the meanings which have been attached to them by the various departments of the government. Perhaps the courts, and especially the Supreme Court of the United States, have been the most potent factors in this development, yet it must ever be kept in mind that the political departments of the government, namely, the legislative and the executive, have also to give final decisions in all political questions; and the first interpretation of the Constitution, in law making, in all questions which may become judicial as well.

There is scarcely a clause of the Constitution which has not been subjected to this process. It may, perhaps, be stated without exaggeration that there is not a clause in the Constitution so clear that varying ideas in regard to its meaning have not been set forth at some time by someone. It is also true that the Constitution as a whole had to have an interpretation placed upon it. Before a final decision was given, the court of armies was called in. The most desperate civil war of all history was needed to decide upon the location of sovereignty. Had it not been for the existence of sectional slavery, it is probable that there would never have arisen the necessity for making the decision. Yet we must notice that when an attempt was made in our Constitution to place some powers in the central government, and to leave others in the states, the line of division drawn was an indefinite one, hence the chance came for such a struggle. We have already noticed the many factors which were tending to localism, and the counter ones which were developing a feeling of nationality as well as the fact. In this paper the larger part of the extracts are to show the varying interpretations of the Constitution connected with this idea of nationality. This discussion played in the main around the question of implied powers, the location of sovereignty, the slavery issue, and the right of determining the institutions of the territories. It would be claiming too much to say that in treating these topics one had exhausted the subject. In the brief space allotted me I can do no more than give a fair insight into the first two, and touch the others.

IMPLIED POWERS.

The doctrine of "implied powers" first arose in connection with the establishment of the national bank in 1791. On this subject I have let Jefferson, Hamilton, and Madison speak. Mr. Jefferson in his letter to President Washington uses the following arguments:

> It is an established rule of construction when a phrase will bear either of two meanings to give it that which will allow some meaning to the other parts of the instrument, and not that which would render all the others useless. Certainly no such universal power was meant to be given them. It was intended to lace them up straightly within the enumerated powers, and those without which, as means, these powers could not be carried into effect. It is known that the very power now proposed as a means, was rejected as an end, by the convention which formed the constitution. . . .

The second general phrase is, "to make all laws necessary and proper for carrying into execution the enumerated powers." But they can all be carried into execution without a bank. . . . .

. . . The constitution allows only the means which are "necessary," not those which are merely "convenient" for effecting the enumerated powers. If such a latitude of construction be allowed to this phrase as to give any non-enumerated power, it will go to every one, for there is not one which ingenuity may not torture into a convenience in some instance or other, . . . It would swallow up all the delegated powers, and reduce the whole to one power as before observed. Therefore it was that the constitution restrained them to the necessary means. Can it be thought that the constitution intended that for a shade or two of convenience, more or less, congress should be authorized to break down the most ancient and fundamental laws?—*Writings of Thomas Jefferson, vol. V (1895 ed.), pp. 286-289.*

Hamilton argues for the constitutionality of the bank, and in doing this struck a great blow for nationality. Some of the most telling points of his argument are these:

Now it appears to the Secretary of the Treasury that this *general principle* is *inherent* in the very definition of government, and *essential* to every step of the progress to be made by that of the United States, namely, that every power vested in a government is in its nature SOVEREIGN, and includes, by *force* of the *term*, a right to employ all the means requisite, and fairly applicable, to the attainment of the *ends* of such power, and which are not precluded by restrictions and exceptions specified in the constitution; or not immoral; or not contrary to the essential ends of political society.

. . . .

It is not denied that there are implied as well as *express* powers, and that the former are as effectually delegated as the latter; and . . . there is another class of powers, which may be properly denominated *resulting* powers. It will not be doubted that if the United States should make a conquest of any of the territories of its neighbors they would possess sovereign jurisdiction over the conquered territory. This would rather be the result from the whole mass of the powers of the government, and from the nature of political society, than a consequence of either of the powers specially enumerated.

Then . . . as a power of erecting a corporation may as well be *implied* as any other thing; it may as well be employed as an *instrument* or means of carrying into execution any of the specified powers, as any other instrument or means whatever.

. . . *Necessary* often means no more than *needful, requisite, incidental, useful,* or *conducive to,* . . . and it is the true one in which it is to be understood as used in the constitution. The whole turn of the clause containing it indicates that it was the intent of the convention, by that clause, to give a liberal latitude to the exercise of the specified powers. The expressions have a peculiar comprehensiveness. They are: "To make all laws necessary and proper for carrying into execution the foregoing powers, and all other powers vested by the constitution in the government of the United States, or in any department or office thereof." To understand the word as the Secretary of State does would be to depart from its obvious and popular sense and to give it a *restrictive* operation, an idea never before entertained. It would be to give it the same force as if the word *absolutely* or indispensably had been prefixed to it.

. . . .

[It is] no valid objection to the doctrine to say that it is calculated to extend the powers of the government throughout the entire sphere of state legislation. The same thing has been said, and may be said with regard to every exercise of power, by *implication* or *construction*. The moment the literal meaning is departed from there is a chance of error and abuse; and yet an adherence to the letter of its powers would at once arrest the motion of government. It is not only agreed on all hands that the exercise of constructive powers is indispensable, but every act which has been passed is more or less an exemplification of it. . . .

That which declares the power of the President to remove officers at pleasure acknowledges the same truth.

. . . .

It leaves, therefore, a criterion of what is constitutional and of what is not so. This criterion is the *end* to which the measure relates as a *mean*. If the end be clearly comprehended within any of the specified powers, and if the measure have an obvious relation to that end and is not forbidden by any particular provision of the constitution, it may safely be deemed to come within the compass of the national authority. There is also this further criterion, which may materially assist the decision. Does the proposed measure abridge a pre-existing right of any state or of any individual? If it does not, there is a strong presumption in favour of its constitutionality; and slighter relations to any declared object of the constitution may be permitted to turn the scale.—*Works of Alexander Hamilton, vol. I, pp. 112-123.*

Madison was in the House at this time, and had at first been the spokesman of the administration. On this question of the bank he separated himself entirely from Hamilton, with whom he had so long worked, and became the leader, with Jefferson, of the newly forming Republican party. In Congress he said:

After some general remarks on the limitations of all political power, he took notice of the peculiar manner in which the Federal Government is limited. It is not a general grant, out of which particular powers are excepted; it is a grant of particular powers only, leaving the general mass in other hands. So it had been understood by its friends and its foes, and so it was to be interpreted.

. . . .

The essential characteristic of the Government, as composed of limited and enumerated powers, would be destroyed if, instead of direct and incidental means any means could be used, which, in the language of the preamble to the bill, "might be conceived to be conducive to the successful conducting of the finances, or might be conceived to tend to give facility to the obtaining of loans. . . .

The Doctrine of implication is always a tender one. The danger of it has been felt in other Governments. . . .

The delicacy was felt in the adoption of our own;

the danger may also be felt if we do not keep close to our chartered authorities.

Mark the reasoning on which the validity of the bill depends! To borrow money is made the end, and the accumulation of capital implied as the means. The accumulation of capital is then the end, and a bank implied as the means. The bank is then the end, and a charter of incorporation, a monopoly, capital punishments, etc., implied as the means.

If implications thus remote and multiplied can be linked together, a chain may be formed that will reach every object of legislation, every object within the whole compass of political economy.

The latitude of interpretation required by the bill is condemned by the rule furnished by the constitution itself.

The danger of implied power does not arise from its assuming a new principle; we have not only practiced it often, but we can scarcely proceed without it; nor does the danger proceed so much from the extent of power as from its uncertainty.—*Benton, Debates, vol. I, pp. 275, 276.*

Fisher Ames.

The doctrine that powers may be implied which are not expressly vested in Congress has long been a bugbear to a great many worthy persons. They apprehend that Congress, by putting constructions upon the constitution, will govern by its own arbitrary discretion; and therefore that it ought to be bound to exercise the powers expressly given, and those only.

If Congress may not make laws conformably to the powers plainly implied, though not expressed in the frame of Government, it is rather late in the day to adopt it as a principle of conduct. A great part of our two years' labor is lost, and worse than lost to the public, for we have scarcely made a law in which we have not exercised our discretion with regard to the true intent of the constitution.—*Ib., p. 279.*

The question of the constitutionality of the bank came before the Supreme Court in 1819, in McCulloch vs. Maryland. Chief Justice Marshall wrote the opinion in the case, and held to the doctrine of implied powers. In this case again the idea of nationality was affirmed. In part he said:

From these conventions the Constitution derives its whole authority. The government proceeds directly from the people; is "ordained and established" in the name of the people; and is declared to be ordained "in order to form a more perfect union, establish justice, insure domestic tranquility, and secure the blessings of liberty to themselves and to their posterity." The assent of the States, in their sovereign capacity, is implied in calling a convention, and thus submitting that instrument to the people. But the people were at perfect liberty to accept or reject it; and their act was final. It required not the affirmance, and could not be negatived by the State governments. The Constitution, when thus adopted, was of complete obligation, and bound the State sovereignties.

This government is acknowledged by all to be one of enumerated powers. The principle, that it can exercise only the powers granted to it, would seem too apparent to have required to be enforced by all those arguments which its enlightened friends, while it was depending before the people, found it necessary to urge. That principle is now universally admitted. But the question respecting the extent of the powers actually granted is perpetually arising, and will probably continue to arise as long as our system shall exist.

Among the enumerated powers we do not find that of establishing a bank or creating a corporation. But there is no phrase in the instrument which, like the Articles of Confederation, excludes incidental or implied powers; and which requires that everything granted shall be expressly and minutely described. . .

Although, among the enumerated powers of government, we do not find the word "bank" or "incorporation," we find the great powers to lay and collect taxes; to borrow money; to regulate commerce; to declare and conduct a war; and to raise and support armies and navies.

But it may, with great reason, be contended that a government intrusted with such ample powers, on the due execution of which the happiness and prosperity of the nation so vitally depends, must also be intrusted with ample means for their execution.

. . . .

Is that construction of the Constitution to be preferred which would render these operations difficult, hazardous, and expensive? Can we adopt that construction . . . which would impute to the framers of that instrument, when granting these powers for the public good, the intention of impeding their exercise by withholding a choice of means? If, indeed, such be the mandate of the Constitution, we have only to obey; but that instrument does not profess to enumerate the means by which the powers it confers may be executed; nor does it prohibit the creation of a corporation if the existence of such a being be essential to the beneficial exercise of those powers. It is, then, the subject of fair inquiry how far such means may be employed.

. . . .

But the Constitution of the United States has not left the right of congress to employ the necessary means for the execution of the powers conferred on the government to general reasoning. To its enumeration of powers is added that of making "all laws which shall be necessary and proper for carrying into execution the foregoing powers, and all other powers vested by this constitution, in the government of the United States, or in any department thereof."

. . . .

Congress is not empowered by it to make all laws which may have relation to the powers conferred on the government, but such only as may be "necessary and proper" for carrying them into execution. The word "necessary" is considered as controlling the whole sentence, and as limiting the right to pass laws for the execution of the granted powers to such as are indispensable, and without which the power would be nugatory. . . .

Is it true that this is the sense in which the word "necessary" is always used?

. . . .

To employ the means necessary to an end is generally understood as employing any means calculated to produce the end, and not as being confined to those single means without which the end would be entirely unattainable.

* * * * * *

A thing may be necessary, very necessary, absolutely or indispensably necessary.

* * * * * *

If the word "necessary" means "needful," "requisite," "essential," "conducive to" in order to let in the power of punishment for the infraction of law, why is it not equally comprehensive when required to authorize the use of means which facilitate the execution of the powers of government without the infliction of punishment? . . . That any means adapted to the end; any means which tended directly to the execution of the constitutional powers of the government, were in themselves constitutional.

* * * * * *

Let the end be legitimate, let it be within the scope of the Constitution, and all means which are appropriate, which are plainly adapted to that end, which are not prohibited, but consist with the letter and spirit of the constitution, are constitutional.—*Thayer, Cases in Constitutional Law, vol. I, pp. 274-285.*

QUESTIONS.

·1. When was the present constitution formed? 2. Is it expressed in general or specific terms? 3. Who interprets the constitution? 4. Who interprets it finally? 5. What do you understand by "implied powers"? 6. Could there be any implied powers under the Articles of Confederation? 7. Over what question did the discussion of the "implied powers" first arise? 8. Summarize Jefferson's argument. 9. Can you give any example to illustrate his first sentence? 10. What did he believe "necessary" meant? 11. What principle does Hamilton start out with? 12. What three kinds of powers does he name? 13. What meanings does he give to "necessary"? 14. What *means* does he claim may be used when the right to the *end* is admitted? 15. Summarize Madison's arguments. 16. Compare arguments of the three men. 17. Give Fisher Ames' argument. 18. Make an outline of the arguments of John Marshall. 19. Of all their arguments, which do you consider the greatest? Why? 20. Was it important to have the doctrine of implied powers prevail? Why?

SOVEREIGNTY. IN NATION OR STATE?

Perhaps the first formal statement of that

interpretation of the Constitution which affirmed the right of the state to be the final judge of its powers was given in the Kentucky Resolutions of 1798. Indirectly out of these resolutions came nullification and secession. Whether this succession was legitimate or not is an open question, but the parentage, as far as use is concerned, is undoubted. The important resolve read as follows:

1. Resolved, That the several states composing the United States of America are not united on the principle of unlimited submission to their general government, but that by compact under the style and title of a Constitution of the United States, and of amendments thereto, they constituted a general government for special purposes, delegated to that government certain definite powers, reserving, each state to itself, the residuary mass of right to their own self-government; and that whensoever the general government assumes undelegate powers its acts are unauthoritative, void, and of no force. . . .

To this resolution several states answered that the final judge of the powers of the federal government rested in the Supreme Court. The legislature of Kentucky replied in 1799 in these words, in part:

Resolved, That this commonwealth consider the Federal Union, upon the terms and for the purposes specified in the late compact, as conducive to the liberty and happiness of the several states; That it does now unequivocally declare its attachment to the Union, and to that compact, agreeably to its obvious and real intention, and will be among the last to seek its dissolution; That if those who administer the general government be permitted to transgress the limits fixed by that compact, by a total disregard to the special delegations of power therein contained, an annihilation of the state governments and the creation upon their ruins of a general consolidated government will be the inevitable consequence; That the principle and construction contended for by sundry of the state legislatures, that the general government is the exclusive judge of the extent of the powers delegated to it, stop nothing short of despotism,—since the discretion of those who administer the government, and not the constitution, would be the measure of their powers. . . . That this commonwealth does, under the most deliberate reconsideration, declare the said alien and sedition laws are, in their opinion, palpable violations of the said Constitution. . . . That, although this commonwealth, as a party to the federal compact, will bow to the laws of the Union, yet it does at the same time declare that it will not now, or ever hereafter, cease to oppose in a constitutional manner every attempt, at what quarter soever offered, to violate that compact. . . .—*Cited in Cluskey, Political Text-Book.*

James Wilson, in the Pennsylvania ratifying convention, in 1787, outlined his opinion in regard to the nature of the Constitution in these words. This description may be contrasted with the preceding:

The very manner of introducing this Constitution, by the recognition of the authority of the people, is said to change the principle of the present Confederation and to introduce a *consolidating* and absorbing government. . . .

In this confederated republic, the sovereignty of the states, it is said, is not preserved. We are told that there cannot be two sovereign powers, and that a subordinate sovereignty is no sovereignty.

. . . .

It has not been, nor, I presume, will it be, denied that somewhere there is, and of necessity must be, a supreme, absolute, and uncontrollable authority.

. . . .

His [Mr. Findley's] position is that the supreme power resides in the states, as governments; and mine is that it resides in the people, as the foundation of government; that the people have not—that the people meant not—and that the people ought not, to part with it, to any government whatsoever.—*Cited in Foster on the Constitution, pp. 104-106.*

I consider the people of the United States as forming one great community; and I consider the people of the different States as forming communities, again, on a lesser scale. From this great division of the people into distinct communities, it will be found necessary that different proportions of legislative power should be given to the government, according to the nature, number, and magnitude of their objects.

. . . .

Whosoever considers, in a combined and comprehensive view, the general texture of the Constitution, will be satisfied that the people of the United States intended to form themselves into a nation for *national purposes*. They instituted for such purposes a national government, complete in all its parts, with powers legislative, executive, and judiciary, and in all those powers extending over the whole nation.—*Ib.*, *107-109*.

Rawle, in his introduction to Blackstone, uses the following phrase. He wrote in 1825:

"The secession of a State from the Union depends on the will of the people of such a State. The people alone, as we have already seen, hold the power to alter their constitution."—*Cited in Foster, p. 113*.

The Massachusetts legislature (Federal), in discussing the annexation of Louisiana, 1803, indicated very clearly its views of the nature of the Constitution.

That the annexation of Louisiana to the Union transcends the constitutional power of the government of the United States. It forms a new Confederacy, to which the States united by the former compact are not bound to adhere.—*Ib., p. 116*.

A most elaborate discussion of the nature of the Constitution took place over the admission of Louisiana. Josiah Quincy, the leader of the Federalists, discussed the subject fully. Extensive extracts are given from his speech, as it sets forth the views of his party at that time most ably and completely.

But, sir, the principle of this bill materially affects the liberties and rights of the whole people of the United States. To me it appears that it would justify a revolution in this country, and that, in no great length of time, it may produce it. When I see the zeal and perseverance with which this bill has been urged along its parliamentary path, when I know the local interests and associated projects which combine to promote its success, all opposition to it seems manifestly unavailing. I am almost tempted to leave, without a struggle, my country to its fate.

. . . .

If there be a man in this House, or nation, who cherishes the Constitution, . . . I fall not behind him in such sentiments. I will yield to no man in attachment to this Constitution, in veneration for the sages who laid its foundations, in devotion for those principles which form its cement and constitute its proportions. What, then, must be my feelings; what ought to be the feelings of a man, cherishing such sentiments, when he sees an act contemplated which lays ruin at the foot of all these hopes.

Mr. Speaker, there is a great rule of human conduct which he who honestly observes can not err widely from the path of his sought duty. It is, to be very scrupulous concerning the principles you select as the test of your rights and obligations; to be very faithful in noticing the result of their application; and to be very fearless in tracing and exposing their immediate effects and distant consequences. Under the sanction of this rule of conduct, I am compelled to declare *it as my deliberate opinion that, if this bill passes, the bonds of this union are, virtually, dissolved; that the States which compose it are free from their moral obligations, and that, as it will be the right of all, so it will be the duty of some, to prepare, definitely, for a separation: amicably, if they can; violently, if they must.*

. . . .

The bill which is now proposed to be passed has this assumed principle for its basis: that the three branches of this national government, without recurrence to conventions of the people in the States, or to the Legislatures of the States, are authorized to admit new partners to a share of the political power, in countries out of the original limits of the United States. Now, this assumed principle, I maintain to be altogether without any sanction in the Constitution. I declare it to be a manifest and atrocious usurpation of power; of a nature dissolving, according to undeniable principles of moral law, the obligations of our national compact, and leading to the awful consequences which flow from such a state of things.

Touching the general nature of the instrument called the Constitution of the United States there is no obscurity; . . . There can be no doubt about its nature. It is a political compact. . . .

It is, we the people of the United States, for ourselves and our posterity; not for the people of Louisiana; nor for the people of New Orleans, or of Canada. None of these enter into the scope of the instrument; it embraces only "the United States of America."

Sir, what is this power we propose now to usurp? Nothing less than a power changing all the proportions of the weight and influence possessed by the potent sovereignties composing this Union. A stranger is to be introduced to an equal share without their consent. Upon a principle pretended to be deduced from the Constitution, this government, after this bill passes, may and will multiply foreign partners in power at its own mere notion; at its irresponsible pleasure; in other words, as local interests, party passions, or ambitious views may suggest.

"But," the gentleman adds, "what shall we do if we do not admit the people of Louisiana into our Union? Our children are settling that country." Sir, it is no concern of mine what he does.

This Constitution never was, and never can be, strained to lap over all the wilderness of the West without essentially affecting both the rights and convenience of its real proprietors.

Suppose, then, that it had been distinctly foreseen that, in addition to the effect of this weight, the whole population of a world beyond the Mississippi was to be brought into this and the other branch of the Legislature, to form our laws, control our rights, and decide our destiny Sir, can it be pretended that the patriots of that day would for one moment have listened to it? They were not madmen. They had not taken degrees at the hospital of idiocy.

It was not for these men [people of Louisiana] that our fathers fought. It was not for them that this Constitution was adopted. You have no authority to throw the rights and liberties and properties of this people into the "hotch-pot" with the wild men of the Missouri, nor with the mixed, though more respectable race of Anglo-Hispano-Gallo-Americans who bask on the sands in the mouth of the Mississippi. I will add only a few words, in relation to the moral and political consequences of usurping this power. I have said that it would be a virtual dissolution of the Union; and gentlemen express great sensibility at the expression. But the true source of terror is not the declaration I have made, but the deed you propose.

New States are intended to be formed beyond the Mississippi. There is no limit to men's imaginations on this subject, short of California and the Columbia River.

The extension of this principle to the States contemplated beyond the Mississippi cannot, will not, and ought not to be borne.—*American Orations, vol. I, pp. 180-202.*

The New England states spoke in these words in the Hartford convention of 1814:

In cases of deliberate, dangerous, and palpable infractions of the Constitution, affecting the sovereignty of a State and liberties of the people, it is not only the right, but the duty, of such a State to interpose its authority for their protection, in the manner best calculated to secure that end. When emergencies occur which are either beyond the reach of the judicial tribunals, or too pressing to admit of the delay incident to their forms, States which have no common umpire must be their own judges, and execute their own decisions. It will thus be proper for the several States to await the ultimate disposal of the obnoxious measures recommended by the Secretary of War, or pending before Congress, and so to use their power according to the character these measures shall finally assume, as effectually to protect their own sovereignty and the rights and liberties of their citizens.—*Cited in Foster on the Constitution, vol. I, pp. 117, 118.*

As late as 1844 and 1845 we find the legislature of Massachusetts using these phrases:

That the project of annexation of Texas, unless arrested on the threshold, may drive these States into a dissolution of the Union.—*Foster, p. 118.*

As the powers of legislation granted in the Constitution of the United States to Congress do not embrace the case of the admission of a foreign state, or foreign territory, by legislation, into the Union, such an act of admission would have no binding force whatever on the people of Massachusetts.—*Ib.*, *p. 118.*

The legislature of Wisconsin (Republican) passed the following in 1859:

Whereas, The Supreme Court of the United States has assumed appellate jurisdiction in the petition of Sherman M. Booth for a writ of habeas corpus presented and prosecuted to a final judgment in the Supreme Court of this State, and . . . assumed the power to reverse that judgment in a matter involving the personal liberty of the citizen. . . .

Resolved, That this assumption . . . is an act of undelegated power, and therefore without authority, void, and of no force.

Resolved, That the [national] Government . . . was not made exclusive or final judge of the extent of the powers delegated to itself, but that . . . each [state] has an equal right to judge for itself, as well of infractions as the mode and measure of redress.

Resolved, That the principle . . . that the general Government is the exclusive judge of the extent of the powers delegated to it, stop nothing short of despotism; since the discretion of those who administer the Government, and not the Constitution, would be the measure of their powers; that the several States which formed that instrument, being sovereign and independent, have the unquestionable right to judge of its infractions; and that a positive defiance of those sovereignties of all unauthorized acts done under color of that instrument is the rightful remedy.—*Cited in Tyler's Life of Taney, p. 307.*

But let us listen to Lincoln to hear what he has to say on this interesting subject. These extracts are from his inaugural, and from his first annual message:

I hóld that in contemplation of universal law and of the Constitution the union of these States is perpetual. Perpetuity is implied, if not expressed, in the fundamental law of all national Governments.

Again, if the United States be not a government proper, but an association of States in the nature of contract merely, can it, as a contract, be peaceably unmade by less than all parties who make it? One party to a contract may violate it, break it, so to speak; but does it not require all to lawfully rescind it?

. . . no State upon its own mere motion can lawfully get out of the Union; that resolves and ordinances to that effect are legally void; and that acts of violence within any State or States, against the authority of the United States, are insurrectionary or revolutionary, according to circumstances.

I therefore consider that in view of the Constitution and the laws, the Union is unbroken; and to the extent of my ability I shall take care, as the Constitution itself expressly enjoins upon me, that the laws of the Union be faithfully executed in all the States.

And this issue embraces more than the fate of the United States. It represents to the whole family of man the question whether a constitutional republic or democracy—a government of the people by the same people—can or cannot maintain its territorial integrity against its own domestic foes.

"Is there in all republics this inherent and fatal weakness?" Must a government of necessity be too strong for the liberties of its own people, or too weak to maintain its own existence?

It might seem, at first thought, to be of little difference whether the present movement at the South be called "secession" or "rebellion." The movers, however, well understand the difference. At the beginning they knew they could never raise their treason to any respectable magnitude by any name which implies violation of law.

They invented an ingenious sophism which, if conceded, was followed by perfectly logical steps, through all the incidents, to the complete destruction of the Union. The sophism itself is that any state of the Union may, consistently with the national constitution, and therefore lawfully and peacefully, withdraw from the Union without the consent of the Union or of any other state. The little disguise that the supposed right is to be exercised only for just cause, themselves to be the sole judges of its justice, is too thin to merit any notice.

Having never been States either in substance or in

name outside of the Union whence this magical omnipotence of "State Rights," asserting a claim of power to lawfully destroy the Union itself? Much is said about the "sovereignty" of the States; but the word, even, is not in the National Constitution, nor, as is believed, in any of the State constitutions. What is "sovereignty" in the political sense of the term? Would it be far wrong to define it "a political community without a political superior?" Tested by this, no one of our States, except Texas, ever was a "sovereignty."

By conquest or purchase the Union gave each of them whatever of independence or liberty it has. The Union is older than any of the States, and, in fact, it created them as States. Originally some dependent colonies made the Union, and in turn, the Union threw off their old independence for them, and made them States, such as they are.

What is now combated is the position that secession is consistent with the Constitution,—is lawful and peaceful. It is not contended that there is any express law for it; and nothing should ever be implied as law which leads to unjust or absurd consequences.

The seceders insist that our Constitution admits of secession.

The principle itself is one of disintegration, and upon which no government can possibly endure.— *Abraham Lincoln, Works, vol. II, pp. 3-63.*

In 1867, Chief Justice Chase, speaking for the Supreme Court in the case of Texas vs. White, formulated this famous description of the Constitution of the United States:

The Constitution, in all its provisions, looks to an indestructible Union, composed of indestructible States.

QUESTIONS.

1. What two views have been held in regard to the location of sovereignty? 2. What do you understand by sovereignty? 3. What doctrine set forth in the Kentucky resolutions? 4. What law did Kentucky hold unconstitutional? 5. How did they regard such a law? 6. Find out who drafted these resolutions. 7. Could the author of the Kentucky resolutions have cited James Wilson to support his views? 8. How did Mr. Rawle regard the Constitution? 9. Was Mas-

sachusetts, from 1803 to 1814, national or States Rights? 10. Find out the reason for its position. 11. Make an analysis of the arguments of Mr. Quincy. 12. Find out why he was so opposed to the West. 13. How would his views and those of Jefferson Davis in 1861 agree? 14. What did he mean by a "political compact"? 15. Was he narrow or broad minded? 16. Was he a good speaker? 17. Point out strong passages. 18. What view did the Hartford convention take? 19. Learn all you can of this convention. 20. Point out all the passages you can find that show a states right doctrine. 21. Gather all the passages which prove the national idea. 22. How do you explain the fact that men could differ so greatly? 23. Could both have been honest in their beliefs? 24. The position of what party surprises you most? 25. Outline Lincoln's arguments. 26. Does he agree with the Wisconsin republicans of 1859? 27. Can you find out the reason for the change? 28. Commit to memory Chase's definition of the Union. 29. Has this study made you any more tolerant than you were before? 30. Write an essay on the doctrine of "implied powers." 31. Write one on the contest between "states rights" and "nationality."

ACQUISITION OF TERRITORY.

Some additional light is thrown on the nature of the Constitution by adding the opinions of a few other men in regard to the right to acquire territory. Jefferson, in 1803, said, in speaking of the Louisiana purchase:

This treaty must, of course, be laid before both Houses, because both have important functions to exercise respecting it. They, I presume, will see their duty to their country in ratifying and paying for it, so as to secure a good which would otherwise probably be never again in their power. But I suppose they must then appeal to the nation for an additional article to the Constitution, approving and confirming an act which the nation had not previously authorized. The Constitution has made no provision for our holding foreign territory, still less for incorporating foreign nations into our Union. The executive, in seizing the fugitive occurrence, which so much advances the good of our country, has done an act beyond the Constitution. The legislature, in casting behind them metaphysical subtleties and risking themselves like faithful servants, must ratify and pay for it, and throw themselves on their country for doing for them unauthorized what we know they would have done for themselves had they been in a situation to do it. It is the case of a guardian, investing the money of his ward in purchasing an important adjacent territory; and saying to him when of age, I did this for your good; I pretend to no right to bind you; you may disavow me, and I must get out of the scrape if I can; I thought it my duty to risk myself for you. But we shall not be disavowed by the nation, and their act of indemnity will confirm and not weaken the Constitution, by more strongly marked lines.

Our confederation is certainly confined to the limits established by the revolution. The general government has no powers but such as the Constitution has given it; and it has not given it a power of holding foreign territory, and still less of incorporating it into the Union. An amendment of the Constitution seems necessary for this. In the meantime we must ratify and pay our money, as we have treated, for a thing beyond the Constitution, and rely on the nation to sanction an act done for its great good, without its previous authority.—*Thomas Jefferson, Writings (ed. 1895), vol. VIII, pp. 262, 512.*

Webster, about 1830, speaks in these words:

It was consistent with the Constitution of the United States, or thought to be so in Mr. Jefferson's time, to attach Louisiana to the United States. A treaty with France was made for that purpose. Mr. Jefferson's opinion at that moment was, that an alteration of the Constitution was necessary to enable it to be done. In consequence of considerations to which I need not now refer, that opinion was abandoned, and Louisiana was admitted by law, without any provision in, or alteration of, the Constitution. My opinion remains unchanged, that it was not within the original scope or design of the Constitution to admit new States out of foreign country.—*Webster, Works, vol. II, p. 551.*

QUESTIONS.

1. How did Jefferson feel in regard to right to buy Louisiana? 2. Why, then, did he make the purchase? 3. Would you expect Webster to take the same view? 4. How do we regard the right now? 5. How explain the change?

ARISTOCRACY VS. DEMOCRACY.

The aristocratic tendencies of a part of the American people at the close of the last century is well illustrated by the following extracts from Fisher Ames, the most eloquent of the Federalists. A few quotations from Jefferson to show the opposite belief must close this paper.

All such men are, or ought to be, agreed, that simple governments are despotisms, and of all despotisms a democracy, though the least durable, is the most violent. . . .

The known propensity of a democracy is to licentiousness, which the ambitious call, and the ignorant believe, to be liberty.

The great object, then, of political wisdom in framing our Constitution was to guard against licentiousness, that inbred malady of democracies, that deforms their infancy with gray hairs and decrepitude. . . .

The Press, however, has left the understanding of the mass of men just where it found it; but, by supplying an endless stimulus to their imagination and passions, it has rendered their temper and habits infinitely worse, it has inspired ignorance with presumption, so that those who cannot be governed by reason are no longer awed by authority. . . .

While it has impaired the force that every just government can employ in self-defence, it has imparted to its enemies the result of that wildfire, that blazes with the most consuming fierceness on attempting to quench it. . . .

It is undoubtedly a salutary labour to diffuse among the citizens of a free state, as far as the thing is possible, a just knowledge of their publick affairs. But the difficulty of this task is augmented exactly in proportion to the freedom of the state; for the more the citizens, the bolder and more profligate will be their demagogues, the more numerous and eccentrick the popular errours, and the more vehement and pertinacious the passions that defend them.

Yet, as if there were neither vice nor passion in the world, one of the loudest of our boasts, one of the dearest of all the tenets of our creed is, that we are a sovereign people—*self-governed,*—it would be nearer the truth to say, self-conceited. For in what sense is it true, that any people, however free, are self-governed? If they have in fact no government, but such as comports with their ever varying and often inordinate desires, then it is anarchy; if it counteracts those desires, it is compulsory. The individual who is left to act according to his own humour is not governed at all; and if any considerable number, and especially any combination of individuals, find or can place themselves in this situation, then the society is no longer free. For liberty obviously consists in the salutary restraint, and not in the uncontrolled indulgence of such humours.

The republick is a creature of fiction; it is everybody in fancy, but nobody in *heart*. Love, to be anything, must be select and exclusive.

A state consisting of a million citizens has a million sovereigns, each of whom detests all other sovereigns but his own.

Are not the wandering Tartars or Indian hunters at least as susceptible of patriotism as these stragglers in our Western forests, and infinitely fonder of glory? It is difficult to conceive of a country which, from the manner of its settlement or the manifest tendencies of its politicks, is more destitute or more incapable of being inspired with political virtue.

Its nature ordains that its next change shall be into a military despotism, of all known governments, perhaps, the most prone to shift its head, and the slowest to mend its vices. The reason is that the tyranny of what is called the people, and that by the sword, both operate alike to debase and corrupt, till there are neither men left with the spirit to desire liberty, nor morals with the power to sustain justice. Like the burning pestilence that destroys the human body, nothing can subsist by its dissolution but vermine.—*Fisher Ames, Works, pp. 382-419.*

Jefferson speaks as follows:

"The basis of our governments being the opinion of the people, the very first object should be to keep that right; and were it left to me to decide whether we should have a government without newspapers, or newspapers without a government, I should not hesitate a moment to prefer the latter. But I should mean that every man should receive those papers and be capable of reading them. . . . Among [such societies] public opinion is in the place of law, and restrains morals as powerfully as law ever did anywhere. . . . Cherish, therefore, the spirit of our people and keep alive their attention. Do not be too severe upon their errors, but restrain them by enlightening them. If once they become inattentive to the public affairs, you and I, and Congress and Assemblies, Judges, and Governors, shall all become wolves."—*To Edw. Carrington, Jan. 17, 1787. Works, vol. IV (1853 ed.).*

"I hold it that a little rebellion now and then is a good thing, and as necessary in the political world as storms in the physical. Unsuccessful rebellions, indeed, generally establish the encroachments on the rights of the people which have produced them. An observation of this truth should render honest republican governors so mild in their punishment of rebellions as not to discourage them too much. It is a medicine necessary for the sound health of government."—*To Madison, Jan. 30, 1787. Works, vol. IV (1853 ed.).*

QUESTIONS.

1. How does Ames regard the people? 2. What does he expect to become of democracies? 3. How would you explain his feeling? 4. Compare his ideas with those of Jefferson. 5. Did Jefferson fear little insurrections? 6. Why not? 7. Which expressed the best doctrines?

American History Studies

No. 6.   FEBRUARY, 1898.

SLAVERY IN THE UNITED STATES
I.

SELECTIONS MADE FROM THE SOURCES

BY

H. W. CALDWELL,

UNIVERSITY OF NEBRASKA.

J. H. MILLER, Publisher,

LINCOLN, NEBRASKA.

Yearly Subscription, 40 cents.   Single Copy, 5 cents.

PUBLISHED MONTHLY, EXCEPT JULY AND AUGUST.

Entered as second-class matter at the Post Office, Lincoln, Nebraska, U. S. A

AMERICAN HISTORY STUDIES.

SLAVERY IN THE UNITED STATES.

IN some respects this has been the most interesting, as, for a time, it was the most important, question in all American history. The great tragedy of the civil war came from it. For years before that event the people of the north and those of the south were unable to understand one another. It may be that they did not try as hard as they might, yet the environments had become so different from the existence of sectional slavery that it was very difficult for the people to see things from the same standpoints.

It will not do to suppose the civil war was wholly due to slavery, yet that it furnished the main causes I believe history will affirm. Neither must we suppose that the contest was the outcome of momentary hatred, nor that one section can be held wholly responsible for its terrible devastation. The factors had been in process of formation for more than two hundred years. The whole history of the white race on this continent must be studied to understand the problem thoroughly. The soil, climate, and resulting industries played an important part. Perhaps the most important thought for the youth of to-day to grasp is that the two sections were equally honest in their views. History, I believe, will affirm, nay, has affirmed, that those who fought for the southern view were wrong, and that the north, in this case, stood for progress and an advancing civilization. However, we should recognize that conditions and circumstances to a great degree determined belief; we should do justice to the devotion, the sacrifices, the courage, and the brilliancy with which they fought for a mistaken view. It is now time to cement the bond of union, to look to the future, to study the past for its lessons, but not to taunt nor to condemn.

In a general way we may note, as it seems to me, about four general periods in this history. From 1619 to 1774, the period of planting. During these years the question was little thought about. Very few saw the dangers. It was not a political question at all. It can hardly be said to have come into the field of ethics, although a few here and there began to question its morality.

From 1774 to 1808 there was a marked movement to put an end to the system. This force was strongest under the immediate influence of the Revolution, and had almost entirely passed away in the south by the end of the period. During these years the northern states freed themselves, and thus laid the foundation for the sectional contest. The almost, if not quite, unanimous expression of opinion during the earlier, at least, of these years was that slavery was an evil which it was hoped might pass away.

The third period extended from 1808 to 1844, and was marked by a gradual recognition of the fact that there was no chance for the system to die out of itself. Gradually there came to be a recognition that the supposed interests of the two sections, socially, politically, and industrially were opposed. The north was coming to the view more positively that the whole system was an evil, and many came to believe it a sin for which all must answer. On the other hand, the south ceased to be apologists for its existence, and finally came to believe almost as one man that it was "a good—a positive good."

The last period was that of contest. It began as a political issue, and ended in a physical struggle such as the world had perhaps never seen before. During these years scarcely a fact in American politics can be mentioned which was not more or less involved with the question of slavery.

This brief outline is given, not because it is strictly in accordance with the laboratory method, but because in the brief extracts which I can give not enough matter can be presented to suggest the classification. A study of the following extracts may give something of a chance to test the truth of the conclusions, but they will hardly be full enough to establish their correctness.

The following extracts from the early laws of the colonies will give us some idea of the state of mind which must have been back of the laws:

[1652.] And itt is further ordered by this Courte and the authoritje thereof, that all Scotchmen, Negroes, and Indjans inhabitting with or servants to the English, from the age of sixteene to sixty yeares, shall be enlisted. . . .—*Records of the Colony of Mass. Bay, vol. IV, part I, p. 86.*

[1680.] Wm. Seete, Governor: There are but fewe servants amongst us, and less slaves, not above 30, as we judge, in the Colony.—*Colonial Records of Connecticutt, 1678-1689, p. 298.*

[1723.] Be it enacted . . . if any negro or Indian servant or slave shall be found abroad from home in the night season, after nine of the clock, without special order from his or their master or mistress, it shall be lawful for any person or persons to apprehend and secure such negro or Indian servant or slave so offending, and him or them bring before the next assistant or justice of peace.—*Ibid, 1717-1725, p. 390.*

[1681. Proposals for the carrying on of the Negroe's Christianity.] Now concerning the Negroe's, . . . The first and great step will be to procure . . . their Owners consent, as being supposed to be averse thereto: not altogether, as is here believed, out of

Interest . . . ; but by reason of the trouble, and the fancied needlessness of the Work; and to prevent all danger from their slaves being furnisht with knowledge, consequent, they conceive thereto.—*Hart, American History Told by Contemporaries, vol. I, p. 299.*

. . . Be it hereby further Declared and Enacted, by and with the Authority, Advice, and Consent aforesaid, That no Negro or Negroes, by receiving the Holy Sacrament of Baptism, is thereby manumitted or set free, nor hath any Right or Title to Freedom or Manumission, more than he or they had before; any Law, Usage, or Custom to the contrary notwithstanding.— *Hening's Statutes of Virginia, 1715, ch. 44, sec. 24.*

Be it further Enacted, . . . That for every Negro imported into this Province, either by Land or Water, the Importer or Importers of such Negro or Negroes shall pay unto the said Naval Officer aforesaid, the Sum of Twenty Shillings Sterling per Poll . . .—*Ibid, 1715, ch. 36, sec. 8.*

Be it therefore Enacted, . . . , That from and after the End of this present Session of Assembly, No Negro, or Mulatto Slave, Free Negro, or Mulatto born of a White Woman, during his Time of Servitude by Law, or any Indian Slave, or Free Indian Natives of this or the neighboring Provinces, be admitted and received as good and valid Evidence in Law, in any Matter or Thing whatsoever, . . . , wherein any Christian White Person is concerned.—*Ibid, 1717, ch. 13, sec. 2.*

[1765.] Be it Enacted, . . . , That the Justices of the several and respective County Courts within this Province, be, and they are hereby impowered and required, . . . , to appoint the Constable of every Hundred, where the said Justices, at their Discretion, shall think proper and expedient, to suppress the Assembling and tumultuous Meeting of Negroes and other Slaves; . . .—*Hening, Statutes of Virginia.*

[1725.] XI. And be it enacted by the Authority aforesaid, That no Master or Mistress of any Negroe shall hereafter, for any Reward, Sum or Sums of Money, stipulated and agreed upon betwixt them, or upon any Pretence whatsoever, permit or suffer his or their Negroes to ramble about, under Pretence of getting Work, nor give Liberty to their Negroes to seek their own Employ, and so go to work at their own Wills, under the Penalty of Twenty Shillings for every such Offence.—*Acts of Pennsylvania.*

[1792.] V. No negro or mulatto shall be a witness, except in pleas of the Commonwealth against negroes or mulattoes, or in civil pleas, where negroes or mulattoes alone shall be parties.

VI. No slave shall go from the tenements of his master or other person with whom he lives, without a pass, or some letter or token, whereby it may appear that he is proceeding by authority from his master, employer, or overseer. . . .

. . . .

XI. Riots, routs, unlawful assemblies, trespasses and seditious speeches by a slave or slaves, shall be punished by stripes . . .—*Acts of the General Assembly of Pennsylvania, Printed by A. Davis, 1794, pp. 196, 197.*

[1793.] II. Be it enacted by the General Assembly, That from and after the passing of this act, every free negro or mulatto, who resides in, or is employed to labour within the limits of any city, borough, or town, shall be registered and numbered in a book to be kept for that purpose by the clerk of the said city, borough, or town, which register shall specify his or her age, name, colour and stature, by whom, and in what court the said negro or mulatto was emancipated, or that such negro or mulatto was born free.—*Ibid, p. 327.*

[1687, New York.] . . . This I observe that they take no care of the conversion of their Slaves.—*Hart, vol. I, p. 548.*

[1650, New York.] There are, also, various other negroes in this country, some of whom have been made free for their long service, but their children have remained slaves, though it is contrary to the laws of every people that anyone born of a Christian mother should be a slave and be compelled to remain in servitude.—*Ibid, p. 535.*

[Rev. John McDowell said in 1762 concerning North Carolina]: We have but few families in this parish, but of the best in the province, viz., His Excellency the Governor, His Honor the President, some of the honorable Council, Col. Dry, the Collector, and about 20 other good families, who have each of them great gangs of slaves. We have in all about 200 families.—*Cited in J. H. U. Studies, 1896, p. 193.*

Every freeman of Carolina shall have absolute power and authority over negro slaves of what opinion and religion whatsoever.—*Ibid, p. 27.*

Be it further enacted, That if any master, or owner of negroes, or slaves, or any other person or persons whatsoever in the government shall permit or suffer any negro or negroes to build on their or either of their lands or any part thereof any house under pretense of a meeting house upon account of worship or upon any pretense whatsoever, and shall not suppress and hinder them, he, she, or they so offending shall for every default forfeit or pay fifty pounds, one-half towards defraying the contingent charges of the government, the other to him or them that shall sue for the same.—*Ibid, p. 50.*

That there were those during these years who held different views from those manifested in these laws may be seen from the following extracts. JONATHAN EDWARDS the younger said:

"To hold a man in a state of slavery, is to be, every day, guilty of robbing him of his liberty, or of man stealing."—*Cited in Goodell, Slavery and Anti-Slavery, p. 28.*

The town meeting of Danbury, Connecticut, in 1774, passed the following resolution:

"We cannot but think it a palpable absurdity so loudly to complain of attempts to Enslave *us* while we are actually Enslaving others."—*American Archives, vol. I, p. 1038.*

The Friends, in their annual meetings, give us their views in the following resolutions:

[1696, Advised the members to] be careful not to encourage the bringing in of any more negroes, and that those who have negroes be careful of them, bring them to meetings, have meetings with them in their families, restrain them from loose and lewd living, as much as in them lies, and from rambling abroad, on First days or other times.

[1774.] All members concerned in importing, selling, purchasing, giving or transferring negroes or other slaves, or otherwise acting in such a manner as to continue them in slavery beyond the term limited by law or custom [for whites] was directed to be excluded fr. membership or disowned.

[1776.] It was enacted by the same meeting That the owners of slaves, who refused to execute proper instruments for giving them their freedom, were to be disowned likewise.—*Goodell, pp. 35, 36.*

In the Virginia convention of 1774 to choose delegates to the Philadelphia convention, Jefferson laid before it an exposition of the rights of British America. A part was as follows:

The abolition of domestic slavery is the great object of desire in those colonies where it was unhappily introduced in their infant state. But previous to the enfranchisement of the slaves, it is necessary to exclude all further importations from Africa; Yet our repeated attempts to effect this by prohibitions, and by imposing duties which might amount to a prohibition, have been hitherto defeated by his Majesty's negative; Thus preferring the immediate advantage of a few African [British] corsairs, to the lasting interests of the American States, and to the rights of human nature deeply wounded by this infamous practice.—*Jefferson, Works, vol. I (Ford), p. 440.*

The convention actually

Resolved, We will neither ourselves import nor purchase any slave or slaves imported by any other person after the 1st day of November next [1774], either from Africa, the W. Indies, or any other place.—*Ib., p. 687.*

The North Carolina Provincial Convention of the same year

Resolved, That we will not import any slave or slaves, or purchase any slave or slaves imported or brought into the province by others, from any part of the world after the first day of Nov. next.—*Ib., p. 735.*

The first General Congress, in 1774, passed the following Articles of Association:

We do, for ourselves and the inhabitants of the several Colonies whom we represent, firmly agree and associate, as follows: . . .

2. We will neither import nor purchase, any slave imported after the first day of December next; after which time, we will wholly discontinue the slave trade, and will neither be concerned in it ourselves, nor will we hire our vessels, nor sell our commodities or manufactures, to those who are concerned in it.

. . . .

11. That a committee be chosen in every county, city, and town, by those who are qualified to vote for representatives in the legislature, whose business it shall be attentively to observe the conduct of all persons touching this association; and when it shall be made to appear, to the satisfaction of a majority of any such committee, that any person within the limits of their appointment has violated this association, that such majority do forthwith cause the truth of the case to be published in the gazette; to the end, that all such foes to the rights of British-America may be publicly known and universally contemned as the enemies of American liberty; and thenceforth we respectively will break off all dealings with him or her.

. . . .

14. And we do further agree and resolve that we will have no trade, commerce, dealings or intercourse whatsoever, with any colony or province, in N. Amer., which shall not accede to or who shall hereafter violate this association, but will hold them as unworthy of the rights of freemen and as inimical to the liberties of this country.—*Journal of Congress, vol. I, 23 f.*

The representatives of the Darien district, in Georgia, in 1775, resolved:

"To show the world that we are not influenced by any contracted or interested motives, but a general philanthropy for all mankind, of whatever climate, language, or complexion, we hereby declare our disapprobation and abhorrence of the unnatural practice of slavery in America (however the uncultivated state of our country, or other specious arguments may plead for it,) a practice founded in injustice and cruelty, and highly dangerous to our liberties (as well as lives,) debasing part of our fellow-creatures below men, and corrupting the virtue and morals of rest, and is laying the basis of that liberty we contend for, (and which we pray the Almighty to continue to the latest posterity,) upon a very wrong foundation. We, therefore, Resolve, at all times to use our utmost endeavors for the manumission of our slaves in this colony, upon the most safe and equitable footing for the master and themselves."—*Am. Archives, vol. I, p. 1136.*

The Declaration of Independence as originally drafted contained the following clause:

he has waged cruel war against human nature itself, violating it's most sacred rights of life & liberty in the persons of a distant people who never offended him, captivating & carrying them into slavery in another hemisphere, or to incur miserable death in their transportation thither. this piratical warfare, the opprobrium of *infidel* powers, is the warfare of the *Christian* king of Great Britain determined to keep open a market where MEN should be bought & sold he has prostituted his negative for suppressing every legislative attempt to prohibit or to restrain this execrable commerce: and that this assemblage of horrors might want no fact of distinguished die, he is now exciting those very people to rise in arms among us, and to purchase that liberty of which *he* has deprived them, by murdering the people upon whom *he* also obtruded them: thus paying off former crimes committed against the *liberties* of one people, with crimes which he urges them to commit against the *lives* of another. —*Jefferson, Works, vol. II (Ford), p. 51, Facsimile.*

Jefferson's draft of the Ordinance of 1784 for the government of the territories of the United States contained this clause in relation to slavery:

After the year 1800 of the Christian era there shall be neither slavery nor involuntary Servitude in any of the said States, otherwise than in punishment of crimes whereof the party shall have been convicted to be personally guilty.

The Ordinance of 1787, which provided for the

government of the northwest territory, had this provision in regard to the subject under consideration:

Art. VI. There shall be neither slavery nor involuntary servitude in the said territory, otherwise than in punishment of crimes whereof the party shall have been duly convicted; . . .

JEFFERSON, in his "Notes on Virginia," in 1782, discusses the subject as follows:

"There must doubtless be an unhappy influence on the manners of our people produced by the existence of slavery among us. The whole commerce between master and slave is a perpetual exercise of the most boisterous passions, the most unremitting despotism, on the one part, and degrading submissions on the other. Our children see this, and learn to imitate it; for man is an imitative animal. . . . If a parent could find no motive either in his philanthropy or his self-love for restraining the intemperance of passion towards his slave, it should always be a sufficient one that his child is present. But generally it is not sufficient. The parent storms, the child looks on, catches the lineaments of wrath, puts on the same airs in the circle of smaller slaves, gives a loose to the worst of passions, and thus nursed, educated, and daily exercised in tyranny, cannot but be stamped by it with odious peculiarities. The man must be a prodigy who can retain his manners and morals undepraved by such circumstances. And with what execration should the statesman be loaded, who, permitting one-half of the citizens thus to trample on the rights of the other, transforms those into despots, and these into enemies, destroys the morals of the one and the *amor patriæ* of the other! . . With the morals of the people their industry also is destroyed. . . . And can the liberties of a nation be thought secure, when we have removed their only firm basis, a conviction in the minds of the people that these liberties are of the gift of God? That they are not to be violated but with His wrath? Indeed, I tremble for my country when I reflect that God is just; that His justice cannot sleep forever; that considering numbers,

nature, and natural means only, a revolution of the wheel of Fortune, an exchange of situation, is among possible events; that it may become probable by supernatural interference! The Almighty has no attribute which can take side with us in such a contest."
—*Works, vol. III (Ford), pp. 266-7.*

The following letters from Jefferson will show how he felt in regard to the institution of slavery:

To Dr. Price, encouraging him and praising the spirit of a pamphlet against slavery, 1785:

Southward of the Chesapeak it will find but few readers concurring with it in sentiment on the subject of slavery. From the mouth to the head of the Chesapeak, the bulk of the people will approve it in theory, and it will find a reputable minority ready to accept it in practice, a minority which for weight and worth of character preponderates against the greatest number, who have not the courage to divest their families of a property which however keeps their conscience unquiet. Northward of the Chesapeak you may find here and there an opponent to your doctrine or you may find here and there a robber and a murderer, but in no greater number. . . . In a few years there will be no slaves Northward of Maryland. In Maryland I do not find such a disposition to begin the redress of this enormity as in Virginia. This is the next state to which we may turn our eyes for the interesting spectacle of justice in conflict with avarice and oppression.—*Works, vol. IV (Ford), pp. 82-3.*

To M. de Meustier, January 24, 1786:

I conjecture there are 650,000 negroes in the 5 Southernmost states, and not 50,000 in the rest. In most of these latter effectual measures have been taken for their future emancipation. In the former, nothing is done toward that. The disposition to emancipate them is strongest in Virginia. Those who desire it, form, as yet, the minority of the whole state, but it bears a respectable proportion to the whole in numbers and weight of character, and is continually recruiting by the addition of nearly the whole of the young men as fast as they come into public life. I flatter myself it will take place there at some period of time not very distant. In Maryland and N. Carolina a very few are disposed to emancipate. In S. Carolina and Georgia not the smallest symptoms of it, but, on the contrary these 2 states and N. Carolina continue importations of negroes.—*Ibid, pp. 145-6.*

To M. DE MEUSTIER, 1786:

What a stupendous, what an incomprehensible machine! Who can endure toil, famine, stripes, imprisonment and death itself in vindication of his own liberty, and the next moment be deaf to all those motives whose power supported him thro' his trial, and inflict on his fellow men a bondage, one hour of which is fraught with more misery than ages of that which he rose in rebellion to oppose. But we must await with patience the workings of an overruling providence. I hope that, that is preparing the deliverance of these, our suffering brethren. When the measure of their tears shall be full, when their groans shall have involved heaven itself in darkness, doubtless a God of justice will awaken to their distress, and by diffusing light and liberality among their oppressors, or at length by his exterminating thunder, manifest his attention to the things of this world, and that they are not left to the guidance of a blind fatality."—*Ibid, p. 185.*

To ST. GEORGE TUCKER, August 28, 1797,

[subscribes to emancipation], and to the mode of emancipation, I am satisfied that that must be a matter of compromise between the passions, the prejudices, and the real difficulties which will each have their weight in that operation. Perhaps the first chapter of this history, which has begun in St. Domingo . . . may prepare our minds for a peaceable accomodation between justice, policy and necessity; and furnish an answer to the difficult question, whither shall the colored emigrants go? and the sooner we put some plan underway, the greater hope there is that it may be permitted to proceed peaceably to it's ultimate effect. But if something is not done and soon done, we shall be the murderers of our own children.—*Ibid, vol. VII, pp. 167-8.*

To EDWARD COLES, 1814:

[His views] have long since been in possession of the public, and time has only served to give them stronger proof. The love of justice and the love of country plead equally the cause of these people, and it is a mortal reproach to us that they should have pleaded so long in vain. . . . The hour of emancipation is advancing in the march of time. It will come and whether brought on by the generous energy of our own minds or by the bloody process of St. Domingo . . . is a leaf in our history not yet turned over. . . . I have seen no proposition so expedient, on the whole, as that of emancipation of those born after a given day. . . . This enterprise . . . shall have all my prayers.

Washington speaks in no uncertain words in regard to his desires and intentions:

To ROBT. MORRIS, April 12, 1786:

I can only say that there is not a man living who wishes more sincerely than I do to see a plan adopted for the abolition of it [slavery]; but there is only one proper and effectual mode in which it can be accomplished, and that is by legislative authority; and this, so far as my suffrage will go, shall never be wanting.—*Works, vol. IX (Sparks), p. 158.*

To JOHN F. MERCER, September 9, 1786:

I never mean, unless some particular circumstances should compel me to it, to possess another slave by purchase, it being among my first wishes to see some plan adopted, by which slavery in this country may be abolished by law.—*Ib., p. —.*

Washington, by his will, freed all his slaves.

WILLIAM PINCKNEY, in Maryland House of Delegates, 1789, says:

Iniquitous and most dishonorable to Maryland, is that dreary system of partial bondage which her laws have hitherto supported with a solicitude worthy of a better object and her citizens, by their practice, countenanced. Founded in a disgraceful traffic, to which the present country lent its fostering aid, from motives of interest, but which even she would have disdained to encourage, had England been the destined mart of such inhuman merchandize, its continuance is as shameful as its origin.—*Elliot's Debates, vol. —, p. —.*

JOHN JAY says:

Till America comes into this measure [abolition] her progress to Heaven will be impious. This is a strong expression but it is just. I believe that God is just, and I believe it to be a maxim in His, as in other courts, that those who ask equity ought to do it. —*Letter from Spain, 1780, Goodell, p. 30.*

THE SLAVE COMPROMISES IN THE CONSTITUTION.

Representatives and direct Taxes shall be apportioned among the several States which may be included within this Union, according to their respective numbers, which shall be determined by adding to the whole Number of free Persons, including those bound to Service for a Term of Years, . . . three-fifth of all other Persons.—*The Constitution, art. I, sec. 2, cl. 3.*

On the above article of the Constitution a long debate took place in the Constitutional Convention. Various opinions in regard to its merits were expressed by the members of the convention. The following extracts will well illustrate the general trend of the debate.

GERRY (MASS.): Why should the blacks, who were property in the South, be in the rule of representation more than the cattle and horses in the North?

PINCKNEY (S. C.): . . . He thought the blacks ought to stand on an equality with the whites; but would agree to the ratio settled by Congress.

BUTLER (S. C.) insisted that the labor of a slave in South Carolina was as productive and valuable as that of a free man in Massachusetts; that as wealth was the great means of defence and utility to the nation, they were equally valuable to it with freemen; and that consequently an equal representation ought to be allowed for them in a government which was instituted principally for the protection of property, and was itself to be supported by property.

WILSON (PA.) did not well see on what principle the admission of blacks in the proportion of three-fifths could be explained. Are they admitted as citizens—then why not admitted on an equality with white citizens? Are they admitted as property—then why not all other property? . . .

RANDOLPH (VA.): He urged strenuously that express security ought to be provided for including slaves in the ratio of representation. He lamented that such a species of property existed. But as it did exist, the holders of it would require this security. It was perceived that the design was entertained by some of excluding slaves altogether; the Legislature therefore ought not to be left at liberty.

PINCKNEY (S. C.) reminded the committee that if the convention should fail to insert some security to the Southern States against an emancipation of slaves, . . . he should be bound by duty to his state to vote against their report.

ROGER SHERMAN (CONN.) did not regard the admission of the negroes into the ratio of representation, as liable to such insuperable objections. It was the freemen of the Southern States who were, in fact, to be represented according to the taxes paid by them, and the negroes are only included in the estimate of the taxes. . . .—*The Madison Papers, pp. 143, 302, 324, 332, 336, 418, 480.*

The Migration or Importation of such Persons as any of the States now existing shall think proper to admit, shall not be prohibited by the Congress prior to the Year one thousand eight hundred and eight, but a Tax or duty may be imposed on such Importation, not exceeding ten dollars for each Person.—*The Constitution, art. I, sec. 9, cl. 1.*

On this clause again a long debate ensued:

RUTLEDGE (S. C.): . . . Religion and humanity had nothing to do with this question. Interest alone is the governing principle with nations. The true question at present is, whether the Southern States shall or shall not be parties to the Union. If the Northern States consult their interest, they will not oppose the increase of Slaves, which will increase the commodities of which they will have become the carriers.

ELLSWORTH (CONN.) was for leaving the clause as it stands. Let every State import what it pleases. The morality or wisdom of slavery are considerations belonging to the States themselves. What enriches a part enriches the whole, and the States are the best judges of their particular interests.

PINCKNEY (S. C.): South Carolina can never receive the plan if it prohibits the slave trade.

SHERMAN (CONN.): He disapproved of the slave trade, yet as the States were now possessed of the right to import slaves, and as the *public good* did not require it to be taken from them . . . he thought it best to leave the matter as we find it. He observed that the abolition of slavery seemed to be going on in the United States, and that the good sense of the several States would probably by degrees complete it, . .

MASON (VA.): This infamous traffic originated in the avarice of British merchants. . . . The evil of having slaves was experienced during the late war, . . . Maryland and Virginia had already prohibited the importation of slaves. . . . All this would be in vain, if South Carolina and Georgia be at liberty to import. . . . The Western people are already calling out for slaves for their new lands; and will fill that country with slaves, if they can be got through South Carolina and Georgia. . . .

BALDWIN (GA.): . . . Georgia could not give up this one of her favorite prerogatives. If left to herself she may probably put a stop to the evil. . . .

WILLIAMSON (N. C.): . . . He thought the Southern States could not be members of the Union if the clause should be rejected.

KING (MASS.): If Southern States would not confederate with the tax on slaves imported, so he thought Northern would not if this clause were omitted.

RUTLEDGE (S. C.): If the convention thinks North Carolina, South Carolina and Georgia will ever agree to the plan, unless their right to import be untouched, the expectation is vain. The people of those States will never be such fools as to give up so important an interest.

MADISON (VA.): Twenty years will produce all the mischief that can be apprehended from the liberty to import slaves. So long a time will be more dishonorable to the American character than to say nothing about it in the constitution. . . .

He thought it wrong to admit in the constitution the idea that there could be property in men.—*The Madison Papers, pp. 577, 578, 581, 582, 603, 610.*

A few extracts from speeches made in the State conventions to consider the adoption of the constitution throw still more light on the views prevailing at the time.

JAS. WILSON (Pa.):

I consider this clause as laying the foundation for banishing slavery out of this country; and though the period is more distant than I could wish it, it will produce the same kind, gradual change as was produced in Pennsylvania. . . . The *new* States which are to be formed will be under *the control* of Congress in this particular, and slavery will never be introduced among them.—*Elliot's Debates, vol. II, p. 452.*

GEN. HEATH (Mass.):

The migration or importation, etc., is confined to the States now *existing only;* new States cannot claim it. Congress by their ordinance for erecting new States some time since, declared that the new States shall be republican, and that there shall be no slavery in them.—*Ib., vol. II, p. 115.*

JOHNSON (Va.):

They tell us they see a progressive danger of bringing about emancipation. The principle has begun since the Revolution. Let us do what we will, it will come round. Slavery has been the foundation of much of that rapacity and dissipation which have been so much disseminated among our countrymen. If it were totally abolished, it would do much good.—*Ib., vol. III, pp. 6-48.*

GOVR. RANDOLPH (Va.):

I hope there are none here who, . . . will advance an objection dishonorable to Virginia, that, at the moment they are receiving the rights of their citizens, there is a spark of hope that those unfortunate men now held in bondage may, by the operation of the general government, be made free.—*Ib., vol. III, p. 598.*

PATRICK HENRY (Va.)

[argued for] the power of Congress . . . to abolish slavery in the States. Another thing will contribute to bring this event about. Slavery is detested. We feel its effects. We deplore it with all the pity of humanity.—*Ib. vol. III, p. 463.*

On the presentation of the Quaker memorial on slave trade to the House of Representatives, March, 1790, JACKSON (Ga.), said:

The situation of the slaves here, their situation in their native states, and the disposal of them in case of emancipation, should be considered. That slavery was an evil habit he did not mean to controvert; but that habit was already established, and there were peculiar situations in countries which rendered that habit necessary. Such situations the states of South Carolina and Georgia were in: large tracts of the most fertile lands on the continent remained uncultivated for the want of population. It was frequently advanced on the floor of Congress how unhealthy those climates were, and how impossible it was for northern constitutions to exist there. What, he asked, is to be done with this uncultivated territory? Is it to remain a waste? Is the rice trade to be banished from our coasts? Are Congress willing to deprive themselves of the revenue arising from that trade, and which is daily increasing, and to throw this great advantage in the hands of other countries? . . .—*Annals, vol. II, pp. 1197-1205.*

Eight years later the territory of Mississippi was organized. On motion to strike out the clause protecting slavery in the territory, MR. HARPER (S. C.), said:

In the Northwest Territory the regulation forbidding slavery was a very proper one, as the people inhabiting that part of the country were from parts where slavery did not prevail, and they had of course no slaves amongst them; but in the Miss. Territory . . that species of property already exists, and persons emigrating there from the Southern States would carry with them property of this kind. To agree to such a proposition would, therefore, be a decree of banishment to all the persons settled there and of exclusion to all those intending to go there . . . It struck at the habits and customs of the people.—*Berton's Debates, vol. II, p. 221 f.*

MR. VARNUM (Mass.)

thought the high-price of lands in the N. W. Territory was due to the absence of slavery "and if the Southern States could get clear of their slaves, the price of their land would immediately rise."—*Ib., p. 221 f.*

MR GILES (Va.)

thought that if the slaves of the Southern States were permitted to go into this Western country, by lessening the number in those States, and spreading them over a large surface of country there would be a greater probability of ameliorating their condition.—*Ib., p. 221 f.*

At the time of the organization of Arkansas as a territory, in 1819, a long and bitter debate took place. These extracts show the spirit:

WALKER (N. C.):

Shall they [the South] be proscribed and prohibited from taking their slaves? Sir, if so, your land will be an uncultivated waste—a fruitless soil; it is further south than the 35th degree of latitude, a low and warm country, that will not support a laboring white population.

Slavery is an evil we have long deplored but cannot cure; it was entailed upon us by our ancestors; it was not our original sin, and we cannot, in our present situation, release ourselves from the embarrassment; and, as it is an evil, the more diffusive, the lighter it will be felt, and the wider it is extended the more equal the proportion of inconvenience.—*Annals, vol. XXXIV, p. 1226.*

MCLANE (Delaware):

The fixing of a line on the West of the Miss., north of which slavery should not be tolerated had always been with him a favorite policy, and he hoped the day was not distant when upon principles of fair compromise it might constitutionally be effected.

If we meet upon principles of reciprocity we cannot fail to do justice to all. It has already been avowed by gentlemen . . . from the South and the West that they will agree upon a line which shall divide the slaveholding from the non-slaveholding states. It is this proposition I am anxious to effect; but I wish to effect it by some compact which shall be binding upon all parties, and all subsequent legislatures; which cannot be changed and will not fluctuate with the diversity of feeling and of sentiment to which this Empire in its course must be destined.—*Ib.*, *p. 1227 f.*

The Missouri question, and line of 36° 30′, 1819-'21.

REID (Ga.):

Slavery is "an unnatural state; a dark cloud which obscures half the lustre of our free institutions! But it is a fixed evil which we can only alleviate. Are we called upon to emancipate our slaves? I answer, their welfare—the safety of our citizens, forbid it."—*Annals, vol. XXXV, p. 1024.*

If you remain inexorable; if you persist in refusing the humble, the decent, the reasonable prayer of Missouri, is there no danger that her resistance will rise in proportion to your oppression? Sir, the firebrand, which is even now cast into your society will require blood—ay; and the blood of freemen—for its quenching. Your Union shall tremble as under the force of an earthquake.—*Ib., p. 1033.*

BARBOUR (Va.):

I am not easily alarmed, nor am I disposed to be an alarmist; but this I will say, that I fear this subject will be an ignited spark, which, communicated to an immense mass of combustion, will produce an explosion that will shake this Union to its center. This portentious subject, twelve months ago, was a little spark scarcely visible above the horizon; it has already overcast the heavens, obscuring every other object.—*Ib., p. 107.*

WHITMAN (Mass.):

In the degree in which you increase the proportion of the free beyond that of the slave population, in the same ratio you increase the chance for emancipation, final and total. . . . The best mode, . . . to promote the cause of a final emancipation would be to suffer the slaves to be scattered thinly over the western States. The permission of slavery in the Territory of Arkansas will afford no additional facilities to the introduction of this unfortunate race from abroad. The natural increase will be the same whether in one part of the Union or the other; or if it would be greater in the Western country, it would be the consequence of an ameliorated condition and therefore not to be regretted.—*Annals, vol. XXXIV, pp. 1274-5.*

Why may we not continue in this way, admitting states off against the non-slaveholding states westerly, with the restriction, and off against the slaveholding States without it? True, sectional lines are to be abhorred: But we have them in relation to this subject already. The line [of the Ohio] is distinctly marked. . . . Having so begun we must continue on.—*Ib., p. 1278.*

JEFFERSON writes:

[1820.] The coincidence of a marked principle, moral and political, with geographical lines, once conceived, I feared would never more be obliterated from the mind; that it would be recurring on every occasion and renewing irritations, until it would kindle such mutual and mortal hatred as to render separation preferable to eternal discord. I have been among the most sanguine in believing that our Union would be of long duration. I now doubt it much.—*Jefferson, Works, vol. VII (Washington ed.), p. 158.*

QUESTIONS.

1. Were negroes subject to military service? 2. What does this imply in regard to their position? 3. Were there many negroes in the north? 4. Why the law against the negroes being abroad at night? 5. How long had they been away from Africa at this time? 6. Why did they question whether the negro

should be Christianized? 7. How did they settle the matter? 8. How about their right to testify? 9. Why do you suppose such a law was passed? 10. Why the acts against assembling of negroes? 11. Make a list of the states that had harsh laws against the negro. 12. Why such laws? 13. Who first began to oppose slavery? 14. What reasons given? 15. Write an essay on the subject of slavery in the colonies. 16. What change of tone at the beginning of the Revolution? 17. From what section does the greatest opposition come? 18. How do you explain the change? 19. Who did they blame for the slave trade? 20. Did they stop it? 21. How were they going to try to stop it? 22. How did Jefferson feel on the subject? 23. Collect all the thoughts you can from Jefferson on the subject. 24. In 1785 how, according to Jefferson, was slavery regarded north of the Potomac? 25. How did the leaders in Virginia feel about emancipation? 26. Did Jefferson predict truthfully in regard to future? 27. Make an outline to show the views, plans, and predictions of Jefferson. 28. What other men opposed? 29. What were their arguments? 30. What do you believe to be the cause of such a radical revolution in thought? 31. Name the compromises in the constitution. 32. Give their terms. 33. Any change in tone in discussion from that of writings just quoted? 34. What does the change mean? 35. What section is strongest against slavery and the slave trade? 36. Write an essay on slavery in the constitution, including therein the debates. 37. Trace the character of the arguments in congress. 38. Gather all the moral arguments you can. 39. Do both sides use them? 40. Note all the industrial points in the arguments. 41. Which side uses such arguments most effectively? 42. What is the political argument? 43. Compare the feeling of 1775 and that of 1820. 44. Mark all the changes. 45. Which section has changed most? 46. What predictions do Adams and Jefferson make about 1820? 47. What is their argument? 48. Did they prove to be correct? 49. Jefferson's thought on compromise of 1820? 50. Write essay on whole subject.

American History Studies

No. 7.   MARCH, 1898.

SLAVERY IN THE UNITED STATES
II.

SELECTIONS MADE FROM THE SOURCES

BY

H. W. CALDWELL,

UNIVERSITY OF NEBRASKA.

J. H. MILLER, Publisher,

LINCOLN, NEBRASKA.

Yearly Subscription, 40 cents.   Single Copy, 5 cents.

PUBLISHED MONTHLY, EXCEPT JULY AND AUGUST.

Entered as second-class matter at the Post Office, Lincoln, Nebraska, U. S. A.

AMERICAN HISTORY STUDIES.

SLAVERY IN THE UNITED STATES.

FOUND it utterly impossible to handle the subject of slavery in a satisfactory manner in one article; and it must be confessed that two numbers even do hardly more than touch the abundance of interesting and valuable matter that lies at hand.

In the last number we had just reached the moment when this question began to absorb a large part of the thought of the American people. This article begins with the struggle over the "Incendiary Publications" and the "Right of Petition," of which J. Q. Adams was the hero, and ends with the inauguration of Lincoln.

The next number will deal with the Civil War and Reconstruction.

J. Q. ADAMS writes, 1820:

Slavery is the great and foul stain upon the North American Union, and it is a contemplation worthy of the most exalted soul whether its total abolition is or is not practicable: if practicable by what means it may be effected, and if a choice of means be within the scope of the object, what means would accomplish it at the smallest cost of human suffering. A dissolution, at least temporary, of the Union, as now constituted, would be certainly necessary, and the dissolution must be upon a point involving the question of slavery, and no other. The Union might then be organized on the fundamental principle of emancipation. The object is vast in its compass, awful in its prospects, sublime and beautiful in its issue, a life devoted to it would be nobly spent or sacrificed.—*J. Q. Adams, Memoirs, vol. IV, p. 531.*

If slavery be the destined sword in the hand of the

destroying angel which is to sever the ties of this Union, the same sword will cut in sunder the bonds of slavery itself. A dissolution of the Union for the cause of slavery would be followed by a servile war in the slave-holding States combined with a war between the two severed portions of the Union. It seems to me that its result must be the exterpation of slavery from this whole continent; and, calamitous and desolating as this course of events in its progress must be, so glorious would be its final issue, that as God shall judge me, I do not say that it is not to be desired.

Never since human sentiments and human conduct were influenced by human speech was there a theme for eloquence like the free side of this question. . . . Oh, if but one man could arise with a genius capable of communicating those eternal truths that belong to this question, to lay bare in all its nakedness that outrage upon the goodness of God, human slavery; now is the time and this is the occasion, upon which such a man would perform the duties of an angel upon earth. —*Ibid, vol. V, p. 210.*

HAYNE speaks on the Panama mission in the United States senate, March, 1826, in these prophetic words:

The question of slavery is one, in all its bearings of extreme delicacy; and concerning which I know of but a single wise and safe rule, either for the states in which it exists or for the Union. It must be considered and treated entirely as a domestic question. With respect to foreign nations, the language of the United States ought to be, that it concerns the peace of our own political family, and therefore we cannot permit it to be touched; and in respect to the slaveholding s.ates, the only safe and constitutional ground on which they can stand is, that they will not permit it to be brought into question, either by their sister states or by the federal government. It is a matter for ourselves. To touch it at all, is to violate our most sacred rights—to put in jeopardy our dearest interests—the peace of our country—the safety of our families, our altars, and our firesides. . . . On the slave question my opinion is this: I consider our rights in that species of property as not even open to discussion, either here or elsewhere; and in respect to our duties, (imposed by our situation,) we are not to be taught them by fanatics, religious, or political. To call into question our rights, is grossly to violate them; to attempt to instruct us on this subject is to insult us; to dare to assail our institutions, is wantonly to invade our peace. Let me solemnly declare, once for all, that the Southern States never will permit, and never can permit, any interference whatever in their domestic concerns; and that the very day on which the unhallowed attempt shall be made by the authorities of the federal government, we will consider ourselves as driven from the Union. Let the consequences be what they may, they never can be worse than such as must inevitably result from suffering a rash and ignorant interference with our domestic peace and tranquillity. But . . . I apprehend no such violation of our constitutional rights. I believe that this house is not disposed and that the great body of our intelligent and patriotic fellow-citizens in the other states have no inclination whatever to interfere with us. . . . If we are true to ourselves we shall have nothing to fear.—*Benton.*

By 1831 the raising of slaves in the northern states for market had become a recognized industry, as may be seen from the following letters and speeches:

HENRY CLAY, in an address before the Kentucky Colonization Society in 1829, said:

It is believed that nowhere in the United States would slave labor be generally employed, if the proprietor was not tempted to raise slaves by the high price of the Southern market, which keeps it up in his own.—*Ibid, p. 257.*

PROF. DEW, president of William and Mary college, in reviewing the debates in the Virginia constitutional convention, in 1831-2, said of the domestic slave trade:

A full equivalent being thus left in the place of the slave, this immigration becomes an advantage to the State, and does not check the black population . . . because it furnishes every inducement to the master to attend to the negroes, to encourage breeding, and to

cause the greatest number possible to be raised. . . .
Virginia is in fact a negro-raising State for other States.
—*Goodell, p. 250.*

CHAS. F. MERCER, in the Virginia constitutional convention of 1829, said:

The tables of the *natural* growth of the slave population demonstrate, when compared with the [actual] increase of its numbers in the Commonwealth for 20 yrs. past, that an annual revenue of not less than a million and a half of dollars is derived from the exportation of a part of this population.—*Ibid, p. 250.*

MR. GHOLSON, in the Virginia legislature, January 18, 1831

[Claimed the right of] the owner of brood mares to their product, and of the owner of female slaves to their increase. The legal maxim of *partus sequitur ventrem* is coeval with the existence of the right of property itself, and is founded in wisdom and justice. It is on the justice and inviolability of this maxim that the master foregoes the services of a female slave—has her nursed and raises the helpless infant offspring. The value of the property justifies the expense; and I do not hesitate to say that in its increase consists much of our wealth.—*Ibid, p. 257.*

Let us now see what views were held in regard to the printing and disseminating of abolition literature by 1835.

The South Carolina legislature passed this resolve in 1835:

Resolved, That the Legislature of South Carolina, having every confidence in the justice and friendship of the non-slaveholding States, *announces her confident expectation,* and she earnestly requests, that the Government of these States will promptly and effectually suppress all those associations within their respective limits, purporting to be abolition societies. . . .—
Cited in Goodell, p. 413.

The North Carolina general assembly [1835]:

Resolved, That our sister States are respectfully requested to enact penal laws, prohibiting the printing, within their respective limits, all such publications as may have a tendency to make our slaves discontented.—*Ibid, p. 413.*

The Alabama legislature [1836]:

Resolved, That we call upon our sister States, and respectfully request them to enact such penal laws as will finally put an end to the malignant deeds of the abolitionists.—*Ibid, p. 413.*

Virginia legislature [1836]:

Resolved, That the non-slaveholding States of the Union are respectfully but earnestly requested promptly to adopt penal enactments or such other measures as will effectually suppress all associations within their respective limits purporting to be, or having the character of abolition societies.—*Ibid, p. 417.*

On learning that the United States mails had been searched for "incendiary documents" at Charleston, South Carolina, on July 29, 1835, POSTMASTER-GENERAL AMOS KENDALL said:

By no act or direction of mine, official or private, could I be induced to aid, knowingly, in giving circulation to papers of this description, directly or indirectly. We owe an obligation to the laws, but a higher one to the communities in which we live, and if the former be permitted to destroy the latter, it is patriotism to disregard them. Entertaining these views I cannot sanction, and will not condemn, the step you have taken. Your justification must be looked for in the character of the papers detained and the circumstances by which you are surrounded.—*Ibid, p. 416.*

PRESIDENT JACKSON, in his annual message, December, 1835, used these words in discussing the subject:

I would therefore call the special attention of Congress to the subject, and respectfully suggest the propriety of passing such a law as will prohibit under severe penalties, the circulation, in the Southern States, through the mail, of incendiary publications, intended to instigate the slaves to insurrection.

THE RIGHT OF PETITION.

KING (Ala.):

We were sent here to do the business of the public and not to set up arbitrary codes for the protection of our dignity, and then be left to determine what dignity means. I consider true senatorial dignity to consist in a straight-forward, independent discharge of our constitutional duties, and not in searching into the language employed by our constituents, when they ask us for a redress of grievances, to see if we cannot find some pretext to commit a fraud upon the constitution.—*Benton, vol. XII, p. 723.*

BUCHANAN (Pa.):

Let it once be understood that the sacred right of petition and the cause of the abolitionists must rise or fall together, and the consequences may be fatal. . . We have just as little right to interfere with slavery in the South as we have to touch the right of petition. . . . Can a republican government exist without it? . . . If the people have a constitutional right to petition, a corresponding duty is imposed upon us to receive their petitions.—*Ibid, pp. 733-5.*

ADAMS:

[A discussion on petitions is bound to be merely] a discussion upon the merits of slavery. Sir, on such a discussion every speech made by a Representative from the north of Mason and Dixon's line, in this House, will be an incendiary pamphlet and what will you do with them? . . . The newspapers report these speeches; every speech is circulated through your whole country; and how can you arrest it? . . . Well, sir, you begin with suppressing the right of petition; you must next suppress the right of speech in this House; for you must offer a resolution that every member who dares to express a sentiment of this kind shall be expelled, or that speeches shall not go forth to the public—shall not be circulated. What will be the consequence then? You suppress the right of petition; you suppress the freedom of speech; the freedom of the press, and the freedom of religion; for, in the minds of many worthy, honest, and honorable men, fanatics, if you please so to call them, this is a religious question . . . and however erroneous may be their conclusions, it is not for me, nor for this House, to judge them.—*Ibid, vol. XIII, pp. 9-10.*

Calhoun was the great apostle of the south, and his words—the words of an honest man—will usually give us the very clearest insight into the thought of his section:

On the right of rejecting abolition petitions, although, in his opinion, one of the clearest that can be imagined, we of the South were, unfortunately for the peace of the country, in a minority. So, also, on the question of the constitutional right of abolishing slavery in this District and the Territories, and also on every other particular question which has been attempted to be raised on constitutional grounds, as a barrier to our rights and security. What remains, then, short of taking our protection into our own hands, but to find some barrier in the general character and structure of our political system? and where can we find that but in the view of the Constitution, which considers it as a compact between sovereign and independent States, formed for their mutual prosperity and security?

He saw (said Mr. C.) in the question before us the fate of the South. It was a higher than the mere naked question of master and slave. It involved a great political institution, essential to the peace and existence of one-half of this Union.

They were there inseparably united, beyond the possibility of separation. Experience had shown that the existing relation between them secured the peace and happiness of both. Each had improved; the inferior greatly; so much so, that it had attained a degree of civilization never before attained by the black race in any age or country. Under no other relation could they co-exist together. To destroy it was to involve a whole region in slaughter, carnage, and desolation; and, come what will, we must defend and preserve it.

This agitation has produced one happy effect at least; it has compelled us of the South to look into the nature and character of this great institution, and to correct many false impressions that even we had entertained in relation to it. Many in the South once believed that it was a moral and political evil; that folly and delusion are gone; we see it now in its true light and regard it as the most safe and stable basis for free institutions in the world.—*Congressional Globe, vol. VI, pp. 29, 61-62.*

. . . It is easy to see the end. By the necessary course of events, if left to themselves, we must become, finally, two peoples. It is impossible under the deadly hatred which must spring up between the two great sections, if the present causes are permitted to operate unchecked, that we should continue under the same political system. The conflicting elements would burst the Union asunder. . . . We of the South will not, cannot, surrender our institutions. . . . But let me not be understood as admitting, even by implication, that the existing relations between the two races in the slaveholding States is an evil:—far otherwise; I hold it to be a good, as it has thus far proved itself to be to both, and will continue to prove so if not disturbed by the fell spirit of abolitionism. [Discusses relations; then says:] But I take higher ground. I hold that in the present state of civilization, where two races of different origin, and distinguished by color, and other physical differences, as well as intellectual, are brought together, the relation now existing in the slaveholding States between the two, is, instead of an evil, a good—a positive good.—*Calhoun, Works, vol. II, pp. 629-30.*

The various "Gag" rules, or rules to prevent the reception and discussion of petitions in regard to slavery, were passed as follows:

[Pinckney's of 5|26|1836. Adopted by 117 to 68 votes in House of Representatives]:

"*Resolved*, That all petitions, memorials, resolutions, and propositions relating, in any way, or to any extent, whatever, to the subject of slavery, shall, without being either printed or referred, be laid on the table, and no further action whatever shall be had thereon."

Hawes', 1|18|'37: enacted by 115 to 47.
Patton's, 12|21|'37: enacted by 122 to 74.
Atherton's, 1|12|'38: enacted by 126 to 78.
Johnson's, 1|28|'40: enacted by 114 to 108, and made a standing rule of the House till 1846.—*Goodell, pp. 422-3.*

William Lloyd Garrison and Wendell Phillips, as the leaders of the Abolitionists, speak in no uncertain tones, as the following extracts will show:

W. L. Garrison in Faneuil Hall, 1843.

Resolved, That the compact which exists between the North and the South is "a covenant with death and an agreement with hell"—involving both parties in atrocious criminality, and should be immediately annulled.

We cannot regard any man as a consistent abolitionist who, while holding to the popular construction of the Constitution, makes himself a party to that instrument, by taking any office under it requiring an oath, or voting for its support.

Resolutions of Wendell Phillips.

That the abolitionists of this country should make it one of the primary objects of their agitation, to dissolve the American Union; [and again] That secession from the present United States Government is the duty of every abolitionist; since no one can take office, or throw a vote for another to hold office, under the United States Constitution, without violating his anti-slavery principles, and rendering himself an abettor of the slaveholder in his sin.

W. L. Garrison, in an address to the Friends of Freedom in the United States, undertook a fresh declaration of its principles—first, as regards slavery:

That it ought to be immediately and forever abolished; and as regards the existing national compact, "That it is a covenant with death and an agreement with hell," and that henceforth, therefore, until slavery be abolished the watchword shall be No UNION WITH SLAVEHOLDERS.

Continued—To accomplish this sublime resolution the Society registers its sacred pledge to continue its agitation on the above lines.—*Life and Writings of William Lloyd Garrison, vol. III, pp. 88, 90, 100.*

PLATFORMS.

Buffalo platform of Free Soil Party of 8-9-1848.

Resolved, That we . . . do plant ourselves upon

the National Platform of Freedom, in opposition to the Sectional Platform of Slavery.

Resolved, That slavery in the several States of this Union which recognize its existence, depends upon State laws alone, which cannot be repealed or modified by the Federal Government, and for which laws that Government is not responsible. We therefore propose no interference by Congress with slavery within the limits of any State.

Resolved, That . . . the entire history of that period [1784-7, etc.] clearly shows that it was the settled policy of the nation not to extend, nationalize, or encourage, but to limit, localize, and discourage slavery; and to this policy, which should never have been departed from, the Government ought to return. . .

Resolved, That we accept the issue which the slave power has forced upon us, and to their demand for more slave States, and more slave Territory, our calm but final answer is, No more slave States, and no more slave Territory. Let the soil of our extensive domains be ever kept free. . . .

From 1845 to 1850 the great question in congress was in regard to the nature of the power of government in the territories. The following extracts suggest several views:

If . . . that experiment [annexation of new soil] shall not prove successful, so as to disprove the asserted possibility of the co-existence of the two races and two colors, side by side, on the same soil, in a relation of freedom and equality of rights, how can any of the friends of either desire to keep them forcibly pent up within the States when every day is tending faster and faster to ferment the discordant elements into a result which threatens to be the dissolution of both—instead of opening this safety valve by which the noxious vapor may pass off harmlessly and insensibly?

Crowd then your population into the Southern States as you may, rapidly and without fear. Texas will open before it as an outlet, and slavery, retiring from the Middle and Southern States of the present confederacy, will find for a time a resting-place there. But only for a time. For the irresistable law of population which decrees that in a densely peopled region slavery shall cease to exist, will emancipate Texas in her turn, and the negro will then pass to a land of political freedom and social dignity under a genial sky. He will pass without convulsion and leaving no domestic ruin in his path. As his labor becomes less and less valuable, emancipation, a gradual, progressive, at last universal, will pass him over the southern border to his own appropriate home in Mexico and the States beyond.—*Democratic Review, vol. XXIII, p. 106, 1848.*

RHETT (S. C.):

The Court declares that the territories belong to the United States. They are tenants in common, or joint proprietors and co-sovereigns over them. As co-sovereigns they have agreed in their common compact, the Constitution, that their agent, the General Government, "may dispose of and make all needful rules and regulations" with regard to them. but beyond this, they are not limited or limitable in their rights. Thus sovereignty, unalienated and unimpaired by this mutual concession to each other, exists in all its plenitude over our territories; as much so as within the limits of the States themselves. Yet there can be no conflict, for none of the States can make any "rules and regulations" separately within the territories, which may bring them in conflict. The "rules and regulations" prevailing will be made by all and obligatory on all, through their common agency, the government of the United States. The only effect and probably the only object of their reserved sovereignty is that it secures to each State the right to enter the territories with her citizens and settle and occupy them with their property—with whatever is recognized as property by each State. The ingress of the citizen is the ingress of his sovereign, who is bound to protect him in his settlement. . . . He is not responsible to any of the co-sovereigns for the nature of his property.—*Globe, 29th Congress, Second Session, App., p. 246.*

SENATOR BUTLER (S. C.):

His advice to his constituents would be, to go to these new territories with arms in their hands; to go as armed communities, and take possession of the lands which they had helped to acquire, and see who would attempt to dispossess them. . . . So help him God

he would so advise his constituents to take with them
their property there and settle at all hazards.—*Globe,
30th Congress, First Session, p. 1060.*

Calhoun (S. C.):

The separation of the North and South is completed.
The South has now a most solemn obligation to perform—to herself—to the Constitution—to the Union.
She is bound to come to a decision not to permit this to
go on any further but to show that, dearly as she prizes
the Union, there are questions which she regards as of
greater importance than the Union.—*Ibid, p. 1074.*

Webster (Mass.):

We certainly do not prevent them [Southern men]
from going into these territories with what is in general
law called property. But these States have by their
local laws created a property in persons, and they cannot carry these local laws with them. . . . No man
can be held as a slave, except the local law shall accompany him.—*Ibid, p. 1078.*

Dickinson (N. Y.):

That no conditions can be constitutionally imposed
upon any territorial acquisition, inconsistent with the
right of the people thereof to form a free, sovereign
State, with the powers and privileges of the original
members of the Confederacy, I deem too obvious for
serious argument. Whatever laws Congress may constitutionally enact for the regulation of the territories of
the United States are subject to be altered or repealed
at pleasure. . . . Every State admitted to the Union
from the moment of its admission, enjoys all the rights
of sovereignty common to every other member of the
Confederacy. . . . If any State is prohibited from
[any of or] all the rights of every other then it is not
. . . a sovereign State. . . . Every State after its
admission, may, in virtue of its own sovereign power,
establish or abolish this institution [slavery] whatever
may have been the conditions imposed, or attempted to
be imposed, upon it during its territorial existence.

Whatever power may or may not rest in Congress
under the Constitution, that instrument could not take
from the people of territories the right to prescribe their
own domestic policy; nor has it attempted any such

office. . . . The republican theory teaches that sovereignty resides with the people of a State, and not with its political organization. . . . If sovereignty resides with the people and not with the organization, it rests as well with the people of a Territory, in all that concerns their internal condition as with the people of an organized State. . . . And if in this respect a form of government is proposed to them by the Federal Government, and adopted or acquiesced in by them, they may afterwards alter or abolish it at pleasure. Although the government of a Territory has not the same sovereign power as the government of a State in its political relations, the people of a Territory have, in all that appertains to their internal condition, the same sovereign rights as the people of a State.—*Ibid, p. 88.*

CALHOUN (S. C.):

The assumption [that the sovereignty resides in the inhabitants of the territories] is utterly unfounded, unconstitutional, without example, and contrary to the entire practice of the government from its commencement to the present time.—*Globe, 31st Congress, First Session, p. 4514.*

Compromise of 1850.

CLAY (Ky.):

It would not be possible to get twenty votes in the Senate, or a proportional vote in the House, Clay said, in favor of the *recognition* of slavery south of 36 degrees 30 minutes. "It is impossible. All that you can get—all that you can expect to get—all that was proposed at the last session—is action north of that line, and non-action as regards slavery south of that line. . . It is better for the South, that there should be non-action as to slavery both north and south of the line—far better that there should be non-action both sides of the line, than that there should be action by the interdiction on the one side, without action for the admission upon the other side of the line."—*Globe, vol. XXII, pt. I, p. 125.*

WEBSTER (Mass.):

There is not at this moment, within the United States, or any territory of the United States, a single foot of land, the character of which in regard to its being free-soil territory or slave territory is not fixed by some law, and some irrepealable law beyond the power of the action of this government.

What, then, have been the causes which have created so new a feeling in favor of slavery in the South—which have changed the whole nomenclature of the South on the subject—and from being thought of and described in the terms I have mentioned . . . it has now become an institution, a cherished institution there; no evil, no scourge, but a great religious, social, and moral blessing, as I think I have heard it latterly described? I suppose this, sir, is owing to the sudden uprising and rapid growth of the cotton plantations of the South.—*Ibid, p. 272.*

Douglas (Ill.):

You cannot fix bounds to the onward march of this great and growing country. You cannot fetter the limbs of a young giant. He will burst your chains. He will expand and grow, and increase, and extend civilization, Christianity, and liberal principles. Then, sir, if you cannot check the growth of the country in that direction, is it not the part of wisdom to look the danger in the face, and provide for an event you cannot avoid? I tell you, sir, you must provide for continuous lines of settlement from the Mississippi Valley to the Pacific Ocean. And in making this provision you must decide upon what principles the territory shall be organized; and in other words, whether the people shall be allowed to regulate their domestic institutions in their own way, according to the provisions of this bill, or whether the opposite doctrine of congressional interference is to prevail. Postpone it, if you will; but whenever you do act, this question must be met and decided.—*Sheahan's Life of Douglas, p. 259.*

Seward (N. Y.):

My position concerning legislative compromises is this, namely: personal, partizan, temporary, and subordinate questions, may lawfully be compromised; but *principles* can never be justly or wisely made the subjects of compromise. By *principles* I mean the elements in public questions of moral rights, political justice, and high national expediency. Does any honorable senator assert a different maxim on the subject of legislative compromise?

There is no peace in this world for compromisers; there is no peace for those who practice evasion; there is no peace in a republican land for any statesman but those who act directly, and boldly abide the popular judgment whenever it may be fairly and clearly and fully ascertained, without attempting to falsify the issue submitted, or to corrupt the tribunal.—*Works, vol. IV, pp. 517, 611.*

A. H. STEPHENS, to his brother Linton, 1850:

In the message received to-day you will see that the policy of General Taylor is that the people inhabiting the new acquisitions shall come into the Union as States, without the adoption of territorial governments. . . . But the bearing of this policy on the great questions of the day is a matter still to be considered. Will the Slavery question be settled in this way? I think not. My deliberate opinion at this time, or the opinion I have formed from the best lights before me, is that it will be the beginning of an end which will be the severance of the political bonds that unite the slave-holding and non-slaveholding States of this Union. I give you this view rather in opposition to the one I ventured to express on the evening of the 25th of December. I then looked to settlement and adjustment and a preservation of the Union; and as far as I then saw on the horizon, I think the opinion was correct. There will, perhaps, be a temporary settlement and a temporary quiet. But I have lately been taking a farther and a broader view of the future. When I look at the *causes* of the present discontent I am persuaded there will never again be harmony between the two great sections of the Union. When California and New Mexico and Oregon and Nebraska are admitted as States, then the majority in the Senate will be against us. The power will be with them to harass, annoy, and oppress. And it is a law of power to exert itself, as universal as it is a law of nature that nothing shall stand still. Cast your eye, then, a few years into the future, and see what images of strife are seen figuring on the boards! In the halls of Congress, nothing but debates about the crimes and the iniquity of slavery and the duty of the General Government to withhold all countenance of the unholy institution of human bondage. Can Southern men occupy seats in the halls of a Legislature with this constant reproach? It is not reasonable. It is more than I expect. It is more than human nature can expect. The present crisis may pass; the present adjustment may be made; but the great question of the permanence of slavery in the Southern States will be far from being settled thereby. And, in my opinion, the crisis of that question is not far ahead. The very palliatives now so soothingly administered do but more speedily develop the stealthly disease which is fast approaching the vitals. . . . My opinion is that a dismemberment of this Republic is not among the improbabilities of a few years to come. In all my acts I shall look to that event. I shall do nothing to favor it or hasten, but I now consider it inevitable. . . . But I should not say much in *praise* of the Union. I see no hope to the South from the Union. . . . I do not believe much in resolutions, any way. . . . If I were now in the Legislature, I should introduce bills reorganizing the militia, for the establishment of a military school, the encouragement of the formation of volunteer companies, the creation of arsenals, of an armory, and an establishment for making gunpowder. In these lies our defence. I tell you the argument is exhausted; and if the South do not intend to be overrun with anti-slavery doctrines, they must, before no distant day, stand by their arms. My mind is made up; I am for the fight, if the country will back me. And if not we had better have no 'Resolutions,' and no gasconade. They will but add to our degradation. . . . My course shall be directed to the future. I shall regard with little interest the events of the intervening years. . . . One other thought. Could the South maintain a separate political organization? On this I have thought a great deal. It has been the most perplexing question to my mind. The result of my reflections is that she could, if her people be united. She would maintain her position, I think, better than the North. She has great elements of power.—*Johnston-Browne, Life of A. H. Stephens, pp. 243-5.*

THE EXCITING YEARS 1850-1860.

They threaten us with a great Northern party, and a general war upon the South. If they were not mere hucksters in politics—with only this peculiarity, that every man offers himself, instead of some other commodity, for sale—we should surmise that they might do what they threaten, and thus bring out the real triumph of the South, by making a dissolution of the Union necessary.

But they will do no such thing. They will threaten and utter a world of swelling self-glorification, and end by knocking themselves down to the highest bidder. To be sure, if they could make the best bargain by distroying the South, they would set about it without delay. But they cannot. They live upon us, and the South affords them the double glorification of an object for hatred and a field for plunder. How far they may be moved to carry their indignation at this time it is impossible to say; but we may be sure they will cool off just at the point when they discover that they can make nothing more out of it, and may lose.—*Charleston Mercury, Quoted by Redpath, Echoes, p. 460.*

It is vain to disguise it, the great issue of our day in this country is, Slavery or no Slavery. The present phase of that issue is, the extension or non-extension of the institution, the foundations of which are broad and solid in our midst. Whatever the general measure— whatever the political combinations—whatever the party movement—whatever the action of sections at Washington, the one single, dominant, and pervading idea, solving all leading questions, insinuating itself into every policy, drawing the horoscope of all aspirants, serving as a lever or fulcrum for every interest, class and individuality—a sort of directing fatality, is that master issue. As in despite of right and reason— of organisms and men—of interests and efforts, it has become *per se* political destiny—why not meet it? It controls the North, it controls the South—it precludes escape. It is at last and simply a question between the South and the remainder of the Union, as sections and as people. All efforts to give it other direction, to solve it by considerations other than those which pertain to them in their local character and fates, to divest it, to confound it with objects and designs of a general nature, is [sic] rendered futile. It has to be determined by the real parties, by their action in their character as sections—inchoate countries.—*Charleston Evening News, Quoted in Redpath, p. 496.*

The North has thus far carried the South on its

shoulders, and this it is bound to do in all time to come. It has purchased its lands, maintained the fleets and armies required for its purposes, and stood between it and the public opinion of the world while maintaining the value of its commodities and giving value to its labor and land. During the whole of this period it has borne unmeasured insolence, and has for the sake of peace, permitted its whole policy to be governed by a body of slaveholders amounting to but little more than a quarter of a million in number. It has made one compromise after another until at length the day of compromise has passed, and has given place to the day on which the South and the North—the advocates of Slave labor on the one side and Free labor on the other—are now to measure strength, and we trust it *will* be measured.—*Redpath, Echoes, p. 512.*

Falstaff was strong in words, but weak in action. So it is with the South, whose every movement betokens conscious weakness. For a quarter of a century past she has been holding conventions, at which it has been resolved that Norfolk, Charleston and Savannah *should* become great commercial cities, which obstinately they refuse to be. She has resolved upon all kinds of expedients for raising the price of cotton, which yet is lower by 1-3d. than it was ten years since. She has resolved to suppress discussion of slavery and the discussion is now more rife than ever before. She has resolved upon becoming strong and independent, but is now more dependent upon the forbearance of the world than in any time past. Under such circumstances, there need be small fear of her secession from the North, which has so long stood between her and ruin. The irritability of our Southern friends is evidence of conscious weakness, and while that irritability shall continue, the danger of dissolution will continue to be far distant.

The Union *must* be continued until at least the South shall have had the opportunity for taxing the North for the accomplishment of its projects. *Until then the Union cannot be dissolved.* Such being the case, the real friend of the Union is he who opposes the annexation of Cuba and Hayti, and the extension of slavery; and the real disunionist is he who advocates compliance with Southern demands. Thus far, all the measures adopted for the promotion of the Southern objects have been followed by increased abuse and increased threats of separation, and such will certainly be the case with all such future ones. To preserve the Union, it is required that the North shall insist on its rights. . . . The only real disunionists of the country, north of Mason and Dixon's line, are the political doughfaces, like Pierce, Douglas, and Richardson, and the commercial doughfaces . . . who sell themselves to the South for those objects on which Southern madmen now are bent.—*Redpath, Echoes, 512-13.*

An extract from an "Address on Climatology," before the Academy of Science at New Orleans:

The institution of slavery operates by contrast and comparison; it elevates the tone of the superior, adds to its refinement, allows more time to cultivate the mind, exalts the standard in morals, manners, and intellectual endowments, operates as a safety valve for the evil-disposed, leaving the upper race power, while it preserves from degradation, in the scale of civilization, the inferior, which we see in their uniform destiny when left to themselves. The slaves constitute essentially the lowest class, and society is immeasurably benefited by having this class which constitutes the offensive fungus—the great cancer of civilized life—a vast burthen and expense to every community, under surveillance and control; and not only so, but under direction as an efficient agent to promote the general welfare and increase the wealth of the community. The history of the world furnishes no institution under similar management, where so much good actually results to the governors and to the governed as this in the Southern states of North America.—*Quoted in Olmsted's "Cotton Kingdom," p. 277.*

As an offset to the preceding let us hear from Wendell Phillips on "The Lesson of the Hour," Brooklyn, Nov. 1, 1859:

. . . Somewhat briefly stated, such is the idea of American civilization; uncompromising faith—in the average selfishness, if you choose—of all classes, neutralizing each other, and tending towards that fair play that Saxons love. But it seems to me that, on all questions, we dread thought; we shrink behind something; we acknowledge ourselves unequal to the sublime faith of our fathers; and the exhibition of the last twenty years and of the present state of public affairs is, that Americans dread to look their real position in the face. . . . They have no idea of absolute right. They were born since 1787, and absolute right means the truth diluted by a strong decoction of the Constitution of 1789. They breathe that atmosphere. They do not want to sail outside of it; they do not attempt to reason outside of it. Poisoned with printer's ink, or choked with cotton dust, they stare at absolute right, as the dream of madmen. For the last twenty years, there has been going on, more or less heeded and understood in various states, an insurrection of ideas against the limited, cribbed, cabined, isolated American civilization interfering to restor absolute right. . . .

Thank God, I am not a citizen. You will remember, all of you, citizens of the United States, that there was not a Virginia gun fired at John Brown. . . . *You* shot him. Sixteen marines to whom you pay $8 a month—your own representatives, . . . sixteen men, with the Vulture of the Union above them—your representatives! It was the covenant with death and agreement with hell which you call the Union of the States, that took the old man by the throat with a private hand. . . .—*Redpath, Echoes.*

Let us hear LINCOLN speak:

If we would first know where we are, and whither we are tending, we could better judge what to do, and how to do it. We are now far into the fifth year since a policy [Kansas-Nebraska bill] was initiated with the avowed object and confident promise of putting an end to slavery agitation. Under the operation of that policy, that agitation has not only not ceased, but has constantly augmented. In my opinion, it will not cease until a crisis shall have been reached and passed. "A house divided against itself cannot stand.", I believe this government cannot endure permanently half slave and half free. I do not expect the Union to be dissolved—I do not expect the house to fall—but I do expect it will cease to be divided. It will become all one thing, or all the other. . . . —*Lincoln, Works, I., p. 240.*

The Lincoln-Douglas debate, 1858:

I do not question Mr. Lincoln's conscientious belief that the negro was made his equal, and hence is his brother, but for my own part I do not regard the negro as my equal; and positively deny that he is my brother or any kin to me whatever. . . . He [Lincoln] holds that the negro was born his equal and yours, and that he was endowed with equality by the Almighty, and that no human law can deprive him of these rights which were guaranteed to him by the Supreme Ruler of the universe. Now, I do not believe that the Almighty ever intended the negro to be the equal of the white man. . . . He belongs to an inferior race, and must occupy an inferior position. I do not hold that because the negro is our inferior, therefore he ought to be a slave. By no means can such a conclusion be drawn from what I have said. On the contrary, I hold that humanity and Christianity both require that the negro shall have and enjoy every right, every privilege, and every immunity consistent with the safety of the society in which he lives. . . . — *Douglas, in the Lincoln-Douglas Debates, Works, Lincoln, I., p. 284.*

While I was at the hotel to-day, an elderly gentleman called upon me to know whether I was really in favor of producing a perfect equality between the negroes and white people. . . . I will say then that I am not, nor ever have been, in favor of bringing about in any way the social and political equality of the white and black races—that I am not, nor ever have been, in favor of making voters or jurors of negroes, nor of qualifying them to hold office, nor to intermarry with white people; and I will say in addition to this that there is a physical difference between the white and black races which I believe will forever forbid the two races living together on terms of social and political equality. And inasmuch as they cannot so live, while they do remain together there must be the position of superior and inferior, and I as much as any other man am in favor of having the superior position assigned to the white race.—*Lincoln, in Lincoln-Douglas Debates, Lincoln's Works, I., p. 369.*

QUESTIONS.

1. What did J. Q. Adams think of slavery? 2. What did he expect to be necessary in order to secure its abolition? 3. Was his plan statesmanlike? 4. Were his predictions in part fulfilled? 5. Did he attempt in later years the work he here lays out for some man? 6. How did Hayne differ from Adams? 7. Did he see danger in the questions? 8. What remedy did he propose? 9. How do you explain the different positions? 10. Investigate to see whether Hayne had a constitutional foundation for his position. 11. Why did the northern slave states desire the continuance of the system? 12. What profit came to Virginia from the system? 13. Would Virginia naturally favor or oppose the slave trade?

1. What is meant by "incendiary documents"? 2. How were they disposed of in the south? 3. Was such a method right, constitutional? 4. What requests did the south make of northern states regarding these documents? 5. Were they right in demanding their suppression? 6. How did President Jackson propose to deal with the question? 7. Would his plan have been constitutional? 8. What was the real difficulty?

1. Find out what the constitution says in regard to the right of petition. 2. Find out the nature of the petitions sent to Congress. 3. What did Mr. King think of the petitions? 4. What mistake did the south make in opposing the reception of petitions? 5. Name points in Calhoun's argument. 6. What view does he take in regard to slavery? 7. Had the south always held the same views? 8. Did he hold slavery in the abstract to be a good? 9. What prediction did he make? 10. Have his predictions been fulfilled? 11. What objection, if any, to the "gag" rule? 12. What conclusion can you draw from the various votes on the "gag" rules?

1. How did Garrison regard the constitution? Why? 2. Was he a secessionist? 3. How does the Buffalo Platform differ in theory from Garrison and Phillips? 4. How did the *Democratic Review* believe slavery would end? 5. What theories are given in various extracts in regard to method of control or government of the territories? 6. How did Webster hold the character of the institutions of the territories had been fixed? 7. How did Seward regard compromises? 8. Was he right? 9. If so what do you say of the men who made the constitution? 10. What end did A. H. Stephens predict for the Union? 11. Compare views of Stephens and Phillips and Garrison. 12. How explain their views?

1. Did the north and the south understand each other? 2. What qualities did the south believe characterized the people of the north? 3. What did the north think of the southern people? 4. Why was Cuba wished? 5. Did the south believe slavery right? 6.

What arguments given to prove their view? 7. What did Wendell Phillips think of the character of the American people in 1859? 8. Was he right? 9. What difference in tone between Lincoln and Phillips? 10. How did Lincoln hope to end slavery? 11. How did Lincoln regard the negro? 12. How Douglas? 13. What difference in view between the two?

1. Make an outline covering this whole period. 2. Write an essay on the reasons for the contradictory views of the northern and southern statesmen.

American History Studies

No. 8.   APRIL, 1898.

THE CIVIL WAR AND RECONSTRUCTION.

SELECTIONS MADE FROM THE SOURCES

BY

H. W. CALDWELL,

UNIVERSITY OF NEBRASKA.

J. H. MILLER, Publisher,
LINCOLN, NEBRASKA.

Yearly Subscription, 40 cents.   Single Copy, 5 cents.

PUBLISHED MONTHLY, EXCEPT JULY AND AUGUST.
Entered as second-class matter at the Post Office, Lincoln, Nebraska, U. S. A.

AMERICAN HISTORY STUDIES.

THE CIVIL WAR AND RECONSTRUCTION.

IN the last two numbers an attempt was made to trace the development of the slavery question in American history. In this number the culmination is reached; the greatest of civil wars opens before us; and finally the Union appears,—or shall we say reappears, reconstructed, with slavery as a reminiscence. However, it must not be thought that the problem is ended. The American people are too much inclined to accept first settlements as if they were finals. Citizenship was conferred on the negro when he was unprepared for it. He must now be fitted for his duties. Education in its broadest terms must be extended to him. The whole country is interested in, and affected by, the solution. The South has to bear the burden, in the main, as she had to bear that of slavery. In this connection, the most important question of the present and of the immediate future, at least, is that the North and the South do not become estranged over the solution of this question as they did in regard to the original cause. Its difficulties should be recognized by the North, and sympathy and aid, not criticism, should be given.

This number opens with the election of Lincoln, and the consequent secession of the Southern States. The winter of 1860-'61 was perhaps the most momentous and deeply interesting of any that has passed over the history of our country. There may have been other moments of more outward excitement, but none, perhaps, of the same intensity. There was a general feeling as the months passed that the crisis had come. The North could hardly be brought to realize that the Southern States intended to act in accordance with their words; the Southern people were possessed with the idea that the North was purely materialistic and would not fight for an ideal. How little the people of the two sections really did or could understand each other the four years from 1861 to 1865 witness!

However, when the end came, and the greater resources,—but only the same, not greater courage and devotion—had given the victory to the free states, and in giving them their triumph had made all free states, the settlement of the terms of reconstruction, was scarcely less difficult and taxing than had been the details of the struggle itself.

During the year 1860-'61 almost the entire history of the United States may be studied by tracing backward to their beginnings the principles that were then in controversy. The nature of the Constitution: were the States sovereignties? Under this heading we might trace the development of the idea back through the Nullification struggle, the Hartford convention, the Virginia and Kentucky resolutions to the Convention of 1787, and then beyond to the forces that were foundational. The position of slavery under the Constitution: its entire history would be necessary to estimate at their true worth the various arguments that were advocated by the many groups into which the people were at the time divided. The powers of the executive: what were their limits in time of war? But it is impossible to attempt an enumeration of the interesting questions that are found in these years of American history. Their settlement distinctly modified the world's history, and was of the greatest moment in determining the character and future of the United States.

Lincoln, in his great Cooper Institute speech of February 27, 1860, discussed the subject of slavery as he saw it from the standpoint of the South and of the North. In the concluding portion he said:

A few words now to Republicans. It is exceedingly desirable that all parts of this great Confederacy shall be at peace and in harmony one with another. . . . Even though the Southern people will not so much as listen to us, let us calmly consider their demands and yield to them if, in our deliberate view of our duty, we possibly can. . . . What will satisfy them? Simply this: we must not only let them alone, but we must somehow convince them that we do let them alone. . . . What will convince them? This, and this only: cease to call slavery wrong, and join them in calling it right. . . . Their thinking it right and our thinking it wrong is the precise fact upon which depends the whole controversy. Thinking it right, as they do, they are not to blame for desiring its full recognition as being right; but thinking it wrong, as we do, can we yield to them?—*Works, I, pp. 611-12.*

December 22, 1860, Lincoln wrote to A. H. Stephens in reply to a letter from Mr. Stephens in these words:

I fully appreciate the present peril the country is in, and the weight of responsibility on me. Do the people of the South really entertain fears that a Republican administration would, directly or indirectly, interfere with the slaves, or with them about the slaves? If they do, I wish to assure you, as once a friend, and still, I hope, not an enemy, that there is no cause for such fears. The South would be in no more danger in this respect than it was in the days of Washington. I suppose, however, this does not meet the case. You think slavery is right and ought to be extended, while we think it is wrong and ought to be restricted. .. . . —*Ibid, p. 660.*

On the way to Washington, in February, 1861, Lincoln made a series of speeches. A few extracts from these will give us an insight into Lincoln's views at the last moment before he assumed office.

At Indianapolis he said:

The words "coercion" and "invasion" are much used in these days. . . . What, then, is "coercion"? What is "invasion"? Would the marching of an army into South Carolina without the consent of her people, and with hostile intent toward them, be "invasion"? I certainly think it would. . . . But if the United States should merely hold and retake its own forts and other property, etc., . . . would any or all of these be "invasion" or "coercion"?—*Ibid, p. 673.*

In Cincinnati he repeated and reaffirmed the words he had used in a speech there the year before. In part he spoke, addressing the people of Kentucky, as follows:

We mean to treat you, as near as we possibly can, as Washington, Jefferson, and Madison treated you. We mean to leave you alone, and in no way interfere with your institutions; to abide by all and every compromise of the Constitution. . . . *Ibid, p. 675.*

At Columbus he used these words in concluding his address:

I have not maintained silence from any want of real anxiety. It is a good thing that there is no more than anxiety, for there is nothing going wrong. It is a consoling circumstance that when we look out there is nothing that really hurts anybody. We entertain different views upon political questions, but nobody is suffering anything. This is a most consoling circumstance, and from it we may conclude that all we want is time, patience, and a reliance on that God who has never forsaken this people.—*Works, I, p. 677.*

At Pittsburgh, on the same idea, he said:

Notwithstanding the troubles across the river [pointing south] there is no crisis but an artificial one. . . I repeat, then, there is no crisis excepting such a one as may be gotten up at any time by turbulent men aided by designing politicians. My advice to them, under such circumstances, is to keep cool. If the great American people only keep their temper on both sides of the line, the troubles will come to an end, and the question which now distracts the country will be settled, just as surely as all other difficulties of a like character which have originated in this government have been adjusted.—*Works, I, p. 678.*

Lincoln urges the same thought at Cleveland; but it is to be noticed that he did not repeat it again. A deeper and graver tone was manifest as he approached Washington.

The foregoing extracts give an insight into the ideas, and, to some extent, the plans of Lincoln and the Republicans. Buchanan's Annual Message states his thoughts fully, if not clearly. The following excerpts will afford something of an idea of his point of view:

. . . . Why is it, then, that discontent now so extensively prevails, and the Union of the States, wh'ch is the source of all these blessings, is threatened with destruction?

The long-continued and intemperate interference of the Northern people with the question of slavery in the Southern states has at length produced its natural effects. The different sections of the Union are now arrayed against each other and the time has arrived, so much dreaded by the Father of his Country, when hostile geographical parties have been formed. . . .

. . . .

How easy would it be for the American people to settle the slavery question forever, and to restore peace and harmony to this distracted country! . . . All that is necessary to accomplish the object, and all for which the slave states have ever contended, is to be let alone and permitted to manage their domestic institutions in their own way. As sovereign States, they, and they alone, are responsible before God and the world for the slavery existing among them. . . .

. . . .

And this brings me to observe that the election of any one of our fellow-citizens to the office of President does not of itself afford just cause for dissolving the Union. . . . In order to justify a resort to revolutionary resistance, the Federal Government must be guilty of "a deliberate, palpable, and dangerous exercise" of powers not granted by the Constitution.

. . . .

In order to justify secession as a constitutional remedy, it must be on the principle that the Federal Government is a mere voluntary association of States. . . . If this be so, the Confederacy is a rope of sand, . . . [which] might be broken into fragments in a few weeks, which cost our forefathers many years of toil, privation, and blood to establish.

Such a principle is wholly inconsistent with the history as well as the character of the Federal Constitution. . . .

. . . .

It [the Union] was intended to be perpetual, and not to be annulled at the pleasure of any one of the contracting parties.

. . . .

It may be asked, then, are the people of the States without redress against the tyranny and oppression of the Federal Government? By no means. The right of resistance on the part of the governed against the oppression of their governments cannot be denied. It exists independently of all constitutions. . . . But the distinction must ever be observed that this is revolution against an established government, and not a voluntary secession from it by virtue of an inherent constitutional right. In short, let us look the danger fairly in the face; secession is neither more nor less than revolution. It may or it may not be a justifiable revolution, but still it is revolution. . . .

. . . .

Then in speaking of the power of Congress or the president to coerce a State, should it attempt secession, he used this language:

The question fairly stated is: Has the Constitution delegated to Congress the power to coerce a State into submission which is attempting to withdraw, or has actually withdrawn from the Confederacy? . . .

Buchanan argues against this power, then says:

But if we possessed this power, would it be wise to exercise it under existing circumstances? . . .

The fact is, that our Union rests upon public opinion and can never be cemented by the blood of its citizens shed in civil war. If it cannot live in the affections of the people, it must one day perish. Congress possesses many means of preserving it by conciliation; but the sword was not placed in their hand to preserve it by force. He then proposes that Congress submit these amendments to the States, as follows:

I. An express recognition of the right of property in slaves in the States. . . .

II. The duty of protecting the right in all the common territories. . . .

III. The like recognition of the right of the master to have his slave, who has escaped from one State to another, restored and "delivered up" to him. . .

—*Buchanan's Message, Dec. 3, 1860, Cited in Curtis' Buchanan, II, pp. 337 f.*

Passing to the South we see that acts are substituted for words. Let us see what South Carolina did.

AN ORDINANCE to dissolve the Union between the State of South Carolina and other States united with her under the compact entitled "The Constitution of the United States of America."

We, the people of the State of South Carolina in convention assembled, do declare and ordain, . . . that the ordinance adopted by us in convention on the twenty-third day of May [1788] whereby the Constitution of the United States of America was ratified, ... [and amendments] are hereby repealed; and that the Union now subsisting between South Carolina and other States, under the name of the "United States of America," is hereby dissolved.

Done at Charleston the twentieth day of December, [1860].   D. F. JAMESON,

Delegate from Barnwell and President of the Convention, and Others.

Attest:

BENJAMIN F. ARTHUR,

Clerk of the Convention.

—*Rebellion Records, Series I, vol. I, p. 110.*

Two days after the passage of the above ordinance the State of South Carolina gave the following commission to Robert W. Barnwell, James H. Adams, and James L. Orr:

> Whereas the convention of the People of South Carolina, . . . did . . . order that their commissioners . . . proceed to Washington, authorized, . . . to treat with the Government of the United States for the delivery of the forts, magazines, lighthouses, and other real estate . . . within the limits of South Carolina; and also for an apportioning of the public debt and for a division of the other property held by the government of the United States as agent of the confederated States, of which South Carolina was recently a member; and generally to negotiate . . . for the continuance of peace and amity between this commonwealth and the Government at Washington: . . .—*Ibid, p. 111.*

On December 28, 1860, the above named commissioners of South Carolina sent a communication to the president, from which the followin extract is made:

> . . . In the execution of this trust it is our duty to furnish you . . . with an official copy of the ordinance of secession, by which the State of South Carolina has resumed the powers she delegated to the Government of the United States and has declared her perfect sovereignty and independence. It would also have been our duty to have informed you that we were ready to negotiate with you upon all such questions as are necessarily raised by the adoption of this ordinance, and that we were prepared to enter upon this negotiation with the earnest desire to avoid all unnecessary and hostile collision, and so to inaugurate our new relations as to secure mutual respect, general advantage, and a future of good will and harmony.
> . . . But the events of the last twenty-four hours render such an assurance impossible. [This was the taking possession of Ft. Sumter by Major Anderson.]
> . . .
> And in conclusion we would urge upon you the immediate withdrawal of the troops from the harbor

of Charleston. Under present circumstances they are a standing menace which render negotiations impossible, and . . . threaten speedily to bring to a bloody issue questions which ought to be settled with temperance and judgment.—*Ibid, pp. 109-110.*

During the winter of 1860-'61 several plans were proposed to secure such amendments to the Constitution as would satisfy the various sections of the country, and thus restore harmony to the Union. Congress tried its hand and outlined six propositions, which, however, were never sent to the states.

On the request of the State of Virginia, a convention of delegates from the States of the Union was held in Washington, commencing February 4th, and closing on the 27th, of the same month, which proposed that Congress submit seven Constitutional amendments to the States for their action. Delegates were present from Maine, New Hampshire, Vermont, Massachusetts, Rhode Island, Connecticut, New York, New Jersey, Pennsylvania, Delaware, Maryland, Virginia, North Carolina, Tennessee, Kentucky, Missouri, Ohio, Indiana, Illinois, Iowa, and Kansas, including, as delegates, such men as W. P. Fessenden, L. M. Morrill, Geo. S. Boutwell, David Dudley Field, David Wilmot, Reverdy Johnson, Ex-President John Tyler, S. P. Chase, James Harlan, and James Guthrie. Ex-President Tyler, as presiding officer, closed the session in a speech from which these words are taken:

. . . But I here declare that it has never been my good fortune to meet with an association of more intelligent, thoughtful, or patriotic men. . . . I cannot but hope and believe that the blessing of God will follow and rest upon the results of your labors, and that such result will bring to our country that quiet and peace which every patriotic heart so earnestly desires. . . .

Gentlemen, forewell! I go to finish the work you

have assigned me, of presenting your recommendations to the two Houses of Congress. . . .

May you all inculcate among your people a spirit of mutual forbearance and concession; and may GOD protect our country and the Union of the States, which was committed to us as the blood-bought legacy of our heroic ancestors.

Congress did not submit the propositions as recommended, but instead the following action was taken:

MR. CORWIN, Republican (O.), in 1861 moved the following amendment to the Constitution. This amendment was adopted in the House by a vote of 133 to 65, and in the Senate 24 to 12. It reads as follows, and was to be numbered thirteen:

No amendment shall be made to the Constitution which will authorize or give to Congress the power to abolish or interfere, within any State, with the domestic institutions thereof, including that of persons held to labor or service by the laws of said State.

Contrast this with the 13th Amendment as adopted in 1865, and one can conceive of the immense distance that the nation had traversed in the four years of the civil war.

Neither slavery nor involuntary servitude, except as a punishment for crime whereof the party shall have been duly convicted, shall exist within the United States, or in any place subject to their jurisdiction.—*Constitution, Article XIII of Amendments.*

When Lincoln was inaugurated as president in 1861, seven of the Southern States had passed articles of secession, similar in terms to those of South Carolina cited above. Already the States had formed a preliminary constitution, and had chosen officers under it. Thus there were two organized general governments in the same territory. Most of the forts and arsenals in the Southern States had been taken possession of by troops of the various States in which they were situated. Under such conditions Lincoln delivered his Inaugural Address, from which the following extracts are taken:

Apprehension seems to exist among the people of the Southern States that by the accession of a Republican administration their property and their peace and personal security are to be endangered. There has never been any reasonable cause for such apprehension. Indeed, the most ample evidence to the contrary has all the while existed and been open to their inspection. It is found in nearly all the published speeches of him who now addresses you. I do but quote from one of those speeches when I declare that "I have no purpose, directly or indirectly, to interfere with the institution of slavery in the States where it exists. I believe I have no lawful right to do so, and I have no inclination to do so" [1860]. Those who nominated and elected me did so with full knowledge that I had made this and many similar declarations, and had never recanted them. And, more than this, they placed in the platform for my acceptance, and as a law to themselves and to me, the clear and emphatic resolution which I now read:

"*Resolved*, That the maintenance inviolate of the rights of the States, and especially the right of each State to order and control its own domestic institutions according to its own judgment exclusively, is essential to that balance of power on which the perfection and endurance of our political fabric depend, and we denounce the lawless invasion by armed force of the soil of any State or Territory, no matter under what pretext, as among the greatest of crimes."

I now reiterate these sentiments, and in doing so, I only press upon the public attention the most conclusive evidence of which the case is susceptible, that the property, peace, and security of no section are to be in anywise endangered by the new incoming administration. I add, too, that all the protection which, consistently with the Constitution and the laws can be given, will be cheerfully given to all the States when lawfully demanded, for whatever cause—as cheerfully to one section as to another. . . . I take the official oath to-day with no mental reservations, and with no purpose to construe the Constitution or laws by any hypercritical rules. . . .

I hold that in contemplation of universal law and of the Constitution, the Union of these States is perpetual. Perpetuity is implied, if not expressed, in the fundamental law of all national governments. . . .

In your hands, my dissatisfied fellow-countrymen, and not in mine, is the momentous issue of civil war. The government will not assail you. You can have no conflict without being yourselves the aggressors. You have no oath registered in heaven to destroy the government, while I shall have the most solemn one to "preserve, protect, and defend it."

. . . .

I am loath to close. We are not enemies, but friends. We must not be enemies. Though passions may have strained, it must not break our bonds of affection. The mystic chords of memory, stretching from every battle-field and patriot grave to every living heart and hearthstone all over this broad land, will yet swell the chorus of the Union when again touched, as surely they will be, by the better angels of our nature.—*Lincoln's Inaugural Address, Works, II, pp. 1-7.*

The first great question to come before the new administration was connected with provisioning Fort Sumter. March 15 the president consulted his cabinet, with results as follows:

SEWARD said:

. . . If it were possible to peacefully provision Fort Sumter, of course, I should answer that it would be both unwise and inhuman not to attempt it. But the facts of the case are known to be that the attempt must be made with the employment of military and marine force, which would provoke combat, and probably initiate civil war. . . .

I have not hesitated to assume that the Federal Government is committed to maintain, preserve, and defend the Union—peaceably if it can, forcibly if it must—to every extremity. . . .

CHASE wrote:

. . . If the attempt will so inflame civil war as to involve an immediate necessity for the enlistment of armies and the expenditure of millions, I cannot advise it in the existing circumstances of the country and in the present condition of the national finances.— *Lincoln's Works, II, pp. 13, 15.*

The other members of the cabinet agreed with the above in general, except Secretary Blair, who was for sending aid and provisions. On March 29, for the second time, a written opinion in regard to the policy of sending an expedition to relieve Fort Sumter, was asked of each member of the cabinet.

MR. SEWARD wrote:

The fact of preparation for such an expedition would inevitably transpire, and would therefore precipitate the war, and probably defeat the object. I do not think it wise to provoke a civil war beginning at Charleston and in rescue of an untenable position.

Therefore, I advise against the expedition in every view. . . .

MR. CHASE wrote:

. . . I am clearly in favor of maintaining Fort Pickens, and just as clearly in favor of provisioning Fort Sumter. . . .

MR. WELLES said:

I concur in the proposition to send an armed force off Charleston with supplies of provisions, and reinforcements for the garrison of Fort Sumter. . . .

MR. SMITH answered:

. . . Believing that Fort Sumter cannot be successfully defended, I regard its evacuation as a necessity, and I advise that Major Anderson's command shall be unconditionally withdrawn. . . .

MR. BLAIR wrote:

. . . It is acknowledged to be possible to relieve Fort Sumter. It ought to be relieved without reference to Pickens or any other possession. South Carolina is the head and front of this rebellion, and when that State is safely delivered from the authority of the United States it will strike a blow against our authority from which it will take years of bloody strife to recover. . . .

MR. BATES wrote:
[Believed in reinforcing Pickens, and] As to Fort Sumter, I think the time is come either to evacuate or relieve it.—*Lincoln's Works, II, pp. 26-28.*

Read the following letter, and think what the end was, and when it came, nay when it will come:

FORT SUMTER, S. C., *April* 12, 1861.—3:20 A. M.

SIR: By authority of Brigadier-General Beauregard commanding the Provisional Forces of the Confederate States, we have the honor to notify you that he will open the fire of his batteries on Fort Sumter in one hour from this time.

We have the honor to be, very respectfully, your obedient servants,

JAMES CHESTNET, JR.,
Aid-de-Camp.
STEPHEN D. LEE,
Captain C. S. Army, Aid-de-Camp.
MAJ. ROBERT ANDERSON,
U. S. Army, Commanding Fort Sumter.
—*Rebellion Records, I, p. 14.*

Congress met on the call of the president, July 4. President Lincoln sent in his first message on that day. Some striking passages are here quoted:

Lest there be some uneasiness in the minds of candid men as to what is to be the course of the government toward the Southern States after the rebellion shall have been suppressed, the executive deems it proper to say it will be his purpose then, as ever, to be guided by the Constitution and the laws; and that he probably will have no different understanding of the powers and duties of the Federal Government relatively to the rights of the States and the people, under the Constitution, than that expressed in the inaugural address.—*Lincoln's Message to Congress in Special Session, July 4, 1861, Works, II, p. 65.*

In the midst of the war, on November 19, 1863, President Lincoln made his Gettysburg Address, an address which probably will live as long as the English language shall be spoken or read.

Fourscore and seven years ago our fathers brought forth on this continent a new nation, conceived in liberty, and dedicated to the proposition that all men are created equal.

Now we are engaged in a great civil war, testing whether that nation, or any nation so conceived and so dedicated, can long endure. We have come to dedicate a portion of that field as a final resting-place for those who here gave their lives that that nation might live. It is altogether fitting and proper that we should do this.

But in a larger sense we cannot dedicate—we cannot consecrate—we cannot hallow—this ground. The brave men, living and dead, who struggled here, have consecrated it far above our poor power to add or detract. The world will little note nor long remember what we say here, but it can never forget what they did here. It is for us, the living, rather, to be dedicated here to the unfinished work which they who fought here have thus far so nobly advanced. It is rather for us to be here dedicated to the great task remaining before us—that from these honored dead we take increased devotion to that cause for which they gave the last full measure of devotion; that we here highly resolve that these dead shall not have died in vain; that this nation, under God, shall have a new birth of freedom; and that government of the people, by the people, for the people, shall not perish from the earth.—*Works, II, p. 439.*

THE EMANCIPATION PROCLAMATION.

After citing part of the proclamation of September 22, 1862, Lincoln says:

Nor, therefore, I, Abraham Lincoln, President of the United States, by virtue of the power in me vested as commander-in-chief of the army and navy of the United States, . . . and as a fit and necessary war measure for suppressing said rebellion, do, on this first day of January, in the year of our Lord one thousand eight hundred and sixty-three, and in accordance with my purpose so to do, . . . order and designate as the States and parts of States wherein the people thereof, respectively, are this day in rebellion against the United States, the following, to-wit [named] . .

And by virtue of the power, and for the purpose aforesaid, I do order and declare that all persons held as slaves within said designated States . . . are and henceforth shall be free. . . .—*Lincoln's Works, II, pp. 287-88.*

The great question of Reconstruction began to agitate the minds of American statesmen as early as 1862. Lincoln's first State paper on this subject outlines his plans in a general way. Other quotations from later papers, which follow, will show the development of his idea.

I recommend the adoption of a joint resolution by your honorable bodies [of Congress], which shall be substantially as follows:

Resolved, That the United States ought to co-operate with any State which may adopt gradual abolishment of slavery, giving to such State pecuniary aid, to be used by such State, in its discretion, to compensate for the inconveniences, public and private, produced by such change of system. . . .

The Federal Government would find its highest interest in such a measure, as one of the most efficient means of self-preservation.—*Works, II, p. 129.* [Both branches of Congress adopted this resolution by large majorities.]

In December, 1862, Mr. Lincoln recommended three resolutions to be adopted as amendments to the Constitution. They were as follows:

I. "Every State wherein slavery now exists which shall abolish the same therein at any time or times before the first day of January in the year of our Lord one thousand and nine hundred, shall receive compensation from the United States [in United States bonds] as follows ...... for each slave shown to have been therein by the eighth census of the United States" . . . [so many dollars].

The measure is both just and economical. In a certain sense the liberation of slaves is the destruction of property—property acquired by descent or by purchase, the same as any other property. It is no less true for having been often said, that the people of the South are not more responsible for the original introduction of this property than are the people of the North; and when it is remembered how unhesitatingly we all use cotton and sugar and share the profits of dealing in them, it may not be quite safe to say that the South has been more responsible than the North for its continuance. If, then, for a common object this property is to be sacrificed, is it not just that it be done at a common charge?

II. "All slaves who shall have enjoyed actual freedom by the chances of the war at any time before the end of the rebellion, shall be forever free; but all owners of such who shall not have been disloyal shall be compensated for them at the same rates as are provided for States adopting abolishment of slavery." . . .

III. "Congress may appropriate money and otherwise provide for colonizing free colored persons, with their own consent at any place or places without the United States." . . .

I cannot make it better known than it already is, that I strongly favor colonization. . . .

This plan is recommended as a means, not in exclusion of, but additional to, all others for restoring and preserving the national authority throughout the Union. The subject is presented exclusively in its economical aspect. The plan would, I am confident, secure peace more speedily, and maintain it more permanently, than can be done by force alone; while all it would cost, considering amounts, and manner of payment, and times of payment, would be easier paid than will be the additional cost of the war, if we rely solely upon force. It is much—very much—that it would cost no blood at all. . . . Other means may succeed; this could not fail. The way is plain, peaceful, generous, just, . . . a way which, if followed, the world will forever applaud, and God must forever bless.—*Ibid, pp. 270-277.*

And it is suggested as not improper that, in constructing a loyal State government in any State, the name of the State, the boundary, the subdivisions, the constitution, and the general code of laws, as before the rebellion, be maintained, subject only to the modifications made necessary by the conditions hereinbefore stated, and such others, if any, not contravening said conditions, and which may be deemed expedient.—*Lincoln's Proclamation of Amnesty and Reconstruction, Aug. 12, 1863, Works, II, p. 444.*

The policy of emancipation, and of employing black soldiers, gave to the future a new aspect, about which hope, and fear, and doubt contended in uncertain conflict. According to our political system, as a matter of civil administration, the General Government had no lawful power to effect emancipation in any State, and for a long time it had been hoped that the rebellion could be suppressed without resorting to it as a military measure. It was all the while deemed possible that the necessity for it might come, and that if it should, the crisis of the contest would then be presented. It came, and, as was anticipated, it was followed by dark and doubtful days. Eleven months having now passed, we are permitted to take another review. The rebel borders are pressed still further back. . . . Maryland and Missouri, neither of which three years ago would tolerate any restraint upon the extension of slavery into new Territories, only dispute now as to the best mode of removing it within their own limits. . . . No servile insurrection, or tendency to violence or cruelty, has marked the measures of emancipation and arming the blacks. These measures have been much discussed in foreign countries, and contemporary with such discussion the tone of public sentiment there is much improved. . . .—*Lincoln's Annual Message, Dec. 8, 1863, Works, II, pp. 453, 454.*

Lincoln's plan of Reconstruction, as formulated December, 1863, continued to be attacked till the end of his life. Two days before his death he made his last public address, which was largely given over to a discussion of this question. In part he said:

We meet this evening not in sorrow, but in gladness of heart. The evacuation of Petersburg and Richmond, and the surrender of the principal insurgent army, give hope of a righteous and speedy peace, whose joyous expression cannot be restrained. . . .

By these recent successes the reinauguration of the national authority—reconstruction—which has had a large share of thought from the first, is pressed much more closely on our attention. It is fraught with great difficulty. . . . Nor is it a small additional embarrassment that we, the loyal people, differ among ourselves as to the mode, etc. . . . [He then discusses what he has done in Louisiana.] [Concerning the question whether the States were ever out of the Union] I have purposely forborne any public expression on it. As it appears to me, that question has not been, not yet is, a practically material one. . . .

We are all agreed that the seceded States, so-called, are out of their proper practical relation with the Union, and that the sole object of the government . . . is to again get them into that proper practical relation. I believe that it is not only possible, but in fact easier, to do this without deciding or even considering whether these States have ever been out of the Union, than with it. Finding themselves safely at home, it would be utterly immaterial whether they had ever been abroad. . . .

. . . .

I repeat the question: Can Louisiana be brought into proper practical relation with the Union sooner by sustaining or by discarding her new State government? . . . So new and unprecedented is the whole case that no exclusive and inflexible plan can safely be prescribed as to details and collaterals. . . . Important principles may and must be inflexible. In the present situation, as the phrase goes, it may be my duty to make some new announcement to the people of the South. I am considering, and shall not fail to act when satisfied that action will be proper.—*Works, II, pp. 672-675.*

RECONSTRUCTION UNDER PRESIDENT JOHNSON.

President Johnson began on May 29, 1865, to carry out a system of reconstruction which he always claimed was the one Lincoln had planned. On that date he issued an amnesty proclamation to all those lately in rebellion, with fourteen excepted classes.

To the end, therefore, that the authority of the Gov-

ernment of the United States may be restored, and that peace, order, and freedom may be established, I, Andrew Johnson, President of the United States, do proclaim and declare that I hereby grant to all persons who have, directly or indirectly, participated in the existing rebellion [exceptions] amnesty and pardon, with restoration of all rights of property, except as to slaves, . ., . upon the condition . . . that such person subscribe the following oath. . . . I, ——
—— do solemnly swear . . . that I will henceforth faithfully support, protect, and defend the Constitution of the United States. . . .—*McPherson, Reconstruction, pp. 9-10.*

On the same day he appointed William W. Holden Provisional Governor of North Carolina, with powers and duties as follows:

. . . I, Andrew Johnson, . . . do hereby appoint William W. Holden Provisional Governor of the State of North Carolina, whose duty it shall be . . to prescribe such rules and regulations as may be necessary and proper for convening a convention, [and also] with authority to exercise . . . all the powers necessary and proper to enable such loyal people of the State . . . to restore said state to its constitutional relations to the Federal Government. . . .

Similar action was taken for the other States.

The president, by proclamation, also provided for the recall of the proclamations establishing martial law, blockade, the suspension of the Habeas Corpus, etc. In other words, during the summer of 1865 he had taken almost all the steps necessary to restore the States to their "practical relation" to the Union, by December, when Congress should come together. Almost immediately on its assembling there were signs that there was to be a struggle between Congress and the President. However the Congressional plan was not fully matured and enacted into law before March 2, 1867. In the meantime the State governments set up under President Johnson's plan continued to exist with some power, but subject to suspension whenever Congress might direct. The first part of the Congressional plan with which the President agreed was the passage of the 13th amendment. The second part was the 14th amendment. The great struggle, however, came over the following law, which contains the substance of the Congressional plan of Reconstruction:

WHEREAS, No legal State governments or adequate protection for life or property now exists in the rebel States [named], therefore,

Be it enacted, etc., That said rebel States shall be divided into military districts and made subject to the military authority of the United States . . . [Five districts provided for.]

SEC. 2. That it shall be the duty of the President to assign to the command of each of said districts an officer of the army . . . and to detail a sufficient military force to enable such officer to perform his duties and enforce his authority. . . .

SEC. 3. That it shall be the duty of each officer . . . to suppress insurrection, disorder . . . and to this end he may allow civil tribunals to take jurisdiction of and to try offenders, or, when in his judgment it may be necessary for the trial of offenders, he shall have power to organize military commissions . . . for that purpose. . . .

SEC. 4. [Speedy trials and no unusual punishments.]

SEC. 5. That when the people of any one of the rebel States shall have formed a constitution of government in conformity with the Constitution of the United States in all respects, framed by a convention of delegates elected by the male citizens of said State, twenty-one years old and upward, of whatever race, color, or previous condition, . . . except such as may be disfranchised for participation in the rebellion, . . . and when such constitution shall provide that the elective franchise shall be enjoyed by all such persons as have the qualifications herein stated for electors . . . and when ratified by a majority vote [accepted by Congress] and when said State . . . shall have adopted the amendment, . . . known as fourteen, and when said article shall have become a

part of the Constitution of the United States . . .
[then the State admitted to privileges of other States].
SEC. 6. [Any existing government provisional only.
. . .]—*McPherson, Reconstruction, pp. 191, 192.*

This bill and all other supplementary bills were vetoed by President Johnson, but all were passed over his veto, and thus became the law of the land. By 1870, under the series of acts of which the one cited is the most important, all the rebel States were again in full operation, and represented in Congress. The final outcome of the struggle was the impeachment of President Johnson. The Senate failed to convict. Congress triumphed, however, in its policy.

QUESTIONS.

1. Was Lincoln anxious to avoid war? 2. Point out the real difference he notes between the North and the South. 3. Did he wish the Republicans to yield their ground? 4. Was it possible for the two sections to agree? 5. What phrase had Lincoln used before this to characterize the nature of the struggle? 6. How had Seward characterized it? 7. How did Lincoln feel toward the South? 8. Give quotations to prove your position. 9. What would be "coercion" of a State according to Lincoln? 10. What did he think the nation might do? 11. How did Lincoln mean to treat slavery in the States? 12. What did he mean by leaving them alone? 13. Did Lincoln seem to think war was necessary? 14. What was the matter? 15. What advice did he give to the people of North and South? 16. Could they take it? 17. Are Lincoln's positions in these extracts and in those given last month consistent with one another?

1. How did President Buchanan explain the troubles? 2. How could the difficulties be settled? 3. Did he believe then in the "irrepressible conflict" doctrine? 4. Which proved to be right? 5. Did he believe the South might secede on account of President Lincoln's election? 6. Did he recognize the *right of secession* at all? 7. How could the States get a redress of grievances? 8. Should anything be done to permit secession? 9. Why not? 10. How did he propose to settle the trouble? 11. Compare ideas of Lincoln and Buchanan.

1. What State passed the first Ordinance of Secession? 2. What relation to the action of the State in 1788? 3. Who acted for the State? 4. Apparently did the State expect war? 5. If not, why not? 6. What did the State offer to do? 7. What was to be the future relation? 8. Judged by the extracts given last

month, why did secession take place? 9. What attempt did Virginia make to prevent secession? 10. How far were many of the Republicans, Lincoln included, ready to go to prevent war? 11. Compare the proposed Thirteenth amendment with the existing one.

1. How did Lincoln attempt to satisfy the South that secession was not justifiable? 2. How did he propose to treat them? 3. Who would be responsible for war if it came? 4. Commit the last paragraph of his inaugural. 5. Can you find another paragraph more eloquent than this?

1. How did the Cabinet feel in regard to aiding Fort Sumter? 2. Why such feelings? 3. Any changes in sentiment between March 15 and March 29? 4. What is the most important letter in this number? Why?

1. How did Lincoln propose to treat the Southern States after the Rebellion was suppressed? 2. What important thought in the Gettysburg speech? 3. Under what power did Lincoln claim the right to issue the Emancipation Proclamation? 4. Would Congress have had the same right? 5. How did Lincoln propose to secure the abolishment of slavery? 6. When would slavery have been ended by his plan? 7. What arguments did he use to sustain his plan? 8. How did the country first receive the Emancipation Proclamation? 9. What did Lincoln believe in regard to the States having ever been out of the Union? 10. When did Lincoln last speak concerning Reconstruction? 11. What policy did President Johnson claim to follow in regard to Reconstruction? 12. What was the great difference between the Congressional plan of Reconstruction and President Johnson's? 13. What do you understand by Reconstruction? 14. Name the principal elements in the Congressional plan. 15. Who could vote in reconstructing the seceded States under President Johnson's plan under the Congressional plan? 16. Write an essay on President Lincoln in the war, using only the material here given.

American History Studies

No. 9.   MAY, 1898.

A STUDY IN AMERICAN FOREIGN RELATIONS AND DIPLOMACY.

SELECTIONS MADE FROM THE SOURCES

BY

H. W. CALDWELL,

UNIVERSITY OF NEBRASKA.

J. H. MILLER, Publisher,
LINCOLN, NEBRASKA.

Yearly Subscription, 40 cents.   Single Copy, 5 cents.

PUBLISHED MONTHLY, EXCEPT JULY AND AUGUST.
Entered as second-class matter at the Post Office, Lincoln, Nebraska.
U. S. A.

AMERICAN HISTORY STUDIES.

A STUDY IN AMERICAN FOREIGN RELATIONS AND DIPLOMACY.

SINCE 1815 the development of American political history has been only slightly modified by foreign influences. To a great extent the reason for this may be found in the geographical situation of the United States. Separated by wide oceans from any other important nation, they have been enabled to pursue a self-directive course, almost as freely as if located on an island in the midst of the sea. American diplomatic history may be said to begin on November 29, 1775, when a motion was made to appoint a committee to correspond with "our friends in England and elsewhere." At the moment of writing this introduction our nation is in the midst of the excitement due to the Cuban question, and the imminence of war with Spain on account of it. In 1775 Spain looked upon us as a band of rebels, if she condescended to think of us at all. Now the United States has more than four times the population, and many times the wealth, of the haughty nation which then owned and controlled the larger part of this western hemisphere. The importance and complexity of the problems arising from our foreign relations in 1776 were almost as nothing compared with those that confront us to-day; yet it is undoubtedly true that the course of our development then was much more influenced by our diplomatic policy than it is now. The really great problems are internal ones, and the American people should ever remember this. The diplomatists as well as the statesmen of the Revolutionary period were men of vigor and power. Franklin, Jay, J. Adams, and Jefferson proved themselves able to meet on equal terms the best men that France and England possessed. A little later we find Clay, J. Q. Adams, and especially A. Gallatin, contending with the English ambassadors over the terms of the treaty of peace in 1814, and winning for our nation a decided victory. Monroe and Adams in the events connected with the promulgation of the so-called Monroe doctrine proved themselves able and skilled diplomatists. Webster, in the Webster-Ashburton treaty of 1842, gained the good will of Europe for the skill and dignity with which he managed the American cause.

It is possible in one article to touch only a very few of the many events in which our nation has come into contact with other nations. I have chosen to take a few important points and give them a fuller treatment, rather than to attempt to cover the whole ground. The reader, therefore, must remember that these extracts do not touch even many of the most interesting questions which have confronted our statesmen in the past. Yet it is hoped that they may arouse an interest so that more of the documentary matter pertaining to our external relations may be called for and used.

November 29, 1775, congress passed the following resolution, which may be said to be the first word ever uttered by the American people with regard to foreign affairs:

Resolved, That a committee of five be appointed for the sole purpose of corresponding with our friends in Great Britain, Ireland, and other parts of the world; and that they lay their correspondence before Congress when directed.

The members chosen were Mr. Harrison, Dr. Franklin, Mr. Johnson, Mr. Dickinson, and Mr. Jay.—*Secret Journals of the Congress of the Confederation, vol. II, p. 5.*

We next find our diplomatic history set forth in the resolutions which follow:'

[June 11, 1776.] *Resolved,* That a committee be appointed to prepare a plan of treaties to be proposed to foreign powers.—*Ibid, p. 475.*

[September 17, 1776.] Congress took into consideration the plan of treaties to be proposed to foreign nations, with the amendments agreed to by the committee of the whole; and thereupon,

Resolved, That the following plan of a treaty be proposed to his most christian majesty: [Plan.]—*Ibid, p. 6.*

Resolved, That Thursday next be assigned for appointing commissioners to transact the business of the United States at the court of France.—*Ibid, p. 31.*

Resolved, That three be appointed. The ballots being taken, Mr. B. Franklin, Mr. S. Deane, and Mr. T. Jefferson, were elected.—*Ibid, p. 31.*

[September 28, 1776.] *Resolved,* That the commissioners should live in such a style and manner, at the court of France, as they may find suitable and necessary to support the dignity of their publick character, keeping an account of their expenses, which shall be reimbursed by the Congress of the United States of America.—*Ibid, p. 33.*

The first alliance made by the United States contains, among others, the following clauses:

The most christian king, and the United States of North America . . . having this day concluded a treaty of amity and commerce, . . . have thought it necessary to take into consideration the means of strengthening those engagements, and of rendering them useful to the safety and tranquility of the two parties; particularly in case Great Britain, in resentment . . . should break the peace with France. . . . And his majesty and the United States, having resolved, in that case, to join their counsels and efforts against the enterprises of their common enemy,

... have ... concluded and determined on the following articles:

* * * * * * * *

ART. II. The essential and direct end of the present defensive alliance is, to maintain effectually the liberty, sovereignty, and independence absolute and unlimited of the said United States, as well in matters of government as of commerce.

* * * * * * * *

ART. XI. The two parties guarantee, mutually, from the present time and forever, against all other powers, to-wit, the United States to his most christian majesty, the present possessions of the crown of France in America, as well as those which it may acquire by the future treaty of peace; and his most christian majesty guarantees, on his part, to the United States, their liberty, sovereignty, and independence, absolute and unlimited, as well in matters of government as of commerce, and also their possessions, and the additions or conquests that their confederation may obtain during the war, from any of the dominions now or heretofore possessed by Great Britain in North America, ... the whole as their possession shall be affixed and assured to the said states at the moment of the cessation of their present war with England.

* * * * * * * *

Done at Paris, this 6th day of February, one thousand seven hundred and seventy-eight.

C. A. GERARD. [L. S.]

          B. FRANKLIN. [L. S.]
          SILAS DEANE. [L. S.]
          ARTHUR LEE. [L. S.]

—*Secret Journal of Congress, vol. II, pp. 82, 86, 88.*

The extracts below from the treaty of peace of 1783 will give much valuable information if duly studied:

In the name of the Most Holy and Undivided Trinity.

It having pleased the Divine Providence to dispose the hearts of ... King George the Third, ... and of the United States of America, to forget all past misunderstandings ... have agreed upon and confirmed the following articles:

ART. I. His Britannic Majesty acknowledges the

United States, viz.: New Hampshire, Massachusetts, Rhode Island and Providence Plantations, Connecticut, New York, New Jersey, Pennsylvania, Delaware, Maryland, Virginia, North Carolina, South Carolina, and Georgia, to be free, sovereign, and independent States; that he treats with them as such; and for himself, his heirs and successors, relinquishes all claims to the government, propriety, and territorial rights of the same, and every part thereof.

. . . .

ART. VII. The navigation of the river Mississippi, from its source to the ocean, shall forever remain free and open to the subjects of Great Britain, and the citizens of the United States.

(Signed.)   D. HARTLEY.
                             JOHN ADAMS.
                             B. FRANKLIN.
                             JOHN JAY.
—*United States Statutes at Large, vol. VIII, pp. 81, 83.*

The treaty of peace of 1783 was completed only after a long and intense struggle between the commissioners of the two countries. John Adams, in his diary, has left us a clear picture of the daily life and disputes, not only between the English and American commissioners, but also among the American commissioners themselves. The negotiations had to do with many subjects. These extracts in regard to the right to fish off the banks of Newfoundland introduce us to their daily "squabbles" as well as any that may be chosen:

Upon the return of the other gentlemen, Mr. Strachey proposed to leave out the word "right" of fishing, and make it "liberty." Mr. Fitzherbert said the word "right" was an obnoxious expression. Upon this I rose up and said, "Gentlemen, is there or can there be a clearer right? In former treaties, that of Utrecht and that of Paris,—France and England have claimed the right, and used the word. When God Almighty made the banks of New Foundland, at three hundred leagues distance from the people of America, and at six hundred leagues distance from those of

France and England, did He not give as good a right to the former as to the latter? If Heaven in the creation gave a right it is ours at least as much as yours. If occupation, use, and possession, give a right, we have it as clearly as you. If war, and blood, and treasure give a right, ours is as good as yours. We have been constantly fighting in Canada, Cape Breton, and Nova Scotia, for the defense of this fishing, and have expended beyond all proportion more than you. If, then, the right cannot be denied, why should it not be acknowledged, and put out of dispute? Why should we leave room for illiterate fishermen to wrangle and chicane?—*Life and Works of John Adams, vol. III, pp. 333, 334.*

I forgot to mention that, when we were upon the fishery, and Mr. Strachey and Mr. Fitzherbert were urging us to leave out the word "right" and substitute "liberty," I told them at last, in answer to their proposal, to agree upon all other articles, and leave that of the fishery to be adjusted at the definitive treaty. I never could put my hand to any articles without satisfaction about the fishery; that Congress had, three or four years ago, when they did me the honor to give me a commission to make a treaty of commerce with Great Britain, given me positive instructions not to make any such treaty without an article in the treaty of peace acknowledging our right to the fishery; that I was happy that Mr. Laurens was now present, who, I believed, was in Congress at the time, and must remember it. Mr. Laurens upon this said, with great firmness, that he was in the same case, and could never give his voice for any articles without this. Mr. Jay spoke up, and said, it could not be a peace, it would only be an insidious truce without it.—*Ibid, p. 335.*

I have not attempted, in these notes, to do justice to the arguments of my colleagues, all of whom were, throughout the whole business, when they attended, very attentive and able, especially Mr. Jay, to whom the French, if they knew as much of his negotiations as they do of mine, would very justly give the title with which they have inconsiderately decorated me, that of *"Le Washington de la negociation"*: a very flattering compliment indeed, to which I have not a right, but sincerely think it belongs to Mr. Jay.—*Ibid, p. 339.*

The X. Y. Z. episode in American history is perhaps well known, but it is doubtful if many of our students ever read an extract from the letters of our ministers in France,—Pinckney, Marshall, and Gerry,—which, when published, roused the American people to the highest pitch of excitement, and led to the production of "Hail Columbia."

Citizen Minister [Mr. Monroe]: I hasten to lay before the Executive Directory the copies of your letters of recall, and of the letter of credence of Mr. Pinckney, whom the President of the United States has appointed to succeed you, in the quality of Minister Plenipotentiary of the United States near the French Republic. The Directory has charged me to notify you "that it will not acknowledge nor receive another Minister Plenipotentiary from the United States, until after the redress of grievances demanded of the American Government, and which the French Republic has a right to expect from it."—*Benton, Abridgment of Debates in Congress, vol. II, p. 390.*

The following extracts may make more evident why the cry "Millions for defense, not a cent for tribute," became such a phrase to conjure with in the years 1797-1800:

In the evening of the same day, M. X called on General Pinckney, and after having sat some time . . . whispered him that he had a message from M. Talleyrand to communicate when he was at leisure. General Pinckney immediately withdrew with him into another room, and said . . . that he had been acquainted with M. Talleyrand, . . . and that he was sure that he had a great regard for [America] and its citizens; and was very desirous that a reconciliation be brought about with France, that, to effect that end, he was ready, if it was thought proper, to suggest a plan, confidentially, that M. Talleyrand expected would answer the purpose. General Pinckney said he would be glad to hear it. M. X replied

FOREIGN RELATIONS AND DIPLOMACY. 203

that the Directory, and particularly two of the members of it, were exceedingly irritated at some passages of the President's speech, and desired that they should be softened, and that this step would be necessary previous to our reception. That, besides this, a sum of money was required for the pocket of the Directory and Ministers, which would be at the disposal of M. Talleyrand; and that a loan would also be insisted on. M. X said if we acceded to these measures, M. Talleyrand had no doubt that all our differences with France might be accommodated. On inquiry, M. X. could not point out the particular passages of the speech that had given offence, nor the quantum of the loan, but mentioned that the douceur for the pocket was twelve hundred thousand livres, about fifty thousand pounds sterling.—*Ibid, p. 393.*

About twelve we received another visit from M. X. He immediately mentioned the great event announced in the papers, and then said, that some proposals from us had been expected on the subject on which we had before conversed; that the Directory were becoming impatient, and would take a decided course with regard to America, if we could not soften them.

. . . .

M. X. again expatiated on the power and violence of France; he urged the danger of our situation, and pressed the policy of softening them, and of thereby obtaining time. M. X. again returned to the subject of money. Said he, you do not speak to the point; it is money; it is expected that you will offer money. We said that we had spoken to that point very explicitly; we had given an answer. No, said he, you have not; what is your answer? We replied no; no; not a sixpence.—*Oct. 27, 1797.—Ibid, p. 395.*

This extract from McMaster's "History of the American People" shows the excitement, and narrates the events which led to the production of "Hail Columbia":

. . . Politics ruled the hour. The city was full of excited Federalists, who packed the theatre night after night for no other purpose that to shout themselves hoarse over the "President's March." He [the player at the theatre] determined to make use of this fact. He would take the March, find some one to write a few patriotic stanzas to suit it, and, on the night of his benefit, sing them to the house. Some Federalists were consulted, were pleased with the idea, and named Joseph Hopkinson as the best man fitted to write the words. He consented and in a few hours "Hail, Columbia" was produced.—*McMaster, History of the People of the United States, vol. II, p. 378.*

This is an example of the "poetry" that the X. Y. Z. affair called forth. There is an abundance of like matter in the newspapers of the day:

> The President, with good intent,
>   Three envoys sent to Paris,
> But Cinq Tetes would not with 'em treat,
>   Of honor France so base is.
>   Yankee Doodle (mind the tune)
>   Yankee Doodle Dandy.
>   If Frenchmen come . . .
>   We'll spank 'em hard and handy
>
> Thro' X. and Y., and Madame Sly,
>   They made demand for money;
> For, as we're told, the French love gold
>   As stinging bees love honey.
>   Chorus.
>
> Bold Adams did in '76
>   Our Independence sign, sir,
> And he will not give up a jot,
>   Tho' all the world combine, sir.
>   Chorus.
>
> —*Ibid, p. 384.*

We may get a few thoughts in regard to the causes of the war of 1812 from the message of President Madison of June 1, 1812, sent to Congress recounting the acts of the British government during the years 1803-1812. He says, in part:

British cruisers have been in the continued practice of violating the American flag on the great highway of nations, and of seizing and carrying off persons sailing under it, not in the exercise of a belligerent right founded on the law of nations against an enemy, but of a municipal prerogative over British subjects.

. . . .

British cruisers have been in the practice also of violating the rights and the peace of our coasts. They hover over and harass our entering and departing commerce. To the most insulting pretensions they have added the most lawless proceedings in our very harbors, and have wantonly spilt American blood within the sanctuary of our territorial jurisdiction.

. . . .

Under pretended blockades, without the presence of an adequate force and sometimes without the practicability of applying one, our commerce has been plundered in every sea, the great staples of our country have been cut off from their legitimate markets, and a destructive blow aimed at our agricultural and maritime interests. . . .

. . . .

Such is the spectacle of injuries and indignities which have been heaped on our country, and such the crisis which its unexampled forbearance and conciliatory efforts have not been able to avert.

. . . .

Other counsels have prevailed. Our moderation and conciliation have had no other effect than to encourage perseverance and to enlarge pretensions. We behold our seafaring citizens still the daily victims of lawless violence, committed on the great common and highway of nations, even within sight of the country which owes them protection.

. . . .

Whether the United States shall continue passive under these progressive usurpations and these accumulating wrongs, or, opposing force to force in defense of their national rights shall commit a just cause into the hands of the Almighty Disposer of events, avoiding all connections which might entangle it in the contest or views of other powers, and preserving a constant readiness to concur in an honorable re-establishment of peace and friendship, is a solemn question which the Constitution wisely confides to the legislative department of the Government. In recommending it to their early deliberations I am happy in the assurance that the decision will be worthy the enlightened and patriotic councils of a virtuous, a free, and a powerful nation.—*Richardson, Messages and Papers of the Presidents, vol. I, pp. 500, 504.*

Henry Clay, in a speech in the House of Representatives on the New Army Bill, January 8, 1813, gives us a good picture of the point of view of the "Young Republicans" of the West and South:

The war was declared, because Great Britain arrogated to herself the pretension of regulating our foreign trade, under the delusive name of retaliatory orders in council—a pretension by which she undertook to proclaim to American enterprise, "thus far shalt thou go and no further"—orders which she refused to revoke, after the alleged cause of their enactment had ceased; because she persisted in the practice of impressing American seamen; because she had instigated the Indians to commit hostilities against us; and because she refused indemnity for her past injuries upon our commerce. I throw out of the question other wrongs. The war in fact was announced, on our part, to meet the war which she was waging on her part. So undeniable were the causes of the war, so powerfully did they address themselves to the feelings of the whole American people, that when the bill was pending before this house, gentlemen in the opposition, although provoked to debate, would not, or could not, utter one syllable against it.—*Mallory, Life of Clay, vol. I, p. 304.*

And who is prepared to say, that American seamen shall be surrendered as victims to the British principle of impressment? And, sir, what is this principle? She contends, that she has a right to the services of her own subjects, and that, in the exercise of this right, she may lawfully impress them, even although she finds them in American vessels, upon the high seas, without her jurisdiction. Now I deny that she has any right, beyond her jurisdiction, to come on board our vessels, upon the high seas, for any other purpose, than in pursuit of enemies, or their goods, or goods contraband of war. But she further contends, that her subjects cannot renounce their allegiance to her, and contract a new obligation to other sovereigns. I do not mean to go into the general question of the right of expatriation. If, as is contended, all nations deny it, all nations at the same time admit and practice the right of naturalization. Great Britain herself does this. Great Britain, in the very case of foreign seamen, imposes, perhaps, fewer restraints upon naturalization than any other nation. Then, if subjects cannot break their original allegiance, they may, according to universal usage, contract a new allegiance. What is the effect of this double obligation? Undoubtedly, that the sovereign, having possession of the subject, would have the right to the services of the subject.—*Ibid, p. 307.*

If Great Britain desires a mark by which she can know her own subjects, let her give them an ear mark. The colors that float from the mast-head should be the credentials of our seamen. There is no safety to us, and the gentlemen have been shown it, but in the rule, that all who sail under the flag (not being enemies) are protected by the flag. It is impossible that this country should ever abandon the gallant tars, who have won for us such splendid trophies.—*Ibid, p. 308.*

The disasters of the war admonish us, we are told, of the necessity of terminating the contest. If our achievements by land have been less splendid than those of our intrepid seamen by water, it is not because the American soldier is less brave. On the one element, organization, discipline, and a thorough knowledge of their duties, exist, on the part of the officers and their men. On the other, almost everything is yet to be acquired. We have, however, the consolation that our country abounds with the richest materials, and that in no instance, when engaged in action, have our arms been tarnished.—*Ibid, p. 312.*

What cause, Mr. Chairman, which existed for declaring the war has been removed? We sought indemnity for the past and security for the future. The orders in council are suspended, not revoked; no compensation for spoliations; Indian hostilities, which were before secretly instigated, are now openly encouraged; and the practice of impressment unremittingly persevered in and insisted upon. Yet the administration has given the strongest demonstrations of its love of peace. On the twenty-ninth of June, less than ten days after the declaration of war, the secretary of the state writes to Mr. Russell, authorizing him to agree to an armistice, upon two conditions only, and what are they? That the orders in council should be repealed, and the practice of impressing American seamen cease, those already impressed being released. The proposition was for nothing more than a *real* truce; that the war should in fact cease on *both* sides.—*Ibid, p. 313.*

No, sir, the administration has erred in the steps which it has taken to restore peace, but its error has been, not in doing too little, but in betraying too great a solicitude for that event. An honorable peace is attainable only by an efficient war. My plan would be to call out the ample resources of the country, give them a judicious direction, prosecute the war with the utmost vigor, strike wherever we can reach the enemy, at sea or on land, and negotiate the terms of peace at Quebec or Halifax. We are told that England is a proud and lofty nation, which, disdaining to wait for danger, meets it half way. Haughty as she is, we once triumphed over her, and, if we do not listen to the councils of timidity and despair, we shall again prevail. In such a cause, with the aid of Providence, we must come out crowned with success, but if we fail, let us fail like men, lash ourselves to our gallant tars, and expire together in one common struggle, fighting for *Free Trade and Seamen's Rights.—Ibid, p. 314.*

The Seminole war and Jackson's invasion of Florida in 1817-18 led ultimately to political animosities among American statesmen that influenced in no slight manner the development of its political history. The following extracts from Clay's speeches on the Seminole war will throw some light on the hatred which in later years existed between him and General Jackson. In part he said, January 17, 1819:

General Jackson says that when he received that letter, he no longer hesitated. No, sir, he did no longer hesitate. He received it on the twenty-third, he was in Pensacola on the twenty-fourth, and immediately after set himself before the fortress of San Carlos de Barancas, which he shortly reduced. *Veni, vidi, vici.* Wonderful energy! Admirable promptitude! Alas, that it had not been an energy and a promptitude within the pale of the Constitution and according to the orders of the chief magistrate.—*Mallory, Life of Clay, vol. I, p. 440.*

That the President thought the seizure of the Spanish posts was an act of war, is manifest through his opening message, in which he says that, to have retained them, would have changed our relations with Spain, to do which the power of the executive was incompetent, Congress alone possessing it. The President has, in this instance, deserved well of his country. He has taken the only course which he could have pursued, consistent with the Constitution of the land. And I defy the gentleman to make good both his positions, that the general was right in taking, and the President right in giving up, the posts.—*Ibid, p. 441.*

Recall to your recollection the free nations which have gone before us, where are they now?

"Gone glimmering through the dreams of things that were,
A school boy's tale, the wonder of an hour."

And how have they lost their liberties?

. . . .

I hope not to be misunderstood; I am far from intimating that General Jackson cherishes any designs inimical to the liberties of the country. I believe his intentions to be pure and patriotic. I thank God that he would not, but I thank Him still more that he could not if he would, overturn the liberties of the republic. But precedents, if bad, are fraught with the most dangerous consequences.—*Ibid, p. 443.*

I hope our happy form of government is to be perpetual. But, if it is to be preserved, it must be by the practice of virtue, by justice, by moderation, by magnanimity, by greatness of soul, by keeping a watchful and steady eye on the executive; and, above all, by holding to a strict accountability the military branch of the public force.

* * * * * * *

Beware how you forfeit this exalted character. Beware how you give a fatal sanction, in this infant period of our republic, scarcely yet two score years old, to military insubordination. Remember that Greece had her Alexander, Rome her Cæsar, England her Cromwell, France her Bonaparte, and that if we would escape the rock on which they split, we must avoid their errors.—*Ibid, p. 444.*

The purchase of Florida was not made without a word of criticism concerning its terms from Clay. In a speech on the treaty, April 3, 1820, he uses these words:

We wanted Florida, or rather we *shall* want it; or, to speak more correctly, we want nobody else to have it. We do not desire it for immediate use. It fills a space in our imagination, and we wish it to complete the *arrondissement* of our territory. It must certainly come to us. The ripened fruit will not more surely fall. Florida is enclosed in between Alabama and Georgia, and cannot escape. Texas may. Whether we get Florida now, or some five or ten years hence, it is of no consequence, provided no other power gets it.—*Mallory, p. 457.*

The next [proposition] was, that it was inexpedient to cede Texas to any foreign power. They constituted, in his opinion, a sacred inheritance of posterity, which we ought to preserve unimpaired. He wished it was, if it were not, a fundamental and inviolable law of the land, that they should be inalienable to any foreign power. It was quite evident that it was in the order of Providence; that it was an inevitable result of the principle of population, that the whole of this continent, including Texas, was to be peopled in process of time. The question was, by whose race shall it be peopled? In our hands it will be peopled by freemen and the sons of freemen, carrying with them our language, our laws, and our liberties; establishing on the prairies of Texas, temples dedicated to the simple and devout modes of worship of God incident to our religion, and temples dedicated to that freedom which we adore next to Him. In the hands of others, it may become the habitation of despotism and of slaves, subject to the vile dominion of the inquisition and of superstition.—*Ibid, p. 459.*

The Monroe Doctrine, so-called, has become so vast that a volume is needed to present it in its entirety. However, it is believed that the following extracts taken from the messages of the Presidents and other documents will serve to throw more light on the subject than can be obtained from our ordinary school history, hence they are given in the hope that every teacher will try to find more illustrative matter. The first extracts are from the articles of agreement of the members of the Holy Alliance:

Their Majesties the Emperor of Austria, the King of Prussia, and the Emperor of Russia, in consequence of the *great events* [of years 1789-1815] . . . have, therefore, agreed to the following articles:

ART. I. In conformity to the words of the Holy Scriptures, which command all men to regard one another as brethren, the three contracting monarchs will remain *united* by the bonds of a true and indissoluble fraternity; . . . and they will lend one another . . . assistance, aid, and support; and, regarding the subjects and armies, as the fathers of their families, they will govern them in the spirit of fraternity with which they are animated, for the protection of *religion, peace,* and *justice.*

ART. II. Therefore, the only governing principle between the above mentioned governments . . . shall be that of rendering *reciprocal services;* of testifying, . . . the mutual affection with which they ought to be animated; of considering all as only the members of one Christian nation, the three allied powers *looking upon themselves as delegated by Providence* to govern three branches of the same family, to-wit: Austria, Prussia, and Russia, confessing . . . that the Christian nations . . . have really no other sovereign than Him to whom alone power belongs of right. . . . Their majesties, therefore, recommend, . . . to fortify themselves every day more and more in the principles and exercise of the duties which the Divine Savior has pointed out to us.

ART. III. All powers which wish solemnly to profess the sacred principles which have delegated this act, and who shall acknowledge how important it is to the happiness of nations, too long disturbed, that *these truths* shall henceforth exercise upon human destinies, all the influence which belongs to them, shall be received with as much readiness as affection, into this *holy alliance.—Cited in American Diplomacy, Snow, p. 243.*

In 1822, at a congress held at Verona, the Holy Allies added secretly the following clauses to their articles of agreement cited above:

The undersigned, specially authorized to make some additions to *The Treaty of the Holy Alliance,* . . . have agreed as follows:

ART. I. The high contracting powers being convinced that the system of *representative* government is equally as incompatible with the monarchical principles as the maxim of the sovereignty of the people with the divine right, engage mutually, . . . to use all their efforts to *put an end* to the system of *representative* governments, in whatever country it may exist in Europe, and to prevent its being introduced in those countries where it is not yet known.

ART. II. As it cannot be doubted that the *liberty* of the *press* is the most powerful means used by the pretended supporters of the rights of nations, to the detriment of those Princes, the high contracting parties promise reciprocally to adopt all proper measures to *suppress* it, not only in their own states, but, also, in the rest of Europe.—*Snow, American Diplomacy, p. 245.*

The Monroe Doctrine may be seen to have been foreshadowed long before its official promulgation by Monroe by a perusal of the following quotation:

Our detached and distant situation invites and enables us to pursue a different course. If we remain one people, under an efficient government, the period is not far off when we may defy material injury from external annoyance; when we may take such an attitude as will cause the neutrality we may at any time resolve upon to be scrupulously respected; when belligerent nations, under the impossibility of making acquisitions upon us, will not lightly hazard the giving us provocation; when we may choose peace or war as our interests, guided by justice, shall counsel.—*Washington's Farewell Address.*

Jefferson, in 1808, speaks as follows:
We consider their interests and ours as the same, and that the object of both must be to exclude all European influence from this hemisphere.—*Jefferson's Works, vol. V, p. 381.*

In 1823 Jefferson writes to Monroe in these words:
Our first and fundamental maxim should be, never to entangle ourselves in the broils of Europe. Our second, never to suffer Europe to intermeddle with cis-Atlantic affairs. America, North and South, has a set of interests distinct from those of Europe, and peculiarly her own. She should therefore have a system of her own, separate and apart from that of Europe. While the last is laboring to become the domicile of despotism, our endeavor should surely be to make our hemisphere that of freedom.—*Jefferson's Works, vol. VII, p. 315.*

Monroe formulates the doctrine in this way in his celebrated message of December 2, 1823:
In the discussion to which this interest has given rise, and in the arrangements by which they may terminate, the occasion has been adjudged proper for asserting, as a principle in which the rights and interests of the United States are involved, that the American continents, by the free and independent condition which they have assumed and maintain, are henceforth not to be considered as subjects for future colonization by any European powers.—*Richardson, Messages and Papers of the Presidents, vol. II, p. 207 f.*

The political system of the allied powers is essentially different in this respect from that of America. This difference proceeds from that which exists in their respective governments. And to the defense of our own, . . . this whole nation is devoted. We owe it, therefore, to candor, and to the amicable relations existing between the United States and those powers, to declare, that we should consider any attempt on their part to extend their system to any portion of this hemisphere as dangerous to our peace and safety.—*Ibid.*

In the war between those new governments and Spain, we declared our neutrality at the time of their recognition, and to this we have adhered, and shall continue to adhere, provided no change shall occur which, in the judgment of the competent authorities of this government, shall make a corresponding change on the part of the United States indispensable to their security.—*Ibid.*

It is impossible that the allied powers should extend their political system to any portion of either continent without endangering our peace and happiness; nor can anyone believe that our southern brethren, if left to themselves, would adopt it of their own accord. It is equally impossible, therefore, that we should behold such interposition, in any form, with indifference.—*Ibid.*

President Cleveland, in his message to Congress December 17, 1895, applied the Monroe Doctrine to the Venezuelan question. Between the farewell message of Washington and the present moment the idea has been in process of development. Trace its evolution.

[It is claimed] that the reasons justifying an appeal to the doctrine enunciated by President Monroe are generally inapplicable "to the state of things in which we live at the present day," and especially inapplicable to a controversy involving the boundary line between Great Britain and Venezuela.

Without attempting extended arguments in reply to this position, it may not be amiss to suggest that the doctrine upon which we stand is strong and sound because its enforcement is important to our peace and safety as a nation and is essential to the integrity of our free institutions and the tranquil maintenance of our distinctive form of government. It was intended to apply to every stage of our national life and cannot become obsolete while our republic endures.

. . . .

It is also suggested in the British reply that we should seek not to apply the Monroe doctrine to the pending dispute, because it does not embody any principle of international law which "is founded on the general consent of nations." . . .

Practically, the principle for which we contend has peculiar if not exclusive relations to the United States. It may not have been admitted in so many words to the code of international law, but since in international councils every nation is entitled to the rights belonging to it, if the enforcement of the Monroe doctrine is something we may justly claim, it has its place in the code of international law as certainly and securely as if it were specifically mentioned. . . . The Monroe doctrine finds its recognition in those principles of international law which are based upon the theory that every nation shall have its rights protected and its just claims enforced.

. . . .

Assuming, however, that the attitude of Venezuela will remain unchanged, the dispute has reached such a stage as to make it now incumbent upon the United States to take measures to determine with sufficient certainty for its justification what is the true divisional line between the republic of Venezuela and British Guiana.

. . . .

In order that such an examination might be prosecuted in a thorough and satisfactory manner, I suggest that the Congress make an adequate appropriation for the expenses of a commission to be appointed by the executive who shall make the necessary investigation. . . . When such report is made and accepted it will, in my opinion, be the duty of the United States to resist by every means in its power as a wilful aggression upon its rights and interests the appropriation by Great Britain of any lands or the exercise of governmental jurisdiction over any territory which after investigation we have determined of right belongs to Venezuela.

. . . .

I am, nevertheless, firm in my conviction that

while it is a grievous thing to contemplate the two great English-speaking peoples of the world as being otherwise than friendly competitors in the onward-march of civilization and strenuous worthy rivals in all the arts of peace, there is no calamity which a great nation can invite which equals that which follows a supine submission to wrong and injustice and the consequent loss of national self-respect and honor beneath which is shielded and defended a people's safety and greatness.—*Nebraska State Journal, December 18, 1895.*

QUESTIONS.

1. Who acted as the first Secretaries of State for the United States? 2. How were they chosen? 3. What their duties? 4. How were treaties to be prepared? 5. Who were the first foreign ministers? 4. Who appointed them? 7. How were they to live? 8. Why were they to live in such a style? 9. With what nation did we form the first treaty? 10. What guarantees did France and the United States mutually make? 11. What was the leading object of the treaty?

1. What peculiar statements do you find in the treaty of peace of 1783? 2. Who were acknowledged independent? 3. Find out why the navigation of the Mississippi river was to remain forever free to both nations. 4. How did John Adams feel in regard to the fisheries. 5. Summarize his arguments. 6. Was he ready to abandon the fisheries? 7. Whom did Adams regard as the ablest of the commissioners? 8. What title had the French given him? 9. Did he believe he deserved it?

1. Why was Mr. Monroe told that France did not intend to receive at present another minister from the United States? 2. Find out who the Directory were. 3. Why the cry "millions for defense, not a cent for tribute"? 4. Why the name X. Y. Z. to the difficulty with France, 1798-'99? 5. How did "Hail Columbia" come to be written? 6. What do you think of the "poetry" of 1798? 7. What did the Americans evidently think of the French at this time? 8. Name the causes of the war of 1812. 9. What does Clay mean by British principle of impressment? 10. Could a person be a citizen of two states at once? 11. If so which should protect him? 12. How did Clay feel in regard to war? 13. How about making peace in 1813?

1. What had Jackson done that made Clay so sarcastic in his speech of January 17, 1819? 2. Did Clay fear Jackson? 3. Where did he get his model for his sentence beginning "Remember that Greece had her Alexander," etc.? 4. Did Clay wish to purchase Florida in 1820? 5. Was there any other territory he preferred; why?

1. What principles did the Holy Allies hold? 2. Who were the Holy Allies? 3. Why had they formed the holy alliance? 4. What principles of government did the Holy Allies intend to destroy? 5. How did they regard the liberty of the press? 6. Who first set forth some of the ideas in the Monroe Doctrine? 7. What idea does Jefferson add? 8. What did Jefferson believe were the differences in government between Europe and America? 9. What doctrines does Monroe set forth in his message of December 2, 1823? 10. What did he mean by their "political system"? 11. How did President Cleveland interpret the Monroe Doctrine? 12. To what question did he apply it? 13. Is is a part of international law? 14. Write a paper on the growth of the Monroe Doctrine. 15. Is it applicable now to the Cuban issue?

American History Studies

No. 10   JUNE, 1898.

A STUDY IN ECONOMIC HISTORY.

SELECTIONS MADE FROM THE SOURCES

BY

H. W. CALDWELL,

UNIVERSITY OF NEBRASKA.

J. H. MILLER, Publisher,

LINCOLN, NEBRASKA.

Yearly Subscription, () cents.   Single Copy, 5 cents.

PUBLISHED MONTHLY, EXCEPT JULY AND AUGUST.

Entered as second-class matter at the Post Office, Lincoln, Nebraska, U. S. A.

AMERICAN HISTORY STUDIES.

A STUDY IN ECONOMIC HISTORY.

THIS last number of our studies for the year will aim to give us a little insight into the history of the tariff, and the movement for internal improvements. It has been thought better to confine our study to these two topics, so that the treatment might be complete enough to give a fair idea of their development, rather than to try to cover in a less thorough manner the whole field. At the best the matter selected can only be held to be supplementary; however it is thought that few, if any, of our ordinary school histories contain as complete a treatment. Besides the chief advantage claimed for these studies is not so much that they give a greater amount of knowledge, but that they afford the means whereby the student may be enabled to work out his history to a great extent for himself. The thought must be present, or the student cannot do anything. He cannot be a mere memory machine.

These studies come down only to the time of the civil war. By leaving out the more recent years it has been hoped that prejudice might play a less important part, and reason and calm judgment a greater part. The tariff has been treated in the main from the standpoint of protection versus free trade. As this is still a controverted question, it needs to be handled with care in order that the student may look at the past from a fair and free minded standpoint. The question of internal improvements has passed so far into limbo that there seems to be no danger in wrong ideas being gained by carrying present prepossessions into a study of past times.

I shall not outline these subjects in my introductory remarks, for I believe the extracts and the questions on them will accomplish the end sought in the general summary; and thus the results will be more completely the student's own work. There is always present a tendency in the pupil to find in the documents what the collator has found, or believes he has found. In this number there will be no suggestions. Each teacher, therefore, may work with his pupils uninfluenced by any suggestions of mine.

I. The Tariff.

The following extracts from the laws of England will help us to understand the early feeling of the statesmen of the United States in regard to any restrictions on the right to manufacture and to trade.

[1699 it was declared to be] unlawful to load wool upon any horse, cart, or other carriage.

[1750.] Whereas, The importation of bar iron from His Majesty's colonies in America, into the port of London, . . . will be a great advantage, not only to the said colonies, but also to this kingdom, by furnishing the manufacturers of iron with a supply of that useful and necessary commodity, and by means thereof large sums of money, now annually paid for iron to foreigners, will be saved to this Kingdom, and a greater quantity of the woolen, and other manufactures of Great Britain, will be exported to America, in exchange for such iron so imported: . . . *Be it therefore enacted*, etc.

Sec. IX. And that pig and bar iron made in his Majesty's colonies in America may be further manufactured in this Kingdom; be it further enacted that . . . no mill or other engine for slitting or rolling of iron, or any plateing forge to work with a tilt hammer, or any furnace for making steel, shall be erected, or after such erection, continue in any part of his Majesty's colonies in America. . . .

Sec. X. And it is hereby enacted . . . that every such mill, engine, forge, or furnace so erected or continued contrary to the directions of this Act, shall be deemed a common nuisance, and within thirty days must be abated.—*Cited in Elliott's Tariff Controversy, p. 13.*

About 1760, when it was proposed by some to restore Canada to France, Franklin protests and uses the following argument to convince the English manufacturing and commercial interests that it will be for their interests to retain Canada. It will be noticed that Franklin speaks as an Englishman:

A people spread through the whole tract of country on this side of the Mississippi, and secured by Canada in our hands, would probably for some centuries find employment in agriculture, and thereby free us at home effectually from our fears of American manufactures. . . . Manufactures are founded in poverty. . . . But no man who can have a piece of land of his own sufficient by his labor to subsist his family in plenty, is poor enough to be a manufacturer and work for a master. Hence while there is land enough in America for our own people, there can never be manufactures to any amount or value.—*Franklin, Works, III, p. 86.*

In 1776, in a letter to Mr. Hartley, in speaking of the terms of peace between England and the United States, Franklin said:

Restraint on the freedom of commerce and intercourse between us can afford no advantage equivalent to the mischief they will do by keeping up ill-humor and promoting a total alienation,—*Works, VIII, p. 337.*

In 1787 he wrote:

We shall, as you suppose, have imposts on trade and custom-houses, not because other nations have them, but because we cannot at present do without them. . . . When we are out of debt we may leave our trade free, for our ordinary charges of government will not be great.—*Works, IX, p. 460.*

Jefferson wrote in his "Notes on Virginia," in 1781, as follows:

Those who labor in the earth are the chosen people of God, if ever he had a chosen people. . . . While we have land to labor, then, let us never wish to see our citizens occupied at bench work, or twirling a distaff. Carpenters, masons, and smiths, are wanting in husbandry; but for the general operations of manufacture, let our workshops remain in Europe.—*Jefferson, Works, VIII, p. 405.*

Seven years later we find these words:

In general, it is impossible that manufactures should succeed in America, from the high prices of labor. This is occasioned by the great demand of labor for agriculture.—*Ibid, II, p. 412.*

John Adams, in 1780, gives us this picture of his expectations:

America is the country of raw materials, and of commerce enough to carry them to a good market; but Europe is the country for manufactures and commerce. Thus Europe and America will be blessings to each other, if some malevolent policy does not frustrate the purposes of nature.—*J. Adams' Works, VII, p. 309.*

Let the following quotation answer whether he believed this "malevolent policy" had triumphed or not. On learning, in 1783, that the English had forbidden all trade with the British West Indies except in British vessels, he wrote:

This proclamation is issued in full confidence that the United States have no confidence in one another; that they cannot agree to act in a body as one nation; that they cannot agree upon any navigation act which may be common to the thirteen States. Our proper remedy would be to confine our exports to American ships.—*Ibid, VIII, p. 97.*

July 19, 1785, he wrote:

Whether prohibitions or high duties will be most politic is a great question.—*Ibid, p. 282.*

August 10, of the same year, he wrote to Jay as follows:

As the French court has condescended to adopt our

principle in theory, I am very much afraid we shall be obliged to imitate their wisdom in practice [and import only in our own vessels] .... We have hitherto been the bubbles of our own philosophical and equitable liberality; ... both France and England have shown a constant disposition to take a selfish and partial advantage of us because of them. ... I hope we shall be the dupes no longer than we must. I would venture upon monopolies and exclusions, if they were found to be the only arms of defence against monopolies and exclusions, without fear of offending Dean Tucker or the ghost of Doctor Quesnay.—*Ibid, 299.*

A few days later he wrote in these words:

Patience under all the unequal burdens they impose upon our commerce will do us no good; it will contribute in no degree to preserve the peace of this country. On the contrary, nothing but retaliation, reciprocal prohibitions and imposts, and putting ourselves in a posture of defence, will have any effect. . . . Confining exports to our own ships, and laying on heavy duties upon all foreign luxuries, and encouraging our own manufactures, appear to me to be our only resource.—*Ibid, 313, cited in Elliott, p. 52.*

From the debate over the tariff act of 1789 we may quote some remarks which will still further help us in understanding the spirit of the time. Madison says:

I am a friend of free commerce, and at the same time a friend to such regulations as are calculated to promote our own interest, and this on national principles. ... I wish we were under less necessity than I find we are, to shackle our commerce with duties, restrictions, and preferences; but there are cases in which it is impossible to avoid following the example of other nations in the great diversity of our trade.—*Annals of Congress, I, pp. 192, 193.*

During the course of the same debate Ames, the leading Federalist from Massachusetts, wrote these words to a friend:

The Senate has begun to reduce the rate of duties.

Rum is reduced one-third. . . . Molasses from five to four. I feel as Euceladus would if Etna was removed. The Senate, God bless them, as if designated by Providence to keep rash and frolicksome brats out of the fire, have demolished the absurd, unpolitic, mad discriminations of foreigners in alliance, from other foreigners.—*Life of Fisher Ames, p. 45.*

Hamilton, in his famous Report on Manufactures, 1792, after noting the arguments for freedom of trade, expresses himself as follows:

This mode of reasoning is founded upon facts and principles which have certainly respectable pretensions. If it had governed the conduct of nations more generally than it has done, there is room to suppose that it might have carried them faster to prosperity and greatness than they have attained by the pursuit of maxims too widely opposite. Most general theories, however, admit of numerous exceptions. . . .—*State Papers and Speeches on the Tariff, p. 3.*

[After discussing the value of manufactures he says:] The foregoing considerations seem sufficient to establish, as general propositions, that it is the interest of nations to diversify the industrial pursuits of the individuals who compose them; that the establishment of manufactures is calculated not only to increase the general stock of useful and productive labor, but ever to improve the state of agriculture in particular. . . *Ibid, p. 25.*

[Again he says:] If the system of perfect liberty to industry and commerce were the prevailing system of nations, the arguments which dissuade a country in the predicament of the United States from the zealous pursuit of manufactures would, doubtless, have great force. It will not be affirmed that they might not be permitted, with few exceptions, to serve as a rule of national conduct. In such a state of things each country would have the full benefit of its peculiar advantages to compensate for its deficiencies or disadvantages. . . .

But the system which has been mentioned is far from characterizing the general policy of nations. . . . The consequence of it is that the United States are, to a certain extent, in the situation of a country precluded from foreign commerce. . . . In such a position of things the United States cannot exchange with Europe on equal terms, and the want of reciprocity would render them the victim of a system which should induce them to confine their views to agriculture, and refrain from manufacture.—*Ibid, pp. 26, 27.*

Hamilton finally sums up in several propositions the advantages which he claims will be secured to the country should it encourage the development of manufactures.

There seems to be a moral certainty that the trade of a country which is both manufacturing and agricultural will be more lucrative and prosperous than that of a country which is merely agricultural. . . .

Another circumstance which gives a superiority of commercial advantages to States that manufacture as well as cultivate consists in the more numerous attractions which a mere diversified market offers. . . .

A third circumstance . . . has relation to the stagnations of demand for certain commodities which at some time or other interfere more or less with the sale of all. . . .

Not only the wealth, but the independence and security of a country appear to be materially connected with the prosperity of manufactures. . . . Our distance from Europe, the great fountain of manufactured supply, subjects us, in the existing state of things, to inconvenience and loss in two ways [Bulkiness of commodities and consequent cost of carriage]. . . .

If, then, it satisfactorily appears that it is the intent of the United States generally to encourage manufactures, it merits particular attention, that there are circumstances which render the present a critical moment for entering with zeal upon the important business. . . .—*Ibid, pp. 52, 53, 55, 56, 60.*

Finally Hamilton suggests eleven means that may be used to encourage the development of manufactures:

(1.) Protective duties. . . .

(2.) Prohibitions of rival articles, or duties equivalent to prohibitions.

(3.) Prohibitions of the exportation of the materials of manufactures.
(4.) Pecuniary bounties [He especially approves of bounties].
(5.) Premiums.
(6.) The exemptions of the materials of manufactures from duty.
(7.) Drawbacks on the duties which are imposed on the materials of manufactures.
(8.) The encouragement of new inventions and discoveries. . . .
(9.) Judicious regulations for the inspection of manufactured commodities.
(10.) The facilitating of pecuniary remittances from place to place.
(11.) The facilitating of the transportation of commodities.—*Ibid, pp. 62-75.*

February 12, 1816, Mr. A. J. Dallas, secretary of the treasury, in obedience to a resolution of the house of representatives, made a report on "a general tariff of duties suitable to be imposed on imported goods." . . . In part he said:

There are few, if any, governments which do not regard the establishment of domestic manufactures, as a chief object of public policy. . . .

. . . .

The American manufactures may be satisfactorily divided into three principal classes; . . . *First class*—Manufactures which are firmly and permanently established, and which wholly, or almost wholly, supply the demand for domestic use and consumption. *Second class*—Manufactures which . . . do not . . . but which, with proper cultivation, are capable of being matured to the whole extent of the demand. *Third class*—Manufactures which are so slightly cultivated, as to leave the demand of the country wholly, or almost wholly, dependent upon foreign sources for a supply. . . .

[*First class*]—Duties might be freely imposed upon the importation of similar articles, amounting wholly, or nearly, to a prohibition, without endangering a scarcity in the supply, or [exorbitant prices]. . . .

The *second class* of manufactures presents considerations of the most interesting, and not of the least embarrassing nature, in the formation of a tariff, . . . for it is respectfully thought to be in the power of the legislature, by a well-timed and well-directed patronage, to place them, within a very limited period, upon the footing which the manufactures of the first class have been so happily placed, . . . and it will soon be understood that the success of the American manufacture which tends to diminish the profit (often the excessive profit) of the importer, does not necessarily add to the price of the article in the hands of the consumer.

The *third class* of manufactures does not require further attention . . . than to adjust the rate of duty to the amount of revenue which it is necessary to draw from them. They have not yet been the objects of American capital, industry, etc., . . . ; and the present policy of the government is directed to protect, and not to create manufactures.—*Niles Register, pp. 437-442.*

In 1824 perhaps the greatest debate of early years over the tariff took place between Clay on the one side and Webster on the other. These speeches ought to be read by every American who wishes to be well informed concerning the history of his country. Clay says, in part:

Two classes of politicians divide the people of the United States. According to the system of one, the produce of foreign industry should be subjected to no other import than such as may be necessary to provide a public revenue; and the produce of American industry should be left to sustain itself, if it can, with no other than that incidental protection, in its competition, at home as well as abroad, with rival foreign articles.

. . . .

In casting our eyes around us the most prominent circumstance which fixes our attention and challenges our deepest regret is the general distress which pervades the whole country.

. . . .

What, again I would ask, is the cause of the unhappy

condition of our country which I have faintly depicted? It is to be found in the fact that, during almost the whole existence of this government, we have shaped our industry, our navigation, and our commerce, in reference to an extraordinary war in Europe, and to foreign markets which no longer exist. . . .

. . . .

Our agricultural is our greatest interest. It ought ever to be predominant. . . . Can we do nothing to invigorate it; . . . ? We have seen the causes. . . . We have seen that an exclusive dependence upon the foreign market must lead to still severer distress, ... We must speedily adopt a genuine American policy. Still cherishing the foreign market, let us create also a home market. . . .

. . . .

The committee will observe, from the table, that the measure of the wealth of a nation is indicated by the measure of its protection of its industry; and that the measure of the poverty of a nation is marked by that of the degree in which it neglects and abandons the care of its own industry, ... Great Britain protects most her industry. and the wealth of Great Britain is consequently the greatest.—*State Papers and Speeches on the Tariff, pp. 253-275.*

April 1 and 2 Mr. Webster replied to this speech of Clay in perhaps the ablest speech that he ever made on the tariff. A few extracts will indicate the scope of the argument:

We are represented as on the very verge and brink of national ruin. So far from acquiescing in these opinions, I believe there has been no period in which the general prosperity was better secured, or rested on a more solid foundation. . . .

. . . .

We have heard much of the policy of England, and her example has been repeatedly urged upon us, . . . I took occasion the other day to remark, that more liberal notions were growing prevalent on this subject; that the policy of restraints and prohibitions was getting out of repute, as the true nature of commerce became better understood; . . .

. . . .

I have never said, indeed, that prohibitory laws did not exist in England; we all know they do; but the question is, does she own her prosperity and greatness to these laws? I venture to say that such is not the opinion of the public men now in England; . . . [Lord Lansdowne, in a recent speech in Parliament said] "No axiom was more true than this: that it was by growing what the territory of a country could grow most cheaply, and by receiving from other countries what it could not produce except at too great an expense, that the greatest degree of happiness was to be communicated to the greatest extent of population." [Webster quoted this with approval, as he did another statement that] "Some suppose that we have risen in consequence of that system [the restrictive]; others, of whom I am one, believe that we have risen in spite of that system." . . .

. . . .

In fine, sir, I think it is clear that if we now embrace the system of prohibitions and restrictions we shall show an affection for what others have discarded, and be attempting to ornament ourselves with cast-off apparel.

We are urged to adopt the system [protective] upon general principles; and what would be the consequence of the universal application of such a principle, but that nations would abstain entirely from all intercourse with one another? I do not admit the general principle; on the contrary, I think freedom of trade to be the general principle, and restriction the exception. . . .

. . . .

We are asked what nations ever attained eminent prosperity without encouraging manufactures? I may ask, what nation ever reached the like prosperity without promoting foreign trade?

. . . .

On the general question, sir, allow me to ask if the doctrine of prohibition, as a general doctrine, be not preposterous? Suppose all nations to act upon it; they would be prosperous, then, according to the argument, precisely in the proportion in which they abolished trade with one another. The less of mutual commerce the better, upon this hypothesis. . . .

The poverty and unhappiness of Spain have been attributed to the want of protection to her own industry. If by this it is meant that the poverty of Spain is owing to bad government and bad laws, the remark is, in a great measure, just. But these very laws are bad because they are restrictive, partial, and prohibitory. If prohibition were protection, Spain would seem to have had enough of it. . . —*State Papers and Speeches on the Tariff, pp. 320-364.*

"The Free Trade Memorial," prepared by Albert Gallatin in 1831, is one of the most famous of American state papers on that side of the question. It is difficult to find any quotable passages in this paper which will show adequately the line of argument followed. In one place he says:

We may, also, before we dismiss this branch of the subject, and in order to rebut those general assertions of the ruin that attends all nations which rely, in any considerable degree, on foreign trade for a market, appeal to that which we know best, which we have seen and enjoyed—to the experience of North America. Assisted only by the ordinary mechanical arts, and with hardly any manufacturing establishments, America, during two centuries, relied almost exclusively on the cultivation of her soil, and on the exportation of her products to foreign ports; and her progress during that period, in population, wealth, and in all the arts of civilization . . . stands unparalleled in the annals of mankind. A change of circumstances may induce a partial and gradual alteration in the pursuits of her citizens, and we may rest assured that, if not diverted by legislative interference, they will, as heretofore, embrace those best adapted to their situation.—*State Papers and Speeches on the Tariff,* p. 156.

The only effect that can possibly be ascribed to a protecting duty is that of encouraging the establishment of manufactures which would otherwise not have existed, or of inducing a greater number of persons to embark in those already existing. The propriety of the duty depends altogether on the probability of speedy success, that is to say, of the manufacture being so far adapted to the circumstances of the country that, after having been assisted by the duty in surmounting the first difficulties to every new undertaking, it will be able to sustain itself, and without such assistance to compete with the foreign article. It has been clearly shown that the manufacture is otherwise a losing concern, productive of national loss. —*Ibid, pp. 161, 162.*

In 1845 Robert J. Walker, secretary of the treasury, in his report to congress, urged that the tariff be reduced to a revenue basis. The following extracts indicate the nature of his report:

In suggesting improvements in the revenue laws, the following principles have been adopted:—

1st. That no more money should be collected than is necessary for the wants of the government, economically administered.

2d. That no duty be imposed on any article above the lowest rate which will yield the largest amount of revenue.

. . . .

4th. That the maximum revenue duty should be imposed on luxuries.

5th. That all minimums, and all specific duties, should be abolished, and ad valorem duties substituted in their place . . . .

6th. That the duty should be so imposed as to operate as equally as possible throughout the Union, discriminating neither for nor against any class or section.

. . . .

A protective tariff is a question regarding the enhancement of the profits of capital. That is the object, and not to augment the wages of labor, which would reduce those profits.

. . . .

The present tariff is unjust and unequal. . . . It discriminates in favor of manufactures and against agriculture, by imposing many higher duties upon the manufactured fabric than upon the agricultural product out of which it is made. It discriminates in favor of the manufacturer and against the mechanic, . . . [also] against the merchant, . . . and against the ship-builder and navigating interest, . . . etc. It discriminates in favor of the rich and against the poor. . . .

. . . .

Legislation for classes is against the doctrine of equal rights, repugnant to the spirit of our free institutions. . . .

. . . .

No prejudice is felt by the Secretary of the Treasury against manufacturers. His opposition is to the protective system, and not to classes or individuals. . . . Whilst a due regard to the just and equal rights of all classes forbids a discrimination in favor of the manufactures by duties above the lowest revenue limits, no disposition is felt to discriminate against them. . . .—*State Papers and Speeches on the Tariff, pp. 219-232.*

II. INTERNAL IMPROVEMENTS.

As early as 1774, at least, Washington saw the great importance of uniting the waters of the Ohio and Potomac, regarding it as "a great and truly wise policy." (Works, IX, 31.) His tour to the western country in 1784 confirmed him in the idea. He wrote, October 10, 1784:

The shortest, easiest, and least expensive communication with the invaluable and extensive country back of us is by one or both of the rivers of this State [Virginia] which have their sources in the Appalachian mountains. . . . I need not remark to you, sir, that the flanks and rear of the United States are possessed by other powers, and formidable ones, too; nor how necessary it is to apply the cement of interest to bind all parts of the Union together by indissoluble bonds, especially that part of it which lies immediately west of us, with the Middle States. . . . The Western States (I speak now from my own observation) stand as it were upon a pivot. The touch of a feather would turn them any way. They have looked down the Mississippi until the Spaniards, very impolitically I think for themselves, threw difficulties in their way, and they looked that way for no other reason than because they could glide gently down the stream and because they have no other means of coming to us but by long land transportations and unimproved roads. . . . But smooth the road and make easy the way for them, and then see what an influx of articles will be poured upon us; how amazingly our exports will be increased by them, and how amply we shall be compensated.—*Works (Sparks) IX, 59-63.*

He urges in various letters the political and commercial possibilities with which such connections are pregnant, and that they are necessary to save the West.

Jefferson wrote to a citizen of Kentucky, May 26, 1788:

I wish to see that country in the hands of people well disposed, who know the value of the connection between that and the maratime states and who wish to cultivate it. I consider their happiness as bound up together and that every measure should be taken which may draw the bands of union tighter.—*Jefferson's Works, V (Ford).*

And to Washington he wrote, May 10, 1789:

I consider the union of [the Potomac and Ohio rivers] the strongest link of connection between the eastern and western sides of our confederacy.—*Ibid, V, pp. 93-94.*

To Madison he wrote, March 6, 1796:

Have you considered all the consequences of your proposition [in Congress for building a road from Maine to Georgia] respecting port roads? I view it as a source of boundless patronage by the executive, jobbing to members of Congress and their friends, and a bottomless abyss of public money. You will begin by only appropriating the surplus of the post office revenues; but the other revenues will soon be called to their aid, and it will be a scene of eternal scramble among the members who can get most money wasted in their state, and they will always get most who are meanest.—*Ibid, VII, pp. 63-64.*

Jefferson wrote to Baron Humboldt:

In our America we are turning to public improvements. Schools, roads, and canals are everywhere either in operation or contemplation. The most gigantic undertaking is that of New York for [the Erie Canal]. . . . Internal navigation by steamboats is rapidly spreading. . . . We consider the employment of the contributions which our citizens can spare, after feeding, and clothing, and lodging themselves comfortably, as more useful, more moral, and even more splendid than that preferred by Europe of destroying human life, labor, and happiness.—*Works (1854 Ed.), VII, p. 75.*

To Gallatin he wrote, June 16, 1817, regarding Madison's recent veto. He thinks the veto fortunate:

Every state will certainly concede the power and this will be a national confirmation of the ground of appeal to them and will settle forever the meaning of this phrase [the "general welfare" clause of article I, section 8] which, by a mere grammatical quibble, has countenanced the General Government in a claim of universal power. . . . It is fortunate for another reason, as the States, in conceding the power, will modify it either by requiring the federal ratio of expense in each state, or otherwise, so as to secure us against its partial exercise.—*Ibid, VII, p. 79.*

To James Madison, December 24, 1825, he said:

I have for some time considered the question of internal improvement as desperate. The torrent of general opinion sets so strongly in favor of it as to be irresistible. And I suppose that even the opposition in Congress will hereafter be feeble and formal. . . . I learn from Richmond that those who think with us there are in a state of perfect dismay, not knowing what to do or what to propose.—*Ibid, VII, p. 422.*

Hamilton, in 1792, shows how he feels on the question in the following words:

The symptoms of attention to the improvement of inland navigation which have lately appeared in some quarters must fill with pleasure every heart warmed with a true zeal for the prosperity of the country. These examples it is to be hoped will stimulate the exertions of the Government and citizens of every state. There can certainly be no object more worthy of the care of the local administration; and it were to be wished that there was no doubt of the power of the National Government to lend its direct aid on a comprehensive plan. This is one of those improvements which could be prosecuted with more efficacy by the whole than by any part or parts of the Union. There are cases in which the general interest will be in danger to be sacrificed to the collision of some supposed local interests. Jealousies in matters of this kind are as apt to exist as they are apt to be erroneous.—*Hamilton's Report on Manufactures, Works (1851 Ed.), III, pp. 255-57.*

He held to the same views in 1801, as may be seen from this extract:

The improvement of the communications between the different parts of the country is an object well worthy of the national purse and one which would abundantly repay to labor the portion of its earnings which may have been borrowed for that purpose. To provide roads and bridges is within the direct purview of the Constitution. In many parts of the country, especially in the Western Territory, a matter in which the Atlantic States are equally interested, aqueducts and canals would also be fit subjects of pecuniary aid from the Government.—*Hamilton's Works, VII, pp. 755-56.*

The improvement of the roads would be a measure universally popular. None can be more so. For this purpose a regular plan should be adopted co-extensive with the Union, to be successively executed, and a fund should be appropriated sufficient for the basis of a loan of a million of dollars. The revenue of the post office naturally offers itself. The future revenue from tolls would more than reimburse the expense, and public utility would be promoted in every direction. . . . An article ought to be proposed to be added to the Constitution for empowering Congress to open canals in all cases in which it may be necessary to conduct them through the territory of two or more States or through the territory of a State and that of the United States The power is very desirable for the purpose of improving the prodigious facilities for inland navigation with which nature has favored this country. It will also assist commerce and agriculture by rendering the transportation of commodities more cheap and expeditious. It will tend to secure the connection, by facilitating the communication between distant portions of the Union, and it will be a useful source of influence to the government.—*Hamilton's Works, VI, pp. 385-87.*

A committee in the House of Representatives reported, March 5, 1806, upon the Chesapeake and Delaware canal, that they "cannot hesitate a moment in deciding on the importance and extensive utility" of the canal.

They consider the project as an opening wedge for an extensive inland navigation which would at all times be of an immense advantage to the commercial as well as the agricultural and manufacturing parts of the community. But in the event of a war its advantages would be incalculable. . . . Did the finances of the country admit of it the committee would feel a perfect freedom in recommending . . . the propriety of . . . such aid. . . .—*American State Papers, I, Miscellaneous, p. 452.*

[The senate committee reported similarly the same year that] it is among the first duties of a Government to promote public improvements of a general nature.—*Ibid, p. 454.*

In Gallatin's famous report on roads and canals, made in 1807, we find the most complete discussion of the subject made in the early years of our history. In part he says:

The general utility of artificial roads and canals is at this time so universally admitted as hardly to require any additional proofs. It is sufficiently evident that whenever the annual expense of transportation on a certain route, in its natural state, exceeds the interest on the capital employed in improving the communication, and the annual expense of transportation (exclusively of the tolls) by the improved route, the difference is an annual additional income to the nation. . . . Some works already executed are unprofitable; many more remain unattempted, because their ultimate productiveness depends on other improvements too extensive or too distant to be embraced by the same individuals. The General Government can alone remove these obstacles. With resources amply sufficient for the completion of every practicable improvement it will always supply the capital wanted for any work which it may undertake as fast as the work itself can progress; avoiding thereby the ruinous loss of interest on a dormant capital, and reducing the real expense to its lowest rate. . . . The inconveniences, complaints, and perhaps dangers, which may result from a vast extent of territory, can no otherwise be radically removed or prevented than by opening speedy and easy communications through all its parts. Good roads and canals will shorten distances, facilitate commercial and personal intercourse, and unite by a still more intimate community of interests the most remote quarters of the United States. No other single operation within the power of Government can more effectually tend to strengthen and perpetuate that Union which secures external independence, domestic peace, and internal liberty. . . . [The improvements he therefore suggests as] most important to facilitate the communication between the great geographical divisions of the United States [are: I, from north to south parallel to the seacoast, canals costing $3,000,000, turnpikes costing $4,800,000; II, from east to west forming communications across the mountains between the Atlantic and western rivers, improvement in Atlantic rivers costing $1,500,000, turnpikes and road improvements costing $3,000,000, canals costing $300,000; III, improvements forming inland navigations between the Atlantic seacoast and the St. Lawrence and Great Lakes, $4,000,000. This total of $16,600,000 is also increased by $3,400,000 for local improvements—a grand total of $20,000,000, which it is proposed to accomplish in ten yearly payments of $2,000,000 each. The public lands may be sold for the purpose and the improvements will, in turn, benefit the purchasers.]

It is evident that the United States cannot, under the Constitution, open any road or canal, without the consent of the State through which such road or canal must pass. In order therefore to remove every impediment to a national plan of internal improvement, an amendment to the Constitution was suggested by the Executive when the subject was recommended to the consideration of Congress [by President Jefferson in Message 11]. Until this be obtained, the assent of the States being necessary for each improvement, the modifications under which that assent may be given, will necessarily control the manner of applying the money. . . . The United States may with the assent of the States undertake some of the works at their sole expense or they may subscribe a certain number of shares of the stock of companies incorporated for the purpose. Loans might also, in some instances, be made to such companies. The first mode would perhaps, by effectually controlling local interests, give the most proper general direction to the work. Its details would probably be executed on a more economical plan by private companies.—*American State Papers, I, Miscellaneous, pp. 724-25, 740-41.*

BENTON (Mo.), May 1, 1828, says:

He was in favor of the federal power to make roads and canals of national importance. . . . He was in favor of the construction of such roads and canals by the Federal Government provided the States through which they would pass consented to it . . . .; not . . . that the consent of a State could confer a power upon Congress not derived from the Constitution; but it was decent and becoming to consult the wishes of the State in all such cases because its assent would do away with all that class of objections to the exercise of the power which were founded upon a real or supposed violation of State sovereignty and a real or supposed violation of State territory.—*Register Debates, IV, p. 718.*

CALHOUN (S. C.) speaks as follows in 1817:

[In times of peace and plenty] to what can we direct our resources and attention more important than internal improvements? What can add more to the wealth, the strength, and the political prosperity of our country? . . . It tends to diffuse universal opulence. . . . When we come to consider how intimately the strength and political prosperity of the Republic are connected with this subject we find the most urgent reasons why we should apply our resources to them. . . . Unless the means of commercial intercourse are rendered much more perfect than they now are we shall never be able in war to raise the necessary supplies . . . and the means by which that [remedy] is to be effected are roads, canals, and the coasting trade. . . . But on this subject of national power what can be more important than a perfect unity in every part, in feelings and sentiments? And what can tend more powerfully to produce it than overcoming the effects of distance? . . . We are great, and rapidly—he was about to say fearfully—growing. This, said he, is our pride and danger—our weakness and our strength. . . . Let us then . . . bind the Republic together with a perfect system of roads and canals. Let us conquer space.—*Annals of Congress, XXX, pp. 851-856.*

At about the same time, February 8, 1817, the House used this language:

Upon mature consideration the facility of commercial and personal intercourse throughout the whole extent of the United States and its Territories is viewed by the committee, as it appears to have been viewed by former committees of both branches of the National Legislature, and by every Executive of the Government since its formation, as an essential ingredient in the general economy of the nation as well in relation to the pursuits of peace as to those of war and also to the perpetuation and integrity of the Republican Union.—*American State Papers, II, Miscellaneous, p. 420.*

Madison vetoes a bill passed by Congress in 1817 to appropriate money for internal improvements, and justifies his veto, in part, in these words:

The legislative powers vested in Congress are specified and enumerated in the eighth section of the first article of the Constitution and it does not appear that power proposed by the bill ["An act to set apart and pledge certain funds for internal improvements"] is among the enumerated powers or that it falls by any just interpretation within the power to make laws necessary and proper for carrying into execution those or other powers held by the Constitution in the Government of the United States. . . . If a general power to construct roads and canals and to improve the navigation of water courses, with the train of powers incident thereto, be not possessed by Congress, the assent of the States . . . cannot confer the power. [But while vetoing the bill he "cherishes the hope" that its beneficial objects may be attained by an amendment to the Constitution.]—*Messages and Papers of the Presidents, I, pp. 584-585.*

Monroe, in his "Views," May 4, 1822, summarized the arguments that have been advanced in favor of the constitutional power of Congress to act. He says:

The advocates of the power derive it from the following sources: First, the right to establish post-offices and post-roads; second, to declare war; third, to regulate commerce among the several States; fourth, from the power to pay the debts and provide for the common defence and general welfare of the United States; fifth, from the power to make all laws necessary and proper for carrying into execution all the powers vested by the Constitution in the Government of the United States or in any department or officer thereof; sixth and lastly, from the power to dispose of and make all needful rules and regulations respecting the territory and other property of the United States. [He denies all successively, his position as to each may be summarized as follows:

[No. 1. merely gives to Congress power to fix the sites of post-offices and the routes on which the mail may be carried.

No. 2, if allowed, would cover the entire country with roads which *might* be useful in time of war but most of which cannot possibly ever be connected with war transportation. And the influences from clause 17 of the Constitution and general reasoning are all against it.

No. 3. Such commercial powers were transferred to the United States whose exercise by the States had proved mischievous and irritating; internal improvements had nothing to do with these, but only the levying of duties and imposts.

No. 4 merely gives to Congress authority to appropriate the public moneys laid and collected by taxes, duties, imposts, and excises. It is the only clause in the Constitution directly giving the right of appropriation; it is evidently not given in class 1 as a distinct grant; if it were, then its vast extent swallows up all the rest of the Constitution and makes it useless. But this power of appropriation is not limited to expenditures under the other specific grants of the eighth section strictly constructed, but is broad, general, discretionary, yet always limited like the Government of the Union to "great national purposes." For internal improvements money might be *appropriated*, but this of itself can do nothing toward securing the land, jurisdiction, building and protecting the works.

No. 5 is of no value unless the power is primarily granted by one of the *other* powers.

No. 6 is shown by an historical argument to have nothing to do with the question.]—*Richardson's Messages and Papers of the Presidents, II, pp. 156-175.*

TRIMBLE (Ky.), January 21, 1825, says:
Public opinion was embodying itself in favor of roads and canals, and during the last year had made so many demonstrations in favor of internal improvements that Congress might consider itself called upon by the nation to begin the work in good earnest.—*Register of Debates, I, p. 319.*

BUCHANAN (Pa.), 1826, uses this language:
If there be any principle of constitutional law which, at this day, should be considered as settled, it is that Congress has the power to aid internal improvement by subscribing for stock in companies incorporated by the States.—*Register of Debates, II, p. 1615.*

CLAY (Ky.), in 1825,
considered the question as to the existence and the

exercise of a power in the General Government to carry into effect a system of internal improvements, as amounting to the question whether the union of these States should be preserved or not. . . . As to the opinion that the carrying on of these improvements belonged to the States in their individual and separate character, it might as well be expected that the States should perform any other duty which appertained to the General Government. You have no more right . . . to ask the individual States to make internal improvements for the general welfare than you have to ask them to make war for the general welfare or to build fortifications for the general defence.—*Register of Debates, I, p. 231.*

In Jackson's veto of the Maysville road appropriation, 1830, we read:

[The first possible line of objection would be upon the question of the sovereignty of the States within whose limits improvements are contemplated if jurisdiction of the territory be claimed by the General Government as necessary to the preservation and use of the improvements; the second would be upon the mere question of right to appropriate public moneys for such objects. So far the Government has never executed the first power—which it does not, in reality, possess. Long practice has sanctioned the second; but always] professedly under the control of the general principle that the works which might be thus aided should be "of a general, not local, national, not State," character. A disregard of this distinction would of necessity lead to the subversion of the federal system. That even this is an unsafe one, arbitrary in its nature, and liable, consequently, to great abuses, is too obvious to require the confirmation of experience. Assuming the right to *appropriate money* to aid in the construction of national works to be warranted by the contemporaneous and continued exposition of the Constitution, its insufficiency for the successful prosecution of them must be admitted by all candid minds. [Whether to enable the Federal Government itself to construct the improvements, or to define the occasion, manner, and extent of its appropriations to works prosecuted by the States, it is true] that a constitutional adjustment of this power upon equitable principles is in the highest degree desirable, . . . nor can it fail to be promoted by every sincere friend to the success of our political institutions.—*Messages and Papers of the Presidents, II, pp. 483-93.*

Jackson's message of December 1, 1834, said:

When the bill authorizing a subscription . . . in the Maysville & Lexington Turnpike Co. passed the two houses, there had been reported by the Committee on Internal Improvements bills containing appropriations for such objects, exclusive of those for the Cumberland road and for harbors and light-houses, to the amount of about 106,000,000 of dollars. In this amount was included authority . . . to subscribe for the stock of different companies to a great extent, and the residue was principally for the direct construction of roads by this Government. In addition to these projects which had been presented . . . there were still pending before the committees and in memorials presented, but not refused, different projects . . . the expenses of which . . . must have exceeded 100,000,000 of dollars. . . .

Since the Maysville veto "no attempt . . . has been made to induce Congress to exercise this power. The applications for the construction of roads and canals . . . are no longer presented; and we have good reason to infer that the consent of public sentiment has become so decided against the pretension as effectually to discourage its reassertion."—*Messages and Papers of the Presidents, III, pp. 120-21.*

Polk, in his veto, 1847, uses these words:

It is not easy to perceive the difference in principle or mischievous tendency between appropriations for making roads and digging canals and appropriations to deepen rivers and improve harbors. All are alike within the limits and jurisdiction of the States. . . . If the power to improve a harbor be admitted it is not easy to perceive how the power to deepen every inlet on the ocean or the lakes and make harbors where there are none can be denied. If the power to clear out or deepen the channel of rivers near their mouths be admitted, it is not easy to perceive how the power to improve them to their fountain head and make them navigable to their sources can be denied. . . . May the General Government exercise power and jurisdiction over the soil of a State consisting of rocks and sandbars in the beds of its rivers? and may it not execute a canal around its waterfalls or across its lands for precisely the same object?—*Ibid, IV, pp. 612-614.*

Buchanan, in his veto of 1860, adds:

The distinctive spirit and character which pervades the Constitution is that the powers of the General Government are confined . . . to subjects of common interest to all the States, carefully leaving the internal and domestic concerns of each individual State to be controlled by its own people and legislature. . . . Besides, the corrupting and seducing money influence exerted by the General Government in carrying into effect a system of internal improvements might be perverted to increase and consolidate its own power to the detriment of the rights of the States. . . . Equality among the States is equity. This quality is the very essence of the Constitution. No preference can justly be given to one of the sovereign States over another. . . . The truth is most of these improvements are in a great degree local in their character and for the particular benefit of corporations or individuals in their vicinity, though they may have an odor of nationality on the principle that whatever benefits any part indirectly benefits the whole. Article I, section 10, paragraph 3, affords a perfectly legitimate mode of acquiring the improvements, in a constitutional manner, by the States.—*Ibid, V, pp. 603-5.*

QUESTIONS.

1. How would the Americans feel towards the law of 1699? 2. Why was bar iron to be imported from America? 3. How would it be helpful to the colonists? 4. Why were the colonists not to manufacture the bar iron into steel? 5. What was to be done with the American mills? 6. How would such laws as these make the colonists feel in regard to the restrictive system?

1. What argument does Franklin use to secure the retention of Canada? 2. What industry does Franklin evidently prefer? 3. What condition results where

manufactures prevail? 4. How does Franklin feel toward the restrictive system? 5. Compare the ideas of Franklin and Jefferson. 6. Why could manufactures succeed in America? 7. Did the statesmen, judged by the ones cited, believe in restraints and discriminations? 8. How would you account for their views? 9. How did they feel after about 1786? 10. Explain the reasons for the change. 11. Did the statesmen like the change, or were they forced to make it?

1. Did Hamilton believe in protection as a general principle? 2. What arguments did he give for protection? 3. What plans did Hamilton propose to encourage manufactures? 4. What position would he probably take now were he living? 5. Outline the plan of Mr. Dallas. 6. To what class of products did he propose to give aid? 7. Why not aid *class three?*

1. What principle did Webster advocate in 1824? 2. What principle did Clay? 3. What condition was the country in according to Clay; to Webster? 4. What remedy did Clay propose for the distress? 5. How would Clay now have to argue in regard to England? 6. Why had England been prosperous, according to Clay; to Webster? 7. What interest was Clay especially speaking for? What Webster? 8. How do you explain the fact that the two men differed so radically both in regard to fact and theory? 9. What new idea does Gallatin bring in? 10. What does he claim protection must accomplish to be beneficial? 11. Name the arguments Dallas makes. 12. Who made, in your opinion, the ablest argument? Why?

1. What good did Washington expect from internal improvements? 2. How did Jefferson expect to join the west to the east? 3. Did he believe in the general government undertaking a system of internal improvements? 4. Compare Jefferson's and Hamilton's views. 5. On which side was Gallatin? 6. Was Calhoun, in 1817, a nationalist or a States Rights man, judging from the extract given? 7. Make a list of all the arguments you find for internal improvements; another list of those against. 8. Into how many classes did Jackson divide internal improvements? 9. In what ways was it claimed the nation might aid internal improvements? 10. Can you give the reasons for so many vetoes of bills for internal improvements? 11. Write a paper on the benefits of a system of internal improvements. 12. Write one on the dangers in it.

www.ingramcontent.com/pod-product-compliance
Lightning Source LLC
Chambersburg PA
CBHW021410230426
43666CB00006B/694